'Katja Schipperheijn provides a helpful and important deep analysis of an area that is rapidly changing our lives. She explains the history and direction of human and behavioural automation clearly and then gives us a framework that we can apply to learn and adapt – a LearnScape. Creating a LearnScape should be on every executive's agenda.'
Julia Cook, CEO of Change Management Group, Deputy Chair of GMC and Chair of Consortium for Street Children US

'As we build an innovation ecosystem to find and nurture new ideas, it is vital to feed it with the most appropriate skills and capabilities to drive growth. Adapting to different learning methods and styles is key to helping the ecosystem thrive. Learning from the intelligent symbioses of humans and technology provides nimble growth opportunities. The method for continuous improvement presented in this book is a useful guide for business leaders who want to innovate together with their team.'
Lisa Perkins, Director of Research and Innovation, BT

'Katja Schipperheijn has one of those unique L&D mindsets that can move your thinking forward. *Learning Ecosystems* is an important book for any serious learning professional or executive who wants to grow with their team through the opportunities that digital innovations have to offer in a world of ever-accelerating change.'
Damien Woods, Chapter Lead, Learning and Growth, 7-Eleven Australia

'Katja Schipperheijn makes a strong case for enabling organization and human development through technology. She takes a fresh look at the latest research in education and the latest technology trends that will develop and amplify humans' abilities. Any leader who wants to unleash the collective experience and knowledge of the organization with engaged employees and wants to meet the challenge of retraining, or nurture a culture of continuous learning, should read *Learning Ecosystems*.'
Regis Chasse, founder and Chief Learning Officer, CLO Advisors LLC, and Dean of the Leadership Institute

'Access to learning opportunities will be one of the key differentiators in adapting to the rapidly changing world. Opportunities for continuous development can be a scarce resource and are not available to everyone to the same extent. Thanks to the evolution of technology, we can build learning ecosystems to provide access to knowledge for learners around the world. Everyone will have a fair chance to develop and grow and not feel limited by a lack of local offerings.'
Sami M Leppänen, Learner Experience Innovation Manager, KONE Corporation

'The turmoil we are going through since the beginning of this century requires companies to grow resilience and people to acquire new skills. In this wonderful book, Katja Schipperheijn shows that competences such as curiosity, openness, optimism, empathy, entrepreneurship, consilience and imagination will make the all the difference needed to thrive, grow and learn. In a world that is becoming increasingly virtual and ever changing, learning architects will find the necessary tools and inspiration to prepare for the future of work.'
Stefan van Hooydonk, founder of Global Curiosity Institute and author of *The Workplace Curiosity Manifesto*

'How does one build a learning organization that constantly collects data, processes it and turns it into actionable information? The answer is simple: understand the science and art of learning and build an organization using those building blocks and dynamics. Connect the dots and create an ecosystem organization. Or in other words: create a LearnScape.'

'Katja Schipperheijn has always been passionate about "learning" and now she has used her scientific understanding of how "learning" works to describe how to create a LearnScape. This fascinating book is a must-read for everybody that not only wants to be ready for the future, but wants to play an active role in shaping it. *Learning Ecosystems* is an instant classic; the book as well as the concept.'
Rik Vera, international keynote speaker, thought leader, business philosopher, author, coach and consultant

'Effective teams need specialized training adapted to their needs, abilities and expectations. This means that a one-size-fits-all approach is no longer working. Leading companies are less interested in hiring people with a lot of knowledge; they recruit people that are highly curious and able to learn fast. They create a learning ecosystem that delivers insights into the strategies, processes and tools that make the difference. For sales organizations too, learning takes place through collaboration, innovation and experimentation supported by AI-enabled technology.'
Gerhard Gschwandtner, founder and Publisher, *Selling Power* magazine

Learning Ecosystems

Creating innovative, lean and tech-driven learning strategies

Katja Schipperheijn

KoganPage

Publisher's note

Every possible effort has been made to ensure that the information contained in this book is accurate at the time of going to press, and the publishers and authors cannot accept responsibility for any errors or omissions, however caused. No responsibility for loss or damage occasioned to any person acting, or refraining from action, as a result of the material in this publication can be accepted by the editor, the publisher or the author.

First published in Great Britain and the United States in 2022 by Kogan Page Limited

2nd Floor, 45 Gee Street	8 W 38th Street, Suite 902	4737/23 Ansari Road
London	New York, NY 10018	Daryaganj
EC1V 3RS	USA	New Delhi 110002
United Kingdom		India

www.koganpage.com

Kogan Page books are printed on paper from sustainable forests.

© Katja Schipperheijn, 2022

The right of Katja Schipperheijn to be identified as the author of this work has been asserted by her in accordance with the Copyright, Designs and Patents Act 1988.

ISBNs

Hardback	978 1 3986 0742 2
Paperback	978 1 3986 0740 8
Ebook	978 1 3986 0741 5

British Library Cataloguing-in-Publication Data

A CIP record for this book is available from the British Library.

Library of Congress Cataloging-in-Publication Data

2022024480

Typeset by Integra Software Services, Pondicherry
Print production managed by Jellyfish
Printed and bound by CPI Group (UK) Ltd, Croydon CR0 4YY

CONTENTS

FOREWORD

BY BRANDON CARSON

Vice President, Learning and Leadership at Walmart, Author, and Founder of L&D Cares

This book comes at a critical time for L&D and you will find it valuable as a resource and catalyst for how to operate a modern learning function. Why? Let me share four key reasons why this book is necessary and important.

1 The pace at which employers are needing to skill their workforce has accelerated exponentially over the last decade. As business continues to reorient itself in this daunting age of transformation and post-pandemic realignment, the workforce is faced with an avalanche of technological advancement, systems and workflow change, as well as heightened customer expectations. Simply stated, every aspect of what we define as work is being reimagined.

2 The next decade will find business and L&D deeply integrating, as every company becomes a technology company and it becomes strikingly critical to have skilled employees at *every level*. L&D is now the central pillar of the business strategy, which is a call to action for L&D to more effectively deliver on business expectations. This newfound responsibility means we need to rethink, reset, and rebuild our practice from the ground up. We need to review our own capabilities, how we are structured, and where we sit in the organization. We must reskill and upskill ourselves to more efficiently, and effectively activate business value through learning. L&D needs digital literacy at every level, deep understanding of data and learning analytics, speed and process efficiency, and business acumen.

3 The most important asset an organization has is its people. To serve the performance needs of both the workforce and the business, L&D needs to deeply understand *how* the work gets done,

not just how it *should* get done. We must become fluent with the existing work systems and environments so we can help facilitate the systemic and structural changes needed to evolve the workplace to a scalable learning model – where both the systems and the environment are harmoniously connected in motivating the workforce to learn and perform while working.

4 L&D must be the disruptor to the status quo. Our job is no longer to be an order taker building content modules on demand. We must take on the complicated work of delivering evidence-based learning solutions that provide real business impact. There's not one business on earth that isn't being disrupted and to successfully navigate this unprecedented age, L&D must shift their operating model accordingly.

In this book, Katja steps you through a pragmatic process to identify a learning strategy that not only aligns to business strategy, but becomes a core component. As we reset, rethink, and rebuild the business of L&D, we have a complicated and immense challenge ahead – we must find nimble, adaptive, and creative ways to deliver scalable learning in near real-time. The days of taking months to deliver learning content are gone. L&D must not only move away from delivering one-size-fits-all learning on its own timeline, it must urgently deliver one-size-fits-one learning in a scalable manner and in near real-time to ensure optimal workforce performance.

PREFACE

I dedicate this book to my children and many others whose lives so far have consisted of learning and longing for the moment when they will finally graduate and start their lives. When I tell them that learning never ends, I see disbelief and horror in their eyes. A tantalizing torment that will never end. What I want to give them are learning ecosystems where learning is not a burden but a gift to create a value-driven future where wellbeing prevails.

For the first book I wrote, *Little Digital Citizens* (2018), I looked at children growing up in today's world. A world that is becoming more and more virtual and therefore may seem less real to some of us. I examined the competences that would support them in finding their place in an increasingly digital society. What struck me is that children often effortlessly pick up the necessary skills because they have the right competences like curiosity and openness. For them, virtual worlds are almost as lifelike for playing and learning together. Something that came in handy during the COVID-19 lockdowns.

When I look back at what I showed the more than 15,000 children in my workshops and inspiration sessions about the future, I notice that this future has often already caught up with us. However, many organizations are absolutely not prepared for it and the urgency is what makes this book necessary.

Nevertheless, I had already started working on a book about learning ecosystems before March 2020. Even then, I was fascinated by the human, team, leadership and cultural challenges these organizations face with regard to technological innovations, knowledge sharing and learning. In doing so, I was looking to make efficient use of the mass of data stored in an organization and also thinking about a value-driven future and wellbeing.

However, at the end of March 2020, I decided to completely delete the manuscript I had finished at that time from my files. I thought my book would no longer be relevant because I was convinced that the 'Black Swan' (the unthinkable suddenly passing by) called COVID-19 would do my job.

So why this book after all? I turned out to be partly right about the impact of COVID-19 on the future of work. For example, according to several studies, including by MIT Sloan, in the first months of COVID-19 we saw an acceleration in digital innovations and learning that was unprecedented. What we expected to see in seven years seemed to happen in seven months. Yet its impact on people's well-being did not turn out as I had hoped.

It started well, though. The resilience I saw in the first months after 'the lockdown' was unprecedented. Yet, almost a year later, I notice that this resilience has often turned into frustration. The temporary solutions proved untenable because we clung to the idea of returning to the old normal. In my opinion, the longer we try to hold on to what we knew, the more we fall back. Fundamentally different thinking about intelligent cooperation between people and technology is needed more than ever. We must dare to make strategic choices at the level of employees and the organization with an extension to the whole ecosystem around it. The ad hoc solutions that we have pulled out of our metaphorical hat have often not been implemented properly. Yet there are also positive points: the hunger for digital change is more than ripe after a year of experimenting with working and learning differently. The time to invest in learning ecosystems has come, or as I will call them: LearnScapes.

ACKNOWLEDGEMENTS

This book would never have come about without my two daughters Farah and Helena and all the other children and young people who took me into their world. By constantly telling me that I did not understand their world, they stimulated my curious mind and I learned to see the world through their eyes.

Without my dear husband Peter Somers, I could not have done this. He has encouraged me to write and sometimes tolerates that I give priority to my work. Above all, I am grateful to him for sharing his knowledge of leadership with me. He is more than once the driving force behind the LearnScapes I envision.

I would also like to thank my father George Schipperheijn and Christine Verhasselt who, even in difficult times, always encourage and challenge me to question everything.

Of course, I am also grateful for the many contributions and inspiration from everyone who has helped me write *Learning Ecosystems*. Andrew Stotter-Brooks, Vice President of Learning and Development Etihad Aviation Group whose enthusiasm for learning is an inspiration to many. Tariq Chauhan, Group CEO and Co-founder of EFS whose leadership and knowledge of engagement is an example to many. Santosh Kher, Managing Director of Human Resources at FedEx Express for whom the future of work is supported by cross-functional teams. Rafael J Grossmann, MD, FACS Surgeon and Digital Health Innovator, Educator and Communicator focused on the convergence of technology and medicine to make healthcare more human. Guy Van Neck, CEO and Founder of Mobietrain who knows better than anyone that as an EdTech entrepreneur you have to connect. Geert Nijs who is a learning architect at KBC and is an expert in social learning environments. Jan Rypers, digital learning expert at Colruyt Group who, like me, does not want to give dogmatic thinking a chance. Anna Tarabasz, Dean of Teaching and Learning, Head of School – Business and

Humanities, Associate Professor at Curtin University who shares her obsession with data and marketing with me. Lieselot De Clerck, founder of d-teach for whom sharing knowledge comes from the heart. Prof. Dr. Nick van Dam who has supported me from the very first concept to continue thinking about lean learning and innovation. Matthew Wilkins, Director of Learning Technology at Biz Group who is the best sparring partner for me to talk about new technologies. Jena Davidson, Founder at Jenson8 who surprised me with her startup and thereby forced me to drop some of my own assumptions about the added value of innovation to support wellbeing. Maarten Van Beek, HR Director at ING and a visionary with regard to talent development and engagement. Marc Mekki, expert of design thinking that demystifies technology and cuts through the hype. Alfred Remmits, CEO of Xprtise and 5 Moments of Need™ specialist for his feedback from mountains of experience with learning strategies. Thierry Geerts, CEO of Google Belgium who made my Digital Citizens grow up to be Homo Digitalis. Lauren Somers, the youngest entrepreneur in this book who, just like my daughter Farah Van Bulck, knows that mindset and competences are the key to success. And of course my examples and inspiration for writing this book with a Forever Frontier in mind; Paul McDonagh-Smith from MIT Sloan, the founder of Algorithmic Business Thinking who I will mention several times and Dr. Steven Shepard with whom I share the passion for Reverse Engineering to build a value driven future. And last but not least, Professor Thomas Malone for inspiring me with the OODAP model.

Introduction

'Executives lack the right focus to develop innovative strategies such as driving the fusion of people and technology.' That's what Deloitte's 2021 *Global Human Capital Trends* report reveals. Only seven per cent of executives internationally would focus on building intelligent forms of collaboration between people and technology. This intelligent collaboration would be about new ways of working that draw on the strengths of both people and technology.

Am I the only one to be surprised to read that thinking about this intelligent collaboration is not obvious to all managers? Why are 93 per cent not looking at technology and the added value it can give us as humans in an intelligent symbiosis where strength of both are combined? Is it fear of change or simply a lack of knowledge of the opportunities that digital transformation can bring in terms of human capital? Is it silo thinking that stands in the way of innovation or is it the skill gap of executives themselves? I decided to search my network for answers and found the motivation to write yet another book. This book is partly a manifesto for the future of work and partly a handbook for building the organization for the future effectively and sustainably.

Those learning ecosystems I call LearnScapes. Those learning ecosystems I call LearnScapes grow through continuous interaction with the larger whole of which they are a part. The inspiration for the name LearnScapes, which is now increasingly used to designate learning ecosystems, I found in an article about agriculture. I learned that agricultural architects built cultural landscapes, called ecosystems or LearnScapes. These LearnScapes were complex systems of relationships, created and maintained by the interactions of living and non-living nature. I saw in this the analogy to the learning ecosystems I wanted to build, where the people are my living nature and the machines are the non-living nature.

So to continue the analogy with agriculture, I was looking for someone who could develop, nurture and grow these complex learning landscapes. Someone with knowledge of people and innovation and above all the right competencies and mindset to connect I would therefore call LearnScaper.

Why would you want to read this book?

You may feel that you are one of the 93 per cent of executives who do not have the right focus to explore innovative strategies based on an intelligent symbiosis between people and technology. You want to support knowledge sharing and growth for employees, the organization and the ecosystem but may lack the knowledge and skills to do so.

On the other hand, you might be the right person to bring new ideas to your organization, based on your expertise and role, and you are looking for tips on how to make your organization grow from its human capital. You might be responsible for integrating new innovations with regard to IT networks. Perhaps you are a start-up entrepreneur looking for a form of organization that can grow along with the people and the innovations that seem to be coming at us ever faster.

I believe this book is for anyone who understands that it is the role of everyone in the ecosystem to create a climate that stimulates knowledge sharing. I want to inspire you to make use of all the potential that is present in the organization and around it.

With this book, I want to inspire you to look beyond the boundaries of your own organization. More than that, I want to make you rise above the silos of our organization that prevent us from growing.

What I want to achieve is that with this book you can be the architect of the new nimble organization where lifelong learning supports the growth mindset of the organization. I call this organization a LearnScape, where learning techniques are tuned to the continuous interaction with the world outside, the ecosystem.

As a LearnScaper, you can help build that place by planting the seeds of a LearnScape. The place where innovation, data-centricity, ecosystem thinking, growth mindset and employee engagement meet.

While I will be assuming some knowledge of strategy, learning and development (L&D for short), technology and marketing and introduce terms and concepts you may not know, I believe lifelong learning, supported by openness, curiosity and many other competences, is the key to future success.

How to read this book?

The book is divided into five parts that provide you step by step with all the information you need to build learning ecosystems or LearnScapes where the symbiosis between people and technology creates added value for everyone.

To do this, it is important to have an understanding of the world around us. Not only the world as we know it, but also the increasingly virtual metaverse that has been the new normal for our children for years. Only when we understand that in many cases the future has already caught up with us, will we understand the context and the urgency to take action now before it is too late.

In the first section, I look very broadly at innovation from different angles such as ever smarter AI that could reach the level of singularity in the coming years. Here, in many circumstances, we as humans would be subordinate to the ability of 'robots'. It is not my intention to go along with hypes. What I do want is to focus attention on an ethical world where we as humans can be human in a world that is becoming increasingly virtual.

When we understand that the technological acceleration is unstoppable, we look at the influence of this on the future of work in a value-driven organization. This section is indispensable for management and HR professionals who want to stand a chance as future employers in the increasingly tight labour market. The organization of the future will not only develop value-driven strategies, they will also have to be more and more data-driven, always taking into account a people first focus.

In the second part of this book, I look at the learner, the employee or even the future employee. Are we as human beings capable of life-long learning with enthusiasm? Is the skill-gap through technology innovations the real challenge or should we focus more on competences that distinguish us as humans from the machine? The essence in this part is to trigger the growth mindset of our employees from motivation and commitment that will be needed for a successful implementation of those projects we want to launch in the last part.

Part 3, which is perhaps the most challenging, is where I look at strategies that have often been ingrained in the culture of our organization for a long time. Yet I wonder if we can still apply them dogmatically in the face of innovation. Here, it is the reader's mindset that will be triggered, because if we abandon old ways of working, what is the role of the guardians of these? In this section, therefore, I will try to link theoretical models and learning analytics to new technologies that support learning.

From the fourth part, we lay the building blocks for the new learning ecosystems or LearnScapes we want to build and new concepts are introduced. For example, we look at the different organizational types that I name in the Learning Maturity Model. In this model, I judge organizations by the way they use technology to share knowledge with the ecosystem they are part of. In addition, I also touch upon the concept of Lean Learning to make learning happen as efficiently as possible without waste of the general principles that underpin lean strategies. In this section, I then conclude with the pillars of social learning in these lean learning ecosystems that I outline. In doing so, we always look at learning from the learner's point of view, who has relevant knowledge at his/her disposal when it can be applied.

Finally, as a LearnScaper, I challenge you to outline your own strategy to achieve continuous improvement in five steps; Discovery, Burning Platform, Path to Improvement, Joint Execution and Future Growth and Improvement. These projects that arise from an opportunity in the future provide nimble innovation that is implemented with a broad base of support from all stakeholders in the ecosystem.

You will notice throughout the book that technology and innovation are central, yet never the essence. I want to take you to a future with a forever frontier where continuous and nimble innovation is essential. Starting from technology is never the answer, starting from people is.

In addition to the concepts and frameworks I provide, I have approached a large number of experts who often have more knowledge of HR, L&D or marketing than I do myself. Their stories contribute to the holistic view I hope to nurture in you as an innovative LearnScaper.

Have fun learning and dare to ask for help!

Reference

Deloitte (2021) 2021 Global Human Capital Trends: Special report, www2. deloitte.com/us/en/insights/focus/human-capital-trends.html (archived at https://perma.cc/FUL8-SVW5)

PART ONE

A world in ever-increasing change

01

The world of human and machine

That the future will be fundamentally different is no surprise, nor is it when I say that machines, or technology, will play an important role there. Or should I say: an even more important role than today.

Intelligent collaborations in a symbiosis of man and machine will enable us to thrive in a world of ever faster change. For business leaders, it is becoming increasingly urgent to align both employees and organizational strategy with the expectations of data- and value-driven organizations of the future.

This may sound very futuristic to many, but in many cases the future has already caught up with us. As a mother of two teenage daughters I regularly hear that I'm not keeping up with the innovations that seem to dominate their lives. For a writer about innovation and learning, that's pretty funny to hear. But they are right, because even though I believe in innovation, I also notice that I easily fall back on the old normal, just because it feels familiar.

Yet even for them, learning is still mostly formal with lessons and tasks organized in a classroom setting. Even in periods of distance learning, technology may have been innovative but the method used had not changed. This school-based approach to learning also tends to dominate the thinking of some workplace L&D practitioners. The fact that learning happens informally through our impressions and interactions with people and technology is too often underestimated. There are advantages for us as humans to learn in a more focused way with knowledge that is relevant in the present, but we shouldn't forget to learn more adaptively together with the environment and to grow as a group.

Learning is inextricably linked to evolution. Formal or informal is not the essence. The essence is the mindset to work intelligently with the knowledge we have. A growth-mindset, where we learn from the past prepares people and organizations to be nimble and positive for the uncertain future. It is this mindset that will prove necessary in the search for opportunities in the future where learning from people and data will give us a head start.

The time to transform your organization has come

The COVID-19 pandemic had, and continues to have, an unprecedented impact on how employees and organizations collaborate and share knowledge. Many organizations have been forced to innovate and to adapt to the world around them. These innovations and investments often turned out to be neither scalable nor adjusted to a permanent reality. Just think of virtual meetings that mirror a real meeting room, but where the participants often have to deal with other things (such as their children) at the same time. It's not really an optimal situation for building the future of collaboration. In many cases, we now see that they are more of a sticking plaster on a festering wound and that frustration with these so-called innovative technologies takes over.

Organizations that really want to make a difference and emerge stronger from the crisis will align their approach with a Forever Frontier. A future of which we cannot see the boundaries and the possibilities. They build a vision for this unknown future and reverse engineer their current strategy from possible expectations.

In this future focussed vision, nimble organizations take into account all the influences from the ecosystem, because long-term strategy in a future where changes roll over us like tsunamis is no longer tenable. Making a difference as a nimble organization is also no longer possible without involving the ecosystem in the strategy. In this ecosystem, every participant influences each other. In an interconnected and increasingly virtual world, any adjustment in the ecosystem can bring about long-term consequences that are difficult to assess or predict.

Upskilling homo digitalis

The 2020 Future of Jobs Survey indicates that 94 per cent of business leaders expect employees to acquire new skills while on the job. That's a sharp increase from 65 per cent in 2018. In doing so, employees are expected to learn more and faster than ever before to succeed in their jobs. Yet organizations from the survey only offer access to retraining and upskilling to 62 per cent of their workforce. They may be expanding that offer to a further 11 per cent of their workforce by 2025, but that's still only 73 per cent.

Organizations that want to focus on knowledge flowing through the organization will therefore look for methods that make the shift from in class or face-to-face training to more hybrid forms that support life-long learning. They will not only look at popular methods like blended and hybrid, or different forms of online and classroom learning, but they will also engage their employees to take ownership of their own learning process and thus directly influence the business results.

This added value of intelligent technologies will also increase employee engagement in learning by allowing them to cater to individual interests and needs. When the above survey mentioned that only 42 per cent of the employees actually make use of the employer-supported retraining and additional training opportunities, there is certainly room for improvement.

A critical question therefore arises about how learning is delivered as the survey also showed that 86 per cent of organizations that respond to the urgency to support learning also adapt the way they provide learning. Short learning in a few minutes a day via *microlearning* is on the rise, as is giving learning a fun experience. While these are nice initiatives, if the tools, the content and the learning culture are not considered together to make knowledge flow effectively and efficiently through the organization, then few investments will pay off.

Thierry Geerts explains very clearly in his book *Homo Digitalis* that we, as humans, have become dependent on the technology that surrounds us. He gives a nuanced view of technology and looks for the impact of these innovations and how they make us more human.

CASE STUDY

The homo digitalis is a homo sapiens in collaborative digital mode who uses technology to be more human

Thierry Geerts, CEO Google Belgium

We are all homo digitalis. We are increasingly surrounded by technology and do not realize its impact on us. The pandemic has reinforced this evolution: imagine if we didn't have these digital tools! They saved us a lot of time. The time freed up allowed us to be more human. We stayed in touch with family and friends via the screen, our children followed distance learning and thanks to e-commerce we were able to make purchases. Businesses also adapted, reinventing themselves and finding new channels to pursue their activities. We suddenly realized the essential place of technology, which we had previously considered a gadget, in our lives. Now we have to ask ourselves what lessons we can learn to avoid getting stuck in our old ways.

That technology would make us less human is a fallacy. Technological tools can help us if we use them correctly. Our jobs evolve, but that need not be a problem if we are positive about change. Technology today enables us to provide solutions for employment and lifelong learning. But we are in a transition phase. That's why an interest in technology is essential, because it will change the way we work.

The digital future also gives us the opportunity to create a world that will be better than the current one: more human, more flexible and more ecological. Less materialistic too, and therefore less polluting in many cases. Just think of Spotify, which has replaced the CD and runs on green energy in Google's date centres.

Once you see the benefits that technology has to offer you for your needs and passions, you're going to be more inclined to take an interest and become better informed. That's a real opportunity to be seized!

Does homo digitalis become homo phygitalis in the metaverse?

That we will all become homo digitalis seems hard to believe for many. Yet, as Thierry Geerts pointed out, the COVID-19 pandemic has had an unprecedented impact on our world. More than that, a virtual or metaverse has emerged alongside, or should I say above, our physical world. In this world, we might even become homo phygitalis, existing simultaneously in the physical and digital world.

Metaverse and phygital seem to have suddenly become hyped since Facebook founder Mark Zuckerberg announced a name change for his company. Meta, which from Ancient Greek means 'after' or 'beside', is now commonly used as 'beyond' or 'at a higher level'. However, he was certainly not the first to come up with this idea. Neal Stephenson was several decades ahead of him by introducing 'the Metaverse' in his 1992 science fiction novel *Snow Crash*. This seemingly rapid rise is obviously causing the necessary controversy and fear among the general public, but also among business leaders. Zuckerberg, and others, see the world on a higher level where lifelike avatars meet in 3D and virtual reality environments.

Microsoft, game developers Epic Games of Fortnite, Roblox and Upland are just a few players who have already made great strides towards the real metaverse. These hyper-real alternative worlds where we can live, work and learn together combine technologies like augmented reality, virtual reality, 3D holographic avatars and video with NFTs and blockchain. Bringing these new digital innovations together gives unprecedented combinations that offer possibilities beyond our imagination. Soon we will enter the virtual world through advanced VR and AR glasses, digital contact lenses or even brain implants like the ones Elon Musk's Neuralink is already experimenting with.

What can the gaming world teach us?

Returning to the present, we see game developers and commercial companies seizing opportunities to reach an often young and trendy audience in the metaverse. This opportunity to connect new 'players' with brands and companies has grown tremendously due to the limitations of the real world during the COVID-19 lockdowns. Tim Sweeney, CEO of Epic Games, for example, saw the ultimate experience in photorealistic digital people that he develops with his MetaHuman Creator. With this he creates your digital double. The fact that this virtual world is a lifelike new dimension for many was demonstrated by the concert series he launched in the meta-world of Fortnite. Stars like Ariana Grande and Travis Scott gave concerts through their lifelike avatars that could never be sold out.

Travis Scott's reached no less than 12.3 million people during his first virtual concert on the gaming platform for a total of 48.5 million engaged visitors over five concerts who were only too happy to pay for it. To realize this in the 'real world' he would have to give 194,000 concerts in the grand concert stage the Great Strahov Stadium in Prague, Czech Republic. Imagine if we could reach and engage as many learners with virtual classrooms.

That the metaverse of Fortnite is bringing the conversion between the physical world and the virtual world ever closer, and that they are making a lot of money with it, was shown by the partnership they announced in September 2021 with the luxury brand Balenciaga. It may seem crazy but for gamers in the virtual worlds their appearance is just as important as in real-life. The outfits, called skins, impart status and personality that facilitate social interactions with other players. This is another take-away for organizing virtual learning experiences. Making the experience so real that we can engage in the same way as we do in the real world will reduce the transactional distance to learning as I discuss in chapter 6 of this book on new technologies for learning.

Another game that is gaining popularity is Roblox where users are able to fantasize, socialize, chat, play, create, interact and relate with others in many ways such as creating their own games or exploring the worlds of their virtual friends. Not that it's new, as the online games platform and game creation system developed by Roblox Corporation founders David Baszucki and Erik Cassel came to market in 2006. For most of their history, Roblox was relatively small, both the platform and the company due to co-founder Baszucki's lack of interest in press coverage. As a result, for a long time it was 'lost among the crowd' due to the large number of platforms coming out around the same time. Roblox only began to grow rapidly in the second half of the 2010s. However, the huge growth of the last few years was, unsurprisingly, achieved during the COVID-19 pandemic due to the need of mostly children for social contacts, experiences and distractions. Today, Roblox is perhaps the most popular platform for children already living in the world of tomorrow. As of April 2021, Roblox had over 202 million monthly active users of which a whopping 80 million registered in 2020. Remarkably, this means that more than half of all children under the age of 16 in the United States already have an alternative 'I' in the metaverse.

What makes Roblox so special? It is partly comparable to Unity or Minecraft from Microsoft, which have greater name recognition. However, Roblox's current success is largely attributed to its passionate community of developers who often start out playing as children, but quickly turn professional like Ben and Matt Horton who first discovered virtual games through play. The twin brothers developed their first big hit on Roblox – a game called Boat Ride – when they were barely 13, a great start to a career at a young age as both brothers now work full-time in the gaming industry. And to say they're making a good living at it is no understatement. Their games are massively played and they earn over 130,000 euros a year from it. Without getting ahead, Roblox might just be the example of a learning ecosystem that has adapted to the future of work.

Non-fungible token, blockchain and the metaverse

If you thought that after reading this the metaverse attracts mainly young people, gamers and developers then you are wrong.

Every NFT is a unique digital file, for example a jpeg-image, a tweet, a meme or a pair of unique Air Jordan sneakers. The price of the most expensive digital artwork as an NFT ever sold in 2021 began with a modest bet at Christies of US $100. The bidding went through the roof in the last few days to a whopping 42,329 Ether (cryptocurrency) or converted 69.3 million dollars paid by Singapore-based programmer Vignesh Sundaresan. This makes *Everydays: the First 5000 Days* not only the most expensive digital artwork but also the most expensive artworks by a living artist: Mike Winkelmann, known professionally as Beeple. The accompanying non-fungible token (NFT) gives Sundaresan the rights to display the artwork, but remarkably, it does not give him the copyright.

For those of you who are not quite familiar with the difference between NFT and cryptocurrencies, both have a virtual application and are linked to the metaverse and blockchain. An NFT is a unique digital item that cannot be replaced, unlike Euros or Cryptocurrencies such as Bitcoins which can be exchanged infinitely. With cryptocurrency you can buy or pay for all kinds of products or services, or if you believe that they will become increasingly valuable, they are also a popular investment tool. Another difference is that NFTs only have their place in the virtual world, while cryptocurrencies are increasingly used in brick and mortar shops.

But not only art and clothing are becoming increasingly popular as NFT. Buildings or more specifically locations are also being tapped using blockchain technology in games such as Upland. And it goes much further now that even cities like Seoul see more and more possibilities in the virtual shadow world.

It is therefore obvious that many organizations, as they accelerate their digital transformation, are looking at the added value that NFTs and the metaverse have to offer. Both for customer loyalty, but also increasingly from the point of view of a learning ecosystem. Therefore, in chapter 6, I give some examples that the metaverse has to offer in terms of learning and knowledge sharing. In addition, I will not shy away from some misconceptions and challenges that are still preventing us from getting real added value from this virtual and connected world.

The robot beats a human on intelligence

The world has taken on a new dimension in which we have been transformed into a digital version of ourselves. In this metaverse, however, we will still make our own decisions. Yet there are increasing indications that artificial intelligence will soon beat us when it comes to making intelligent decisions.

It may seem hard to believe that we would put our lives in the hands of robots, but it is already happening. Futurists like Ray Kurzweil have predicted that by 2030 it will be possible to connect our brains directly to the Cloud, and thus the metaverse, via our neocortex. This means that we will literally be pumping data into our heads via a cable. Does that mean that our children won't have to go to school anymore, but just 'log on' and gain the knowledge they need? Looking at the rapid steps that 'computers' have taken in recent years, one would be inclined to believe that there is some possibility in the future visions regarding artificial intelligence and the connection with the human brain.

What is AI already capable of

It recently appeared that AI has taken another step forward to beat people in the race to make intelligent decisions. Libratus, the 'computer' (or rather: artificial intelligence robot) from the American university Carnegie Mellon won a poker tournament against professional human players for the first time on 31 January 2017. Libratus picked up over US $1.7 million in chips after an impressive and especially very long game of poker no-limits Texas Hold'em, lasting 19 days and involving 120,000 rounds! You might think it was an endurance battle that the four human opponents could not physically withstand, but that was not the basis on which Libratus won after 19 days. The robot won on 'intelligence' by making very thoughtful choices.

The fact that a computer beats a human on intelligence is not so spectacular in itself: on February 10, 1996, Deep Blue, the supercomputer of IBM, won against the Russian chess master Kasparov. In 2017, the ancient Asian strategic board game Go was won by AlphaGo, developed by Google.

Why is this recent Libratus victory different from the previous ones, and why does it affect those competencies that make us unique as humans? Poker is a game that revolves around strategy and game insight, but above all, bluffing and seeing through an opponent's bluff. The latter is very difficult for a computer to deal with. Human emotions expressed in very subtle facial expressions – a *tell* in poker jargon – cannot be recognized by a computer.

So how did Libratus manage to beat a human and what can we learn from this? The first important reason is the difference between human and artificial intelligence, with the latter's computing power being many times faster. The second aspect that makes Libratus unique is the way it handles data. To win poker, you cannot rely on reactive technology, in other words, on intelligence that comes from previous data. Libratus had an improved algorithmic approach to the game through the way it dealt with imperfect or hidden information.

So how did that work? According to Noam Brown of Carnegie Mellon University who helped develop the algorithm for Libratus as a doctoral student, they didn't 'teach' him how to play poker, they gave him the rules and instructed him to 'learn by himself'. The bot started playing randomly, but over the course of playing, trillions of hands were able to refine its approach and arrive at a winning strategy.

Late each day, after the poker game was over, Brown connected Libratus to the Bridgescomputer at the Pittsburgh Supercomputer Centre to run algorithms to improve the strategy overnight. In the morning, he would spend two hours getting the newly improved bot working again. Looking at the collaboration that Brown and Libratus had in this way to learn ever better based on imperfect information opens up many possibilities for human-machine partnerships.

Artificial intelligence could already make better decisions in crisis situations, such as military conflicts, by taking into account much more data without human feelings. AI could also enable the medical community to make rapid progress in research where not all the data is known. It is clear that a whole new world is opening up to us, a world that many cannot comprehend.

When we think of the symbiosis between man and machine to create added value, the ever-faster evolution of AI already holds promise. Yet, as we will see in the next chapters, it also holds potential threats.

Confusion regarding AI

The impact of artificial intelligence on our lives is growing at an ever-increasing rate. However, we must be careful when talking about artificial intelligence because not all innovative products that claim to use AI actually do so. This is partly due to the perceived added value of AI for innovative solutions. As a result, startups often claim something they are not yet able to deliver. On the other hand, we also see that there is a lot of confusion because sometimes people talk about machine learning, deep learning, AI and so on. It may therefore be useful to understand the terms.

Artificial intelligence (AI) is an old and overarching term that originated in 1956 and was introduced by the American computer scientist John McCarthy. It was originally a term for machines that perform tasks based on instructions given by humans. Still a long way from the interpretation we now give to super-AI. Simply put, the computer did no more than read, catalogue or process a set of data based on an algorithm written by humans. Think of recognition software to tell dogs and cats apart. In this context of rule-based systems, 'intelligent technology' takes no action unless it is predefined. Useful, but irrelevant when it comes to technology that would let us learn better from our own intelligence.

Machine learning (ML) goes one step further. The system learns from the many data it processes and adapts itself without any instruction from the programmer. This allows it to respond to situations that could not have been predicted beforehand, as I mentioned earlier with the example of Libratus.

Next, we often hear that neural networks are related to the complex way of reasoning that human brains do. Our brains are made up of neural networks of layers of neurons; they do nothing but pass information from one layer of neurons to another. This is exactly what we are trying to do with machine learning, by connecting as many layers of data sets as possible. The more layers, the deeper the system, hence the term deep learning. Simple, but not yet to be confused with super-AI which is referred to when we think of singularity. Machines that become smarter than people. At present, we are still in the phase of strong artificial intelligence where AI systems can already transfer knowledge from one domain to another, but still lack those competences that make us uniquely human as cited in chapter 4.

That the singularity sounds very futuristic and dangerous is understandable, and so are the concerns of many specialists and governments who are trying to constrain it, as we will see later in this chapter.

Bias and ethical issues for AI

Returning to what Brown did with Libratus and how it dealt with 'imperfect information', there are some other challenges we need to look at. As I mentioned earlier, the question arises whether we want algorithms and automation to determine what is an interesting learning or career path for us. Amazon noticed that artificial intelligence isn't always without bias when they ran into trouble with the ethics test after launching their recruitment tool in 2014.

At first glance, the tool would have been more capable than humans to select the best candidates without bias based on data. In reality, Amazon's system taught itself that male candidates preferred technical jobs. Resumes with references that the candidate was a woman were thereby excluded from further selection. Although the resumes did not always explicitly contain this information, the AI system would learn itself based on *deep learning techniques* and linked datasets. As a result, the system started to discriminate based on mentions of 'captain of women's chess club' and indirect references to women-only schools.

Amazon modified the algorithm, but could not guarantee that the unsupervised system would not discriminate in any other way. This makes us think about the degree of automation via artificial intelligence that we would like to see in learning platforms. In addition, we should not lose sight of the privacy aspect which will be explored in chapter 3.

AI and innovation, ethics and governance

Since May 2018, there has been a wave of new regional data privacy regulations aimed at making our digital experiences safer and more secure. For example, there's GDPR – Europe's General Data Protection Regulations, CCPA – California Consumer Privacy Act, LGPD – Brazil's Lei Geral de Proteção de Dados and POPI – South Africa's protection of personal information, yet when it comes to rules regarding the use of AI and the ethical issues surrounding it, there's still precious little to report.

The need for a clear framework was arguably raised more than 75 years ago by Isaac Asimov, author and professor of biochemistry at Boston University. In his science fiction novel, he published his 'three laws' to protect humans from interactions with robots.

1 A robot must not injure a human being or, by inaction, place a human being in danger.

2 A robot must obey the commands of humans, except when those commands violate the first law.

3 A robot must protect its own existence as long as this protection does not violate the first or second law.

When Asimov spoke of robots he was not yet thinking of AI but rather of androids or human-like humanoid robots. He envisioned a world where these humanoid robots would behave like servants and require a set of programming rules to prevent them from doing harm. But in the 75 years since the first story with its ethical guidelines was published, there have been significant technological advances. We now have a very different idea of what robots might look like and how we will interact with them. More to the point, the simple programming rules are smart algorithms that may be able to replicate, augment or replace human intelligence.

AI typically relies on large amounts of different types of data to develop insights. When algorithms are poorly designed or rely on faulty, inadequate or biased data they can have unintended harmful consequences, as noted in the Amazon example. In addition, with the rapid advancement of algorithmic systems, in some cases, we don't even know how these systems arrive at a decision. When we rely on this intelligence that we do not control and/or understand, it is a risk to our society that we cannot factor in.

Policies and frameworks

That this ethical framework needs to be in place, or should have been in place already, is also known by President of the European Parliament Von der Leysen who on February 21, 2021, presented a proposal for a regulation of the European Parliament and the Council laying down harmonized rules on artificial intelligence (Artificial Intelligence Act) and amending certain legislative acts of the union. With this proposal, the President wants the Commission to present legislation for a coordinated European approach to the human and ethical implications of AI.

Previously, the Commission published the *White Paper on Artificial Intelligence – A European approach based on excellence and trust.* This white paper outlines policy options to achieve the dual objective of facilitating the deployment of AI and addressing the risks associated with certain uses of such technology. The present proposal aims to achieve the second objective of developing an ecosystem of trust by proposing a legal framework for trustworthy AI. Based on the values and fundamental rights of the EU, the proposal aims to give people and other users the confidence to embrace AI-based solutions and encourage companies to develop them. AI should be a tool for people and a positive force in society, with the ultimate goal of increasing human wellbeing. The rules for AI applications available on the Union market or otherwise affecting individuals in the Union should therefore be people-centric, so that the public can trust that the technology is used in a safe way, in accordance with the law and respecting fundamental rights.

This is still one of the only initiatives to define an ethical framework for AI. This ethical framework that AI developers should already adhere to is important in order to achieve a system of moral principles and techniques for the responsible use of AI. However, in my opinion, every organization and stakeholder should already take responsibility now and not wait for legal frameworks. Therefore, I would like to give some guidelines that can be taken into account from a social responsibility perspective.

- **Explainability.** Organizations using AI should be able to explain what the source data is, the expected results and what the algorithms are doing to get there. This is necessary so that when there is damage it can be traced to a cause and lessons can be learned.

- **Fairness and Bias.** It seems like the obvious thing to do, but in data collections containing personally identifiable information, it is extremely important to ensure that there is no racial, gender or ethnic bias or other factors that have no place in an inclusive society.
- **Abuse.** Security of AI will be a big challenge therefore from the development stage an analysis should be made if the AI algorithms can be used for other non-ethical projects. All possible situations and security measures should be taken to mitigate this.
- **Responsibility.** When something goes wrong we want to assign blame and that is no different with AI especially when the outcome can be catastrophic like self-driving cars. The ethical issue of who is better able to make the *right* choice in an impossible life or death decision has occupied many for years as well as the question of who is responsible when things go wrong. The driver who handed over the steering wheel to AI or the creator of the car?

From the above, we see that technology is becoming increasingly intelligent and that this is also having an impact on how we as humans deal with it. Frameworks and agreements will therefore become increasingly important in order to always put the wellbeing of people first. In doing so, we must certainly not forget the competences (chapter 4) that still make us unique as human beings.

Fear of the future? Moore's law

Fear of technological innovation is normal. Charlie Chaplin's *Modern Times* from 1936, assumed that we would all be slaves to machines. And now, more than eighty years later, we say the same thing. The fear of the 'machine' taking over our work is still there. The big difference with the factory equipment in those times is that they have become sophisticated self-thinking robots.

The acceleration with respect to innovations is lightning fast and we are only at the beginning. This became very clear to me when Moore's law (ever faster innovations) was associated with a story about mathematics and a chessboard.

How the inventor of the chessboard taught us about ever faster innovation

The story of the chessboard is said to have been first written down in 1256 by Ibn Khalikan. The origin in itself is not relevant, but the story of the inventor of the chessboard and the computing power it describes are. The many sources tell us that an ancient Indian emperor was so impressed by the invention of chess that he let the inventor choose his prize to thank him.

The clever inventor asked for a simple grain of rice for the first square on the chessboard and a doubling for each subsequent square to represent how much rice he wanted as a prize. The emperor initially laughed at the question, but he would later see the error of his ways as soon the number of grains of rice would be about 1.4 trillion cubic tons (more than 2,500 times the annual world production in 2021). With 64 squares on a chessboard, if you double the number of grains on consecutive squares, the sum of the grains on all 64 squares is: 1 + 2 + 4 + 8 + ... and so on. The total number of grains is equal to 18,446,744,073,709,551,615 (eighteen trillion four hundred forty-six trillion, seven hundred forty-four trillion, seventy-three billion, seven hundred nine million, five hundred fifty-one thousand six hundred fifteen). Converted that gives more than 1.4 trillion cubic tons. Not bad as a price for simply inventing a game.

What Moore's law of 1965 predicted is similar to the calculation of the grains of rice on the chessboard. In his prediction, the number of components on an integrated circuit, a chip, would also double each year to an astonishing 65,000 by 1975, which amounts to doubling every 12 months. His prediction would later outline the trajectory of technological innovations in general, and in many ways progress itself. Today, this comparison is still often made, and reflects the ever-faster progress of innovation even though its relevance has diminished in the face of new ways to measure processing power.

Ever-faster innovation is also associated by futurists with the chessboard to describe the impact. Technological innovations would not even have reached the second half of the chessboard today. In other words, the flying start for innovation has yet to make its take-off.

Looking into the future may not be possible, but if we dare to look back at the last few years, we cannot deny the acceleration. For example the rise of, AI, Internet of Things (IoT), Virtual Reality (VR), which will all be covered later in the book.

The symbiosis between man and machine, hype or hope?

Predictions of *singularity*, the point where artificial intelligence surpasses human intelligence and will be able to improve itself, keep many awake. Yet it is still rather a hypothetical vision of the future even though futurists like Ray Kurzweil predict it could be achieved as early as 2045.

Like Kurzweil, Elon Musk has ambitions to link brains and computers with the aim of improving people's cognitive abilities. For example, in 2017 he announced that he wanted to treat serious brain diseases in the short term, with the ultimate goal of human enhancement or transhumanism. Elon Musk took his inspiration for this from the Neural Lace from the Science Fiction novels *The Culture* by Iain M. Banks. This 'neural layer' that Musk envisioned would then ideally place an implant in the human brain via simple surgery to achieve 'symbiosis with artificial intelligence'.

From the chip, a series of tiny wires, each about 20 times thinner than a human hair, fans out into the patient's brain. These wires, which are equipped with 1,024 electrodes, are capable of both monitoring brain activity and, theoretically – as there is not yet much evidence for this – electrically stimulating the brain. All this data is then sent wirelessly via the chip to computers where it can be studied by researchers in order to further develop the innovation. Testing has been done with some success in pigs and monkeys. Neuralink's next target is trials on humans, where use cases are being investigated in quadriplegics, or people who are paralysed in all four limbs. And what is perhaps even more remarkable is that Musk is now working on robots to perform the operations. So it seems that humans are increasingly being replaced by innovations in the world of the future.

It all seems very futuristic, yet according to Professor Andrew Jackson of Newcastle University, experiments with a brain-computer interface (BCI) were already carried out in 2002. What's more, these investigations date back to the 1960s. Elon Musk is not unique either, because Synchron was already given permission by the FDA in 2021 to test its BCI device, Stentrode, on human patients.

When we think of all these innovations, we naturally look for the added value that these implants have for people's wellbeing. Good examples here are certainly IpsiHand, developed by the University of Washington Neurolutions startup. This wearable is designed to help people who have been disabled by a stroke regain control of their arm and hand function by using their minds. Cochlear implants also date back to the 1970s. These stimulate the auditory nerve in people with (near) deafness who could not be helped sufficiently by classic hearing aids.

However, not all implants seem to have an immediate added value for human wellbeing. The Polish start-up Walletmotor, for example, saw opportunities in the fintech sector. The idea of creator and developer Wojciech Paprota is simple: why would you still pay contactless with (a chip in) a bank card, smartphone or smartwatch when you can have a biologically produced, accepted payment implant. That way, you would always have your money – literally – at hand and, unlike other contactless payments, this ultimate payment convenience would not be traceable, hackable or copyable.

In this chapter we saw that the future sometimes seems to have caught up with us. Not embracing the possibilities that intelligent cooperation, or the symbiosis between man and machine, has to offer can have consequences for us as a citizen, organization and society. We are in danger of creating an ever-widening gap between us and others who are already up to speed.

References

Asimov, I (1950) 'Runaround' I, Robot (The Isaac Asimov Collection) Doubleday New York

BBC (2021) Roblox: We paid off our parents' mortgage making video games, www. bbc.co.uk/news/business-56354253 (archived at https://perma.cc/9LY8-38J3)

Brown, A (2021) Beeple NFT Sells For $69.3 Million, Becoming Most-Expensive Ever, www.forbes.com/sites/abrambrown/2021/03/11/beeple-art-sells-for-693-million-becoming-most-expensive-nft-ever/ (archived at https://perma.cc/W8P4-VQJZ)

Business Insider (2022) Elon Musk's Neuralink wants to embed microchips in people's skulls and get robots to perform brain surgery, www.businessinsider.com/neuralink-elon-musk-microchips-brains-ai-2021-2 (archived at https://perma.cc/D9ZF-6MQ2)

Campbell, C (2020) Campbell Academy, Moore's Law and the Chessboard, www. campbellacademy.co.uk/blog/moores-law-and-the-chess-board (archived at https://perma.cc/7NDF-EW64)

Dean, B (2022) Roblox User and Growth Stats 2022, backlinko.com/roblox-users (archived at https://perma.cc/SXR5-AFYT)

Diamandis, P H (2015) Ray Kurzweil's Wildest Prediction: Nanobots Will Plug Our Brains Into the Web by the 2030s, singularityhub.com/2015/10/12/ray-kurzweils-wildest-prediction-nanobots-will-plug-our-brains-into-the-web-by-the-2030s/ (archived at https://perma.cc/69S4-NNUD)

European Commission, White Paper on Artificial Intelligence – A European approach based on excellence and trust, COM (2020) 65 final, 2020

Forbes (2020) A Staggering Number of People Saw Fortnite's Travis Scott 'Astronomical' Event, www.forbes.com/sites/davidthier/2020/04/28/a-staggering-number-of-people-saw-fortnites-travis-scott-astronomical-event/ (archived at https://perma.cc/4EL3-JCQL)

Futurism (2017) Kurzweil Claims That the Singularity Will Happen by 2045 Get ready for humanity 2.0, futurism.com/kurzweil-claims-that-the-singularity-will-happen-by-2045 (archived at https://perma.cc/Q59U-6GA7)

Geerts, T (2021) Homo Digitalis, Leuven: LannooCampus, www.lannoo.be/nl/homo-digitalis (archived at https://perma.cc/UE7R-BL43)

Meta (2021) Introducing Meta: a social technology company, about.fb.com/news/2021/10/facebook-company-is-now-meta/ (archived at https://perma.cc/69LJ-H4CX)

IBM (2022) Deep Blue, www.ibm.com/ibm/history/ibm100/us/en/icons/deepblue/ (archived at https://perma.cc/6N7R-D9RQ)

Reuters (2018) Amazon scraps secret AI recruiting tool that showed bias against women, www.reuters.com/article/us-amazon-com-jobs-automation-insight-idUSKCN1MK08G (archived at https://perma.cc/4T7J-6SUS)

Statista (2022) Milled rice production volume worldwide 2008/09-2021/22, www. statista.com/statistics/271972/world-husked-rice-production-volume-since-2008/ (archived at https://perma.cc/X39H-3MLQ)

The Business Standard (2020) Culture: The sci-fi series that shaped Elon Musk's ideas, www.tbsnews.net/feature/panorama/culture-sci-fi-series-shaped-elon-musks-ideas-133537 (archived at https://perma.cc/422F-VHUX)

The Editors of Encyclopaedia Britannica (2022) *Moore's law: computer science,* www.britannica.com/technology/Moores-law (archived at https://perma.cc/8PRQ-S5D7)

Walletmor (2022) Walletmor, walletmor.com/ (archived at https://perma.cc/UB2M-ZCXP)

Wired (2017) Inside Libratus, the Poker AI That Out-Bluffed the Best Humans, www.wired.com/2017/02/libratus/ (archived at https://perma.cc/5R5Z-YMSX)

World Economic Forum (2020) The Future of Jobs Report 2020, www.weforum.org/reports/the-future-of-jobs-report-2020 (archived at https://perma.cc/7RZ5-J6PL)

02

The value driven organization

The world around us is changing at an unprecedented rate due to the technological innovations I discussed in the Introduction. These have an impact on us as human beings and on the society in which we live. Organizations that want to survive, or even more, want to grow in this rapidly changing world will have to adapt. The days of hierarchical and silo structured companies where the HiPPO (*highest paid person in the organization*) is in charge, are over. Wanting to hold on to old organizational forms like these is predicting a certain end.

When organizations are steered by a HiPPO, there is more than a good chance that they are not yet relying on data, let alone reaping the benefits of it to inform their decision making. These leaders are the absolute epitome of the 93 per cent who don't believe in intelligent collaborations between humans and machines and the possibility of including artificial intelligence in their human capital portfolio.

Just as the hierarchical top-down controlled organization is rapidly disappearing, physical walls are making way for virtual spaces without boundaries in space or functionality. Why should departments like marketing, communication and L&D still be in their own boxes without looking over the wall when they share the same mission and have the same tools to achieve it? Using data and digital channels, they try to convince internal and external stakeholders of the ecosystem to behave or act in a certain way, something that is discussed in the last part of this book. The popular *neuroscience techniques* from marketing have already spread to L&D departments.

When we break down the walls, we quickly see that teams find added value in an environment and culture where collective knowledge is shared. Organizations that focus on the integration between units benefit from a clear long-term vision for digitalization and efficient use of data. Organizations that embrace benefits of collaboration don't just have an internal focus. They understand that they are a cog in a wider ecosystem. Based on shared values, these teams build a healthy organization that in turn helps to build the ecosystem.

For this value-driven organization, the mission is also to increase turnover and profit, but it combines this by respecting its ecosystem and society. Through data-driven interactions, it actively listens, invests and manages the trends that shape today's world. In this value-driven organization, everyone takes responsibility as a citizen, role model and colleague. Together they form a team that promotes a high degree of cooperation at every level of the ecosystem.

In this chapter, we look at trends that have an impact on the learning and value-driven organization. We already see influences that will affect the future of work. In addition, there are also challenges for the learning organization to remain attractive as an employer in times where the labour market shortages make it difficult to find employees with the right skills and competencies.

The future of work

The future of work has inspired many futurists and consultants to write lengthy books and articles. Without quoting them all here, we can see some overlap that I want to give attention to.

Organizations that take a nimble view of the future of work are responding to the world around them, the ecosystem I mentioned earlier. However, they also have an 'internal view' regarding the challenges their employees face at work, at home and in society. To respond to the needs of their employees, they look at health, safety, essential needs and the virtualization of work and life that is an ongoing reality particularly since COVID-19. They aim to humanize the future of work, including through the smart collaboration of humans and machines.

In summary, there are three domains that will influence the Future of Work:

- the workplace and hybrid working environments
- a job for life in the flex-economy
- cross-functional and project teams.

The workplace and hybrid working environments

There is no more 'waiting for better times'. COVID-19 was that Black Swan, the highly improbable, that suddenly pushed homework, distance work and virtual work into the 'new normal', assuming that the before situation of being in the office all together was more than normal. From one day to another, we had to invent the new virtual workplace. Depending on the job, the collaborative workplace was a physical or virtual choice made by virologists and other experts who normally exert their influence far outside the organization's ecosystem. This had extensive consequences for the employees themselves, the way in which knowledge was shared and collaborated. Before the summer of 2020, many of us hoped that we could return soon to 'normal' and catch up over coffee, but that utopia became less and less of a reality the more we experienced the consequences of COVID-19.

People seem more ready to redesign fixed values such as a workplace. Hybrid working went from being a rare and abstract concept to a fixed value for optimizing workplaces. Thanks in part to the rapid adoption of digital innovations, it seemed for a while that many office buildings would remain empty forever.

Whether offices will remain empty and hybrid working will become the new normal is a debate that is still ongoing in many organizations. It is not an either/or situation between office and remote work. Hybrid, in my view, is optimization of the engine of the company, the employees. Like the engine of a hybrid car, it adapts to conditions and constantly searches for optimal performance. It is nimble and flexible instead of thinking in boxes and silos, taking into account the advantages and disadvantages of both.

Research by WEF in the summer of 2021 found that two-thirds of people around the world would like to work flexibly after the COVID-19 pandemic. More so, almost a third are willing to quit their jobs if the boss forces them to go back to the office full-time. Research conducted with employees from 29 countries in different jobs also found that people have begun to cope with working from home better than some had feared.

The study also refuted some gloomy predictions about the effects of remote working. While experts had expected employees to miss their colleagues, be less productive and suffer from burn-out, only a minority of employees supported these views. Just over half of those surveyed missed their colleagues, 64 per cent said they were more productive with a flexible work schedule and only a third complained of burnout. Only one in three said they did not feel involved in work when working remotely.

Very interesting data that I found in other studies were similar. However, as I will repeat many times in this book, data to push someone towards a strategic choice is very easy to find. Every organization has its own culture, with personal preferences of its employees. Work content within an organization is often very diverse and even factors such as the location of the organization (think of traffic) can often have a substantial influence on the result for a certain organization.

HYBRID WORK IS NOT THE SOLUTION IN EVERY SITUATION

Some of the factors that determine whether an employee and the organization will benefit from certain forms of hybrid or flexible work include time savings next to flexibility and family needs, productivity, nature of work and forms of collaboration, culture and cost savings, etc. Mapping these for, and with, the employees helps to make a choice based on the values of the organization and relevant data.

It goes without saying that employees who commute for two hours to their workplace, or travel to other cities or countries for work, suddenly have much more time available when they start working remotely. Not just for work, but especially for family and leisure activities. When used consciously, this has a positive influence on the employee's wellbeing and, in many cases, on the productivity of his or her job because the time gained is used to get more work done.

However, hybrid working is not always a time saver. In particular, we saw that working from home, or hybrid working, resulted in a loss of time for families with young children. Combining family and work was often a stressful challenge to them. In addition, other family needs sometimes come under pressure when working flexibly or from home. For example, some parents lose the right to childcare when they are at home, working or not. Or lose the private benefits of the car that is no longer provided by the employer.

Productivity, another key factor, depends very much on the nature of the work and the various forms of collaboration. Flexible or hybrid working cannot be determined by rules that are the same for everyone. For example, we will see that location and a 'Glocal' strategy is important for multinationals such as Fedex (chapter 6). However, not only the location, but also the nature of the job is an important indicator to determine whether flex or hybrid working is feasible. For example, Alphabet CEO Sundar Pichai announced that all Google employees would be flexible as of April 2022. Some employees would work completely remotely, yet the vast majority of employees would come in around three days a week to work purposefully together. This would include meetings, collaboration with colleagues in other divisions, brainstorming sessions, meeting with customers and suppliers and building community. Yet, he does not see this as a rule either and says in interviews that he believes that as time goes by, people and teams will find the best solutions together.

When we think of the future of work today, we must dare to think of a distant future. We need to develop a vision that does not respond to ad hoc pains that are merely problem-solving. Short-term solutions that are not in line with the corporate culture, nor take into account the wellbeing of employees and their added value, often turn out to be a breeding ground for frustration rather than an answer to renewed forms of collaboration.

When we talk about LearnScapes in this book, we dare to look at a future where added value is not created by the workplace, but by the way we work together. This means that we literally look outside the boxes and silos for added value through technological innovation and intelligent collaborations supported by people and machines.

A job for life in the flexible and gig-economy

A job for life is one of the last things Millennials and Generation Z are looking for. People now want to see their own values and standards reflected in their jobs. In other words, they want to work for an organization with a vision that is compatible with their beliefs and values. Moreover, the job they want to do must fit their personality, interests and family situation. Authenticity is key here. A job is seen by many as an extension of themselves and what they stand for. According to some, young people might therefore be more demanding. Yet you could say that they are more flexible in dealing with the current zeitgeist. Working overtime is not a problem, but there has to be something in return. These young people are looking for a balance between work and private life.

When organizations want to attract young people, they will have to take into account what drives them and how that can also add value to the organization and its ecosystem. As I mention later in this chapter, corporate social responsibility is one of the principles of the value-driven organization. The contribution that these young people make to society will also benefit the internal culture of the organization.

In addition to young people, technological advances through automation, AI and other emerging technologies are impacting the nature of work and employment. There are often fears that the rise of artificial intelligence (AI) will have a negative impact on employment, but GlobalData notes that increasingly rapid digitisation and Industry 4.0 have actually boosted available jobs and will continue to do so. The data and analytics company points out that the number of active AI-related jobs has increased by 165 per cent since July 2020. This impressive increase shows that technology is unlikely to replace jobs, but will transform the world of work into one where humans and machines work together in intelligent symbiosis.

Besides and partly because of this we see that other influences relate to our choice of employer and workplace, or not having an employer in the ever-growing freelance and gig economy. This economy represents a free market system in which organizations and independent workers enter into short-term work arrangements in which they both add value to the growth of themselves and the entire ecosystem. The meteoric rise of this gig economy has been caused in part by the digital age disrupting labour markets and changing the need for skills.

PLATFORMIZATION OF WORK

These new jobs, or gig jobs, are often cognitively more complex, more collaborative, more dependent on technological competence, more mobile and less dependent on geography and are hugely influenced by the platformization of work. This means that in the gig economy, jobs are mostly chosen on an ad-hoc basis via online platforms based on one's own knowledge, competencies, skills and time frame in which the job should take place. These platforms can be divided into four groups, taking into account the distinction between the mode of service provision (physical versus online) and the customer (collective versus individual):

- **Physical delivery of service to individual customer** like Uber where you can book a driver and RingTwice which is an ecosystem in itself where everyone can help each other. This platform is the very first platform that has been approved by the Belgian government to offer an advantageous tax regime to its service providers. The fact that these new platforms are often also the idea of young entrepreneurs who see the similarities in the differences is something I'd like to explain further when we talk about growth-mindset with a case study of Lauren Somers in chapter 4.

- **Online services to individual through platforms.** Platforms like these offer freelancers a marketplace for their services by the hour/day all over the world. These include professions such as web designers and programmers, writers, analysts, legal counsel and of course programmers, but also more and more jobs in sales, marketing, business and finance. These jobs were mostly performed by an organization's own employees but are now outsourced on platforms such as Guru.

- **Online services for collective clients** are complementary to online services for individual clients, which are increasing via platforms.

Here, use is often made of the added value of collective knowledge from a diverse group of specialists. A telling example of this is Clickworker which saw a doubling since 2017 from 1 million users to 2 million with a variety of specializations ranging from writing, translating, researchers and data processors.

- **Physical services to collective clients,** is similar to RingTwice. Yet we see that this market is not only attractive for full-time gig workers but for anyone looking for an extra income. A nice example of this is the German AppJobber, a place-based microtasking platform. Here, customers look for gig workers to carry out small tasks on the spot for a (usually small) fee of 1 to 15 euros. These tasks often include taking pictures of things in certain places, for example displays in stores, product prices or infrastructure such as parking garages.

The fact that the 'platform economy' is growing in segments like the example of AppJobber and RingTwice is due to the rise of the sharing economy and is largely driven by certain demographic groups: the emerging middle class, women and the elderly. In Europe, an estimated 11 per cent of the adult population has already used online platforms to provide some sort of employment services.

GIG ECONOMY PER SECTOR AND IMPACT ON LEARNING ECONOMY

That the gig economy will make no small contribution to the future of work can be seen from the figures that have been growing exponentially worldwide in recent years. According to a study by Mastercard in 2019, the total global gig economy will reach 347 billion dollars by 2021. Within this growth we find, without surprise, that the majority of this contribution is made in transportation-based services (TRNS) such as Uber and asset-sharing platforms (ASSET) such as Air-bnb. Both amount to US $115.8 billion and US $68.1 billion respectively or 57.8 per cent and 30.3 per cent of the total. A much smaller segment is found in the sector of Handmade Goods, Household and Miscellaneous (HGHM) now still account for US $16.7 billion or 8.2 per cent.

For now, the smallest segment is that of professional services (PRFS), accounting for US $7.7 billion or 3.8 per cent of the total. It should come as no surprise that this latter segment still has a lot of growth potential due to the digital age and the need for new skills. The freelance and gig economy in relation to professional service providers is gaining momentum, with a compound annual growth rate of no less than 17.4 per cent by 2023. This group in the knowledge-intensive industries and creative professions would also be the largest and fastest growing segment in the overall freelance economy, according to McKinsey.

This group also offers the most opportunities for learning ecosystems as we will see in part 4 as they are used to working very flexibly on different platforms and systems. Organizations that want to reap the benefits will therefore open up their systems from what I call in chapter 8, data repositories to LearnScapes that use AI and expert location to provide each project with the right knowledge and competences.

MOTIVATION AND OPPORTUNITIES FOR GIG AND FLEX WORKERS

This fast-growing group seeking self-development also recognizes that there are many personal, social and economic anxieties without the cover and support of a traditional employer. Yet, for them, independence and the benefits are more decisive than the worries of unpredictable schedules and finances.

People who are not in permanent employment find that they have accumulated more courage and live a richer life than their colleagues in the corporate world. Independent of managers and corporate norms, freelancers can choose assignments that make the most of their talents and reflect their true interests. They feel ownership over what they produce and over their entire professional life, which is reflected in their personal wellbeing.

The price of this freedom, however, is an insecurity that does not seem to disappear over time. Even the most successful, established freelance professionals still worry about money and reputation and sometimes feel that their identity is at stake. As a writer, of course, I can empathize with that. After all, you become your job and the day you can no longer produce new material, you lose income. For many freelancers and gig workers, therefore, discipline is the competency that sets them apart from those who fail. Yet this sometimes seems like a paradox in the life of a freelancer. On the one hand, they want to maintain their independence because that gives them peace of mind, but on the other hand, they also need the restlessness that comes with it. It is this restlessness that drives them to keep searching for what gives them an edge over others.

Another motivation of freelancers that I recognize is that they can work where and when they want. Moreover, they feel that they are always doing something that has a positive impact on the ecosystem we are part of. According to a survey by Harvard Business Review (HBR), for the vast majority of respondents, purpose is one of the most important motives for taking on a project. This purpose would be the bridge between their personal interests and motivations and purpose for society.

This bridge between personal interests and motivations and the fulfilment of a need in the world, goes hand in hand with discipline and the restlessness that also drives them to embrace lifelong learning. And that is an enormous added value for the organizations that employ temporary workers. These employees always bring new knowledge for the next assignment. Therefore, gig workers and freelancers provide cross-fertilization that connects different organizations in the larger ecosystem.

I spoke with Marc Rummens who, as a human capital expert, has over 30 years of experience with project workers. He told me about his Golden Triangle and ambition to make project staffing more professional and enjoyable with a view to corporate social responsibility.

CASE STUDY

The golden triangle, added value from knowledge sharing

Marc Rummens, CEO Human Capital Group

The basis of the golden triangle is value driven commitment and knowledge exchange between clients and experts. I am convinced that long-term partnerships are necessary to achieve sustainable and innovative technological projects. Shared values, respect, trust and accountability are the basis. Technical study and project staffing agencies have years of relevant expertise. It is through continuous improvement, however, that experts achieve knowledge leadership. This knowledge exchange is facilitated by the agency, its employees and its clients. This golden triangle forms the basis for a challenging career and provides clients with relevant and accurate knowledge that is essential for innovative projects. In my opinion, it is no longer sufficient to complete training courses in order to offer lifelong excellence. Learning should be embedded in our daily actions and takes place in a hybrid way, independent of where, when and with whom. It is a shared responsibility that can be facilitated by the academy of study and project staffing agency

Remaining an expert requires commitment and motivation. That means being the owner of your own development, but also actively looking for learning opportunities, creating learning habits, expanding your network and sharing knowledge. Digitalization already offers us the possibility to have knowledge at our disposal whenever we need it in order to excel in our job. But without employee involvement, many formal and informal learning moments are lost over time. That's why I think we need to build an ecosystem from employee and customer engagement. To me, this is the golden triangle of learning.

This is the time to envision new ambitions and expectations for future work. From this vision, strategic initiatives can then be launched that seek opportunities for what we can achieve using technology to enhance rather than replace human capabilities.

Cross-functional and project teams

The days when colleagues only interacted within the walls of their silos are long gone. Teams today have become as virtual as the inter- actions in the metaverse. Working relationships are in this context determined by the projects and the results that must be achieved together.

An example of this is discussed by General Stanley McChrystal in his book *Teams of Teams* from his experience as a leader in war situations and the benefits of temporary teams in an increasingly complex world. This approach involves the flexible creation of cross-functional teams for specific assignments based on the competencies and skills needed.

Where previously employees often worked from silos in finance, operations, IT, marketing and HR, we see that the walls have been flattened and at the start of new projects everyone is involved at the same time. An approach based on stakeholder involvement that will show its added value in the last part of this book.

When we scale up this cross-functional approach to the ecosystem, this results in very flexible collaborations beyond the walls of our own organization. The added value of technology ensures better cooperation and optimisation of the project.

LEADERSHIP IN CROSS-FUNCTIONAL TEAMS

Another important added value for organizations that use flexible teams is the vision of leadership. For them, it is no longer about leading or micro-managing. They create a climate of trust and cooperation, where the strength of the leader lies in the freedom from threats that they can influence. In this project-based approach, leadership becomes a changing role that everyone takes on out of commitment to the overall vision and strategy that is jointly formulated.

For these cross-functional teams, it is no longer relevant to be an employee of the organization when it comes to leading a particular project. No hierarchical organizations, but value-driven network organizations that organically adapt to the circumstances and opportunities that arise. This approach is not new for some departments, such as IT and HR, which have long relied on the temporary added value of experts.

An example of this is given at the beginning of chapter 5 where Santosh Kher CHRO of Fedex MEA and the Indian continent explains how they use local experts who understand the culture and the way of working in their regional approach. When they roll out new projects, they are not managed centrally but supported by dotted lines to the local departments. When setting up new projects, the local business needs, specific local culture, infrastructure and all other variables that can affect the success of the project are taken into account, but with the overall value and vision of Fedex. The Fedex approach to transcending silo thinking also extends to the learning organization and the roll-out of learning strategies, as will be discussed in chapter 5.

From this, we see that the impact of the future at work is already noticeable in cooperation within an organization. However, there is still much room for improvement and this will also be necessary when the demand for specific project-related knowledge increases in an increasingly complex world. Organizations that are already adapting with regard to technology and leadership will take the lead in the learning ecosystem.

Employer branding

General Stanley McChrystal described the future of work from his experiences in the Gulf War. However, the comparison with war also applies when we talk about finding talent in an increasingly complex and competitive world. Under pressure from new innovations, finding employees with the right competencies and skills is becoming a war for talent between organizations looking for the same profiles.

Today, as a result of this fierce *war for talent*, another concept has gained importance: *employer branding*. This concept describes the reputation of an organization as a place to work. It starts from the value proposition for employees, as opposed to the more general reputation of the company brand expressed and a value proposition for customers. Just as the value proposition and the brand of the company determine commercial success in the goods and services market, the employer brand determines the attractiveness of the organization in the job market. The stronger the employer branding specialists can put this brand in the spotlight as a great place to work, the more successful the organization will be in the *war for talent*.

Employer branding brings together techniques from Marketing and HR in a cross-functional approach first described by Simon Barrow and Tim Ambler in 1996 in *Journal of Brand Management*. Yet, we see that many organizations are not yet taking full advantage of this cross-silo collaboration for internal and external branding. However, HR can learn a lot from marketing with regard to the use of data, technology, neuroscience and the psychology of persuasion. A view I also share with Dr Anna Tarabasz who in chapter 14 discusses the benefits of collaboration for projects related to building LearnScapes. When we dare to look outside the known box, we will see that both departments have more in common than we would suspect without a holistic view of both.

Employer branding is often even more relevant for younger employees such as Generation-Z and Millennials who are not looking for a job for life. As described earlier, they look for employers and/or projects that reflect their own norms and values.

In this new reality, the job seeker increasingly takes the initiative as traditional job announcements often fail to appeal to them. No empty words, but a reputation that speaks for itself from all channels available to the organization. If they do not all convey the same authentic message, the job announcement may seem attractive, but it will often not be very successful. Even more so, we see that those organizations that promote a value-driven mission with a focus on future employment expectations often do not even have to post job announcements and candidates apply spontaneously. In addition, organizations that have a good reputation as an employer often do not have to convince candidates with high salaries.

A conscious approach to employer branding from a cross-functional collaboration therefore has positive consequences that can even significantly reduce recruitment costs. Yet we see even more advantages when an organization can also propagate its distinctive learning culture. This propagation attracts candidates who have a positive attitude towards learning and knowledge sharing.

Employee engagement as a driver of learning

How frustrating would it be if the efforts for employer branding from the collaboration between marketing and HR were successful, but on the other hand more people leave the organization.

For many organizations, especially the smaller ones, staff turnover is a major problem. If companies cannot meet basic staffing needs, this often has serious consequences such as delays in the delivery of products or services to customers. Add to this that the cost of finding and hiring new employees and we understand that turnover has a financial impact. However, it is not only the financial impact that causes concern. A direct consequence of colleagues leaving also manifests itself within the team and undermines company morale. That employee retention is therefore high on the agenda of company managers should come as no surprise, and rightly so.

That COVID-19 would also be partly responsible for this big resignation or drop in employee engagement is often assumed, yet the figures from Gallup that were recorded one year after the lockdowns indicate that the impact is almost negligible, moreover, 36 per cent is the highest engagement figure that Gallup has published since they started measuring in 2000. But what do all these figures mean and, above all, what should we look for in our own employees?

When we say that 36 per cent are truly engaged, it means that they are excited by their contribution to the organization and feel that their efforts are making a difference. In contrast, 51 per cent of employees who are not engaged are not doing their job badly or harming the organization, they are just not happy. This group is therefore a potential risk of leaving the organization, yet they are not what we should be most concerned about. Research just after the crisis would show that 13 per cent of employees are actively disengaged. They feel miserable at work and spread negativity among their colleagues. Remarkably, however, that 13 per cent is not actively disengaged. The question that therefore arises is on which group do we focus and where do our efforts get the most return, both in terms of numbers with regard to staff turnover and the impact on other employees.

Focus of employee engagement initiatives   Employee engagement initiatives seem to be a hot topic thereby creating new positions within organizations such as employee engagement officer, chief of wellbeing or chief of happiness officer. However, in contrast to the creativity with which the positions are named, many initiatives often turn out to be unsuccessful. The emphasis of these initiatives often lies on a general approach that reaches precisely those target groups who are already involved.

When I talk about employee engagement, I try to look holistically and with the help of innovation and based on data, at possible risks of employees who are at risk of being less engaged or actively not engaged anymore.

From the focus of this book I want to highlight a stimulus for engagement that is often overlooked. Sharing knowledge with employees and relevant information about the organization's vision, strategy and goals so that employees know why they are doing something, and especially how their actions contribute to the organization's results. A recent study shows, for example, that 85 per cent of employees say they are more engaged when they regularly receive this relevant information. Yet, it is remarkable that 74 per cent of employees feel they miss out on company information and news. Furthermore, only 21 per cent of internal communicators believe that employees have a good understanding of why senior leaders make the decisions they do. A study that is certainly relevant to those organizations I call broadcasters of news in chapter 8.

To look at it from another perspective: managers think their messages are understood and employees assume they understand them, but the gap is huge. If we can find opportunities for a quick win project in part 5 of this book, this is certainly an aspect that can be looked at.

Some of the things that support knowledge and information sharing:

- Build habits that support continuous improvement through resilience and knowledge sharing.
- Provide informative communication channels to avoid uncertainty.
- Measure relevant data related to engagement and knowledge sharing.

Internal communication is the key to increased employee engagement and business growth. Simply saying that something must be done because the HiPPO says so, does not work anymore. By explaining to someone why it is important to do something completely different, because it will benefit the individual and therefore the organization. The resistance to do it differently will decrease and there will be a greater follow-through.

Tools such as those from Gallup or Great Place to Work can support this as can many other global startups that offer simple assessments for measuring engagement. If selected properly, these tools will also provide insight into the underlying causes of lower engagement.

Measuring relevant employee engagement data

Finally, employee engagement is all about measurement and yet, according to Gartner, only 16 per cent of organizations surveyed would use technology to measure employee engagement. However, this does not have to be expensive tools from vendors whose surveys are also often published. In recent years, not only are EdTech tools becoming more popular to support learning, but more and more HRTech startups are going far beyond monitoring employees from a control perspective. These startups not only want to collect data, but also get a better understanding of the employee experience. In doing so, they are trying to go a step further and not only look at internal employees, but also the added value of temporary and flex workers who are increasingly part of the future of work.

Measuring the engagement of all employees from a holistic perspective has other benefits. Even more than internal co-workers, gig workers are stakeholders who are part of the larger ecosystem. Their high engagement is a driving force for the organization. They are brand advocates who enhance the attractiveness of the organization as employer branding and also the brand of the organization in the entire ecosystem.

Employee engagement and the value driven organization are closely intertwined, but they are also essential to the learning ecosystem. Throughout this book we will see examples of employee engagement driving craftsmanship (chapter 4), social learning networks (chapter 10) and learning culture (chapter 14).

Corporate social responsibility

Value-driven organizations that present themselves as attractive employers must also live up to their branding. They therefore pay more and more attention to CSR or corporate social responsibility. CSR is a form of self-regulation by companies aimed at contributing to social objectives of a philanthropic, activist or charitable nature. In recent years, however, we have seen that this self-regulatory aspect in particular is increasingly shifting from often individual and voluntary projects to almost compulsory arrangements at regional, national and international level that support ethical business strategy.

Unfortunately, in many organizations CSR is still mainly window dressing that does not connect with employees, the customers or even by extension the ecosystem. For example, we see business leaders choosing to support a local sports club with money. This can be a good initiative in itself. However, if this is not done on the basis of a well thought-out strategy, it can turn against the organization's attractiveness as an employer. I am not a real football fan, yet I can imagine that some fans would go so far as to refuse to work for an organization that says it will support the rival sports club of their team.

Corporate social responsibility or value-driven entrepreneurship must fit within the organization's strategic objective. Everyone, including the executive team, must contribute to this, something which Tariq Chauhan endorses.

Tariq Chauhan, CEO of EFS Facilities Services, proves that executives must set a good example. For more than 20 years, EFS has been providing integrated facilities services in 21 key countries of the Middle East, Africa, South Asia and Turkey. With an equally international population of mostly blue-collar workers, value-driven business is a priority that supports rapid growth. These values: honesty, ethics, teamwork, transparency, trust, integrity, mutual respect, corporate ownership, responsibility are not isolated words. It is deserved that Tariq and EFS won many awards for their practices and authentic leadership, but it shows even more in the results.

When I was invited by Tariq to speak about the value-driven learning organizations, it struck me how much similarity EFS has with the value-driven LearnScapes I have in mind for this book. His ideas on engaged leadership, employee engagement, purpose-driven organizations, employer branding and CSR all came together in his talk with a striking focus on self-actualization.

CASE STUDY
The need for self-actualization and 'Abhaar' to serve the immediate and long-term interest and aspirations of the migrant workers

Tariq Chauhan, Group CEO of EFS Facilities Services Group

A right leadership role demands to cement the vision based on strong values that are co-shared and owned mutually by all. These values, in fact, bind the team with a common resolve to succeed and lead their teams and their colleagues.

From my perspective, self-good in a high values organization will automatically promote the larger good of the company. Therefore, employee wellbeing is a conventional approach to building outstanding organizational sustainability. However, suppose it is focused on self-development and overall wellbeing from all aspects of self-actualization such as health, family, happiness, financial security and professional development. In that case, this brings a quantum leap in employee engagement.

LEADERSHIP ESSENTIALS
Altruism for business leaders and companies is no more just an attribute, but a requirement to keep employees fully engaged and help the organization to realize its wider goals. Conventional employee engagement methods are no longer sufficient to maintain a healthy connection between employees and the organization.

It is equally essential that organizational values concerning leadership – especially those that focus on the inclusivity element – are retained while the company is in a transformative mode. The communication strategy from the board has to be emphatic to ensure that all policies are well articulated across all levels.

A company must build an effective communication strategy based on inclusivity and not just media showcasing. It must not focus only on an external audience to support the brand but cater to its internal channels to boost employee engagement.

SELF-ACTUALIZATION GOALS AND ENGAGEMENT INITIATIVES FOR BLUE-COLLAR WORKERS

Initiatives on employee engagement in context for organizations with a sizeable blue-collar population is a pressing need. To gain their trust is of utmost importance as their self-actualization goals are quite different and complex from white-collar staff.

Their concerns about living conditions, family connectivity, and finances are paramount to building an apt engagement strategy. Encouraging health and wellbeing awareness supporting financial planning and discipline among the less privileged employees are initiatives that can significantly influence employees' engagement and inspiration.

Many blue-collar workers that come to this region from across the world have very low self-actualization levels. To gain their confidence, leaders need to devise strategies that are focused on elevating their holistic needs. Building employee trust and instilling faith in the organization was the principal task that we addressed. As a leadership team, we not only mapped their needs and their perspective but also sought to understand the key issues that were focal to their interests.

It is often specific sensitivities that matter. Their personal living conditions and their day-to-day upkeep needs to be of an appropriately comfortable level, along with the provision of good facilities and amenities. For instance, telephone and WIFI, family demands and finance management are essential factors. This drives their work engagement to higher levels. There needs to be an internal communication strategy in place so that workers can interact with their site leadership and apply for training and development opportunities. These all play a critical role in bridging the gap to gain trust.

On the global stage, the onset of COVID-19 added to the imbalance in their socio-economic structure wherein the migrant workers witnessed life-altering challenges such as job losses, salary cuts, repatriation on very short notices, no employment opportunities in their own home countries, deprivation of basic needs such as fair living standards, timely wages and access to public health infrastructure.

ABHAAR INITIATIVE FOR MIGRANT WORKERS

As a 'people's first' organization across the MEASA region (Middle East, Africa South Asia), EFS Group identified the need for self-actualization concerning the welfare of these workers in the larger society.

In response, the leadership took the initiative to create programs that will serve the immediate and long-term interests and aspirations of the migrant workers. To this end, EFS conducted surveys across the group's regional operations to identify and encourage migrant workers to submit ideas for their incubation projects for their future.

Abhaar is one of those CSR initiatives. It has its main base in India and plans to expand its footprint in the near future to the communities in Nepal, Pakistan, Bangladesh, Sri Lanka, the Philippines and countries in Africa. This initiative understands the concerns and underpinning challenges of the unskilled and semi-skilled migrant workforce. The initiative stands firmly to support their cause for sustainable living with economic and social impact for them, their families, and society.

As EFS leadership, we believe in helping these migrant workers by improving their financial security and self-development. By educating, retraining and informing them about their options to build a better life for themselves and their families.

The above case demonstrates that leadership goes hand in hand with engaged employees in the future of work. Also for blue-collar employees who, as migrants far from home, are temporarily working on a better future for themselves, but even more for their families and the society they temporarily left behind. For them, too, we see that skills alone are not important, but that competencies (chapter 5) such as entrepreneurship can make the difference in a learning society.

References

Forbes (2022) The Future Of Work Is Flexible: Google will transition to hybrid work by April 4, www.forbes.com/sites/jackkelly/2022/03/03/the-future-of-work-for-google-is-hybrid-as-the-company-tells-its-workers-to-return-to-the-office-by-april-4/ (archived at https://perma.cc/2VU3-Q2JV)

Global Data (2021) AI-related jobs have increased by 165% since July 2020 due to rapid rise of digitization, says GlobalData, www.globaldata.com/ai-related-jobs-increased-165-since-july-2020-due-rapid-rise-digitization-says-globaldata/ (archived at https://perma.cc/Q2CB-9MWR)

Harvard Business Review (2018) Thriving in the Gig Economy, hbr.org/2018/03/thriving-in-the-gig-economy (archived at https://perma.cc/933F-RDT8)

Manyika, J et al (2016) Independent work: Choice, necessity, and the gig economy, www.mckinsey.com/featured-insights/employment-and-growth/independent-work-choice-necessity-and-the-gig-economy (archived at https://perma.cc/63DJ-PRL4)

Mastercard and Kaiser Associates (2019) The Global Gig Economy: Capitalizing on a ~$500B Opportunity, newsroom.mastercard.com/wp-content/uploads/2019/05/Gig-Economy-White-Paper-May-2019.pdf (archived at https://perma.cc/37QG-ZXC7)

McChrystal, S (2015) *Team of Teams. New rules of engagement for a complex world,* Penguin Books, New York

Taleb, N N (2010) *The Black Swan: The impact of the highly improbable.* 2nd edn. Penguin Books, New York

World Economic Forum (2021) Home or office? Survey shows opinions about work after COVID-19, www.weforum.org/agenda/2021/07/back-to-office-or-work-from-home-survey/ (archived at https://perma.cc/UTG7-25VT)

03

The data driven organization

We have been hearing for years that data is the new gold. If that is so, then I wonder why so few organizations are making use of this precious resource. As it turns out, data is massively stored in organizations and heavily guarded by the guardians of this golden pot. Not just in the data repository companies, which I will describe further in the Learning Maturity Model, chapter 7, of organizations, but everywhere. Yes, even you reading this now are probably a hoarder when it comes to storing data and never using it again. We store business and private data en masse for when it might be relevant. The question is when is data relevant, and more importantly, can we use all the data we store, however relevant, from an ethical standpoint?

In addition to internal data, we see that a lot of data from outside our own systems including social media is also relevant to the learning organization, both for recruitment on LinkedIn as well as for creating personas for brand advocates. In fact, we now see organizations scanning social media data to gauge the mood among their employees. Even more than internal data that we generate ourselves, this social data is often not integrated into the business analyses on which decisions for growth are based.

In this chapter, we look at the organization from a data-driven approach. For this, we look at the importance of usable and relevant data as well as the impact on performance measurement. In addition, as with AI, we will look at the ethical issues that also arise from the use of different forms of data and their deployment.

The importance of humanizing data

A learning organization or LearnScape grows from learning from the symbiose of humans and technology, and of course, the data it generates. If it's not used or if it's used wrongly, this data is considered mostly waste. As described in chapter 8 we can avoid this by introducing lean learning development.

The question I am often asked is which data is relevant for a learning organization, but these are questions to which no one, least of all I, can or wants to give an unequivocal answer. If you do get a textbook answer, then I would be especially careful to adjust your business operations accordingly. Factors that determine which data are relevant are as diverse as the data itself that we want to measure.

Another important comment I would like to make about organizations or data analysts who collect all the data, store it and present it in often ingenious graphs and tables, is that data must not only be relevant but also understandable. The latter, sometimes called the humanization of data, aims to process information in such a way that even non-technical stakeholders around the table can derive clear and useful insights from Big Data analyses, with the aim of using them intelligently as the basis for decision-making, business insights and strategies for a nimble future. This also means a new skill set is expected of data analysts to hone their craft. They need to become experts in performing independent analyses that they translate into stories that are understandable. In doing so, they become the 'translators' who succeed in bridging the gap between machines and humans. Looking ahead to what I further describe as the competences for the future, they will in fact become data artists with a Master's degree in curiosity, openness, positivity and consilience, among others.

When I take you through the steps a learning organization takes to create a LearnScape in part 4, relevant, understandable and measurable data will be an important part of determining whether the project is contributing to the expectations it was set up for.

Not surprisingly, the method I use and recommend is one of continuous improvement that starts with due diligence and brings all stakeholders around the table. This means data analysts, involved leaders and stakeholders of the project, and if necessary translators who can translate the data and innovation into clear and usable actions. In addition, someone with knowledge of international and local privacy regulations can't be missing in multinational organizations.

Data analytics for people-driven organizations

As mentioned, HR teams are sitting on a wealth of data that is often unused. And, if it is used at all, it is often cast from formulas of a previous century into charts and tables that do not integrate with other systems for future-oriented strategies.

The fact that I make fairly harsh statements about working methods and data collection by HR teams is partly due to working methods that are no longer attuned to a world in constant and rapid change. Expectations of today's employees and flexible/gig employees, are different than a few years ago. Where in the past cost of hiring, keeping employees involved and keeping up with new skills was less relevant, we see that in the current economic climate and the 'war for talent' this is becoming more and more important.

Taking the future of work into account, HR must also dare to throw old systems overboard. It's more important than ever to place previously important data in a current context. I've outlined a few of these in the following list:

1 **Cost per hire** gives us insight into how much it costs an organization to hire one person. However, I notice that in many organizations no analysis is made of the benefits of not having staff. Freelance workers often don't even enter the HR budgets but are assigned to project costs.

2 **Employee turnover** is still often seen as a negative factor and is used to understand whether retention strategies are working, which is certainly important from a recruitment cost perspective. However, intelligent analyses could take into account the added value of project-based and therefore temporary employees and that a high turnover of personnel can oxygenate certain projects.

This in turn can be related to reduced training costs when we deploy experts on temporary projects.

3 **Satisfaction and/or involvement** at work has received a lot of attention since the COVID-19 pandemic turned the world upside down. Rightly so, because the wellbeing of many employees came under enormous pressure. Still, measurements were often made with questionnaires from another era that are often only used once a year. Snapshots that serve to adjust a strategy which in itself takes a lot of time are also actions that often lag behind the facts.

4 **Absence of employees** is still one of the key metrics to measure wellbeing or employee engagement, among others. However, I think that in times when working from home has become mandatory in many countries and sectors, this concept needs a whole new approach. Should we measure when someone is productive rather than absent? Are time clocks still of this era or do we need to assign new metrics for many sectors and certainly knowledge workers?

5 **Productivity,** building on the previous point, is the challenge many organizations struggle with. Understandably, because while every unit of production can be measured for a worker, measuring the productivity of an executive is quite difficult, especially when meetings and emails are considered unproductive as a tech start-up tried to make me believe they could measure productivity with complex algorithms. Apparently, they hadn't understood that a manager's time can often consist mainly of meetings. Capturing relevant data and linking it to individual KPIs is the challenge, especially if you only work with spreadsheets and have more than a handful of employees.

CALCULATING THE RETURN ON INVESTMENT OF HUMAN CAPITAL IS NOT OF THESE TIMES

I want to make it clear that we need to think out-of-the-box and that collaboration with other teams is more relevant than ever. Therefore, I hesitated whether I would talk about the ROI of human capital.

However, after many conversations with HR managers, I'm extremely surprised that this has survived the evolution of the profession. Simply put, it is a measure used to compare the value of the employee to the expenditure.

$$\text{Human Capital ROI} = (\text{Revenue} - \text{Operating Expenses} - \text{Employee Benefits}) / \text{Employee Benefits}$$

This, in turn, is used to see how much each investment in people yields. These investments include salaries, health insurance premiums, contributions to pension schemes and training. In this approach, it is relevant to 'invest' as little as possible in people. I hope it does not surprise only me that many renowned consultants and HR leaders still include ROI as one of the key metrics in their analyses.

The challenge for the future will therefore be for many organizations to collect data across the silos that supports decisions with a focus on employee wellbeing. To optimize processes related to employees, to provide insights related to all employees (internal and external to the organization) and thus deliver value to the organization from a human capital perspective.

Collecting data and linking it to a strategy that translates into Key Performance Indicators is a huge challenge for many organizations. However, also here, a learning organization can benefit from intelligent technology. After talking to many experts in the field, I came into contact with the Singapore-based company Entomo, which introduced me to one of their customers, the largest conglomerate groups in Indonesia, Sinar Mas. The challenge for Sinar Mas was to redefine their KPI strategy to engage and retain the right talent, while making their performance management process more transparent, action-oriented, and accountable.

CASE STUDY
Reinventing KPIs for the future of work

Swasono Satyo, Chief Human Resources Officer, Sinar Mas

Like many other companies, Sinar Mas realized that its system for evaluating the performance of employees – and then training them, promoting them, and paying them accordingly – was increasingly out of step with its objectives.

It searched for something nimbler, real-time, and more individualized – something squarely focused on fueling performance in the future rather than assessing it in the past.

One of the major challenges that Sinar Mas was facing with its performance management was the inability to reward its talent right, and hence, impacting the overall motivation of the top performers. This in turn translated into three-pronged challenges:

1 Unstructured KPIs

2 Readiness to adopt KPI in a clear and transparent manner

3 Inability to measure right performance due to unstructured KPIs.

The journey to building the right performance management strategy for the future of work started by building effective knowledge around KPIs. At Sinar Mas, each Performance Management Officer (PMO) represents different functions and departments. They selected specific training for each department's PMO on setting up and structuring KPIs. During the process, the team also realized that they cannot have a one-size-fits all approach for KPIs, and hence, it took about one month to have company-wide KPIs, which were clear, transparent, and measurable.

The next phase was to introduce the software to track KPIs. And hence the immediate step was to introduce the team to how to use the software and its application. The software and application were also used for engagement between supervisor and employee to evaluate their performance. Entomo had also integrated additional design features called 'coach-in' for supervisors to provide continuous feedback. Once these steps were completed, Entomo introduced the team to the software and delivered training on how to use the software and application.

HOW TECHNOLOGY HAS A GREAT ROLE TO PLAY IN SHAPING KPIS FOR THE NEXT-GENERATION OF WORK

Sinar Mas required a system that was dynamic enough to be able to handle uncertain performance scenarios and at the same time reflect and drive towards the overall strategic growth of the company. The performance management technology by Entomo offered the company a dynamic system that can handle its comprehensive workflow system and mechanism of setting KPIs, conducting their annual reviews, and also 360 feedback.

They developed several dashboards for Sinar Mas' internal use that helps them in forecasting and analysing the data which is being monitored by Sinar Mas' change management team. The dashboards not only allow tracking and measuring the performance at the individual level but also at business unit level. It allowed key business stakeholders to monitor the performance of different entities and helped them to make quick and fast decisions based on the analysis of the data. Furthermore, they are exploring additional capabilities, such as embedding project or program management tools within the system along with other features like gamification.

The platform allows for performing basic activities like task management, assigning tasks between colleagues, tracking the additional task performed beyond the scope of work, etc. This enables measuring or tracking of the work and productivity within the system which would have earlier been done by emails sent.

The system not only helps the manager by simplifying the overall process of tracking employees' goals easier but also empowers employees and managers to keep track of the performance in real-time and hence, make the performance reviews and bonus conversation fair and transparent.

HOW SINAR MAS MOVED THE PERFORMANCE NEEDLE IN THE RIGHT DIRECTION
Millennials constitute the majority of the workforce today and they strive for instant gratification and feedback. Hence, Sinar Mas added the gamification feature where people can earn points and rewards as an acknowledgment of the great work they did. We added another feature that offered employees the opportunity to receive instant and comprehensive feedback from the people they work with.

Some of the key achievements observed from the Sinar Mas performance management transformation was the ability to reward the right person for the right performance – the company was able to separate the social performer, the top performer, and the nonperformer. Further, they could relate that directly with the compensation and benefits within the company.

Through the successful implementation of IMPAC, a platform-based and mobile performance management system from Entomo, Sinar Mas shifted to a meritocracy-based and nimble organization. The system, along with a core team of performance management change agents, facilitated the alignment of business objectives throughout our organization and more importantly, engaged our people toward meeting the objectives through a series of meaningful interventions that are built into the process.

We achieved our goals with a new system which is based on the one-size-fits-all constant learning, all underpinned by a new way of collecting reliable performance data.

The example of Sinar Mas shows that it bridges the gap between business objectives, performance management and learning. One of the challenges of organizations that want to focus on hyper-responsiveness in a world that is changing ever faster.

The future of learning analytics

From the above, we see that by measuring the relevant data we have valuable information on which to base performance management. This will also be one of the main drivers for selecting technology in part 4. However, the relevance of data is often the biggest challenge. We also see that due to the very rapid rise of learning-supporting technologies (EdTech) learning measurability and analytics is developing very fast. Where we used to have Net Promoter Scores as the only reference, we can now go very far.

For example, we see that today startups like AttentivU use eye tracking. This device, in the form of a pair of glasses, measures both brain activity (electroencephalography – EEG) and eye movements (electrooculography – EOG) to measure various cognitive processes in real time, including cognitive load, fatigue, engagement and focus. These multimodal learning analytics can then be used for passive or active interventions. Useful perhaps for the easily distracted dreamers among us, as gentle audio or haptic feedback literally keeps us on our toes. This ability to detect cognitive overload therefore seems very interesting when thinking about solutions that support learning in the workplace in order to reduce risks in the workplace and thus increase productivity.

Other examples focus on the added value of automated online dialogue analysis. These could support the training of communication skills or be used for recruitment purposes. However, many of these innovations raise the question of whether they support wellbeing and are ethically correct. Something AttentivU also took into account because, unlike others, they can work standalone, without a network, to ensure the privacy of the data collected.

Returning to NPS scores, I would not go so far as to say they are not useful. On the contrary, if used intelligently, they certainly add value. An interesting case study on the good use of NPS could have added value here – after all, sometimes we learn more from when things are not going well. The fact that I found no-one willing to share a case study about a less than ideal experience should come as no surprise. Therefore, as I will do more often, I tell a story with respect for the teams involved.

CASE STUDY
A missed opportunity with NPS

A few years ago (before the pandemic broke out) I attended an HR conference for executives. The managing director on stage proudly announced that they had recently introduced the 'new way of working'. The example he gave related, among other things, to call centres and their employees.

Not only were the offices equipped with ergonomic furniture and a colour expert was hired to create an environment that supports wellbeing, working hours were also flexibly adapted to the preferences of the employees themselves. Employee engagement was of paramount importance to this organization.

The MD proudly told us that they were keeping Net Promoter Scores (NPS) for every call and that since the introduction of the new way of working, the NPS had risen for everyone. However, for a learning organization (which he claimed to be building) it seemed to me that he missed the most important relevance of that data. For example, only a general projection was made at individual and team level. Rising and falling of the score was the only thing that was measured and further analysis was not seen to be needed. Data that indicated whether a service agent scored better depending on the time of a customer contact (morning or evening), with which demographics of customers they achieved better results (age, gender, …) or on which questions and topics they scored best, were relevant data that could be measured. Yet, these data were not used to adjust the hours or to initiate coaching and learning programmes. I found it a missed opportunity.

I cannot repeat enough that the measurement of data should primarily support the employee to grow. From there, the organization and the ecosystem can also grow. Whether this is measured using innovative technology or NPS is therefore less relevant.

The ethical use of data and stakeholder involvement

I mentioned it earlier, and this book often brings up ethics. Data and ethics is therefore one of the biggest challenges today that not only organizations but also society is struggling with.

Let's return to the example of AttentivU. This startup already took into account privacy about the data they collect. However, they are the exception rather than the norm. As described earlier, there are currently no international rules regarding data and privacy of employees. There are therefore a growing number of organizations that have large amounts of data about which they are not transparent at all. The question then arises as to what clear, transparent standards should be applied to the way they use that data.

If international governments and corporate governance rules don't have an answer to this, then I certainly don't dare. Still, I would like to try to persuade you to enter into the debate, even if only in your own organization, to see what opportunities and pitfalls learning data has for the wellbeing of your people.

CASE STUDY

The ethical debate that is not conducted on the same basis for all employees

At this innovative player in the manufacturing industry, highly trained technical staff and engineers operate highly complex machines. Everything is monitored down to the smallest detail in order to use lean principles to reduce errors to zero and work more effectively and efficiently. Every action the operator takes is recorded and analysed for improvement. A recent error by the operator was corrected by the machine and reported to the person responsible for the department. Not to punish the employee but to make sure that similar situations would not happen again.

The opportunity I saw here, analogous to the call centre NPS I mentioned earlier, was to use this data to turn it into formal micro-learning or coaching moments. These could anticipate possible wrong actions to share with the operator at the right time. Lean learning at the moment of need. Yet in this organization, the data was not used. That is, the production manager received the data but was not allowed to do anything with it. Why? Well, this organization, which is based in a European country with very strong trade unions, is literally restricted by these trade unions. No personal data about the workers may be stored or used for any positive or negative follow-up.

However, there is a different example with different technology in another department, in the same organization, namely the commercial department that is useful to cover here.

The sales skills of the employees were tracked for years for training purposes. At least once a month, the sales team was called to the sales manager and the sales funnel was minutely examined. For those who have no experience with this, I can tell you that not every salesperson has all the skills to guide a customer through the seven steps of the sales process. It goes without saying that not everyone is equally good at preparing a presentation for the customer, and that negotiating is also not everyone's cup of tea.

Where previously these meetings were mainly based on Excel spreadsheets, the organization invested in a tailor-made salesforce solution that was geared to the seven-step sales process. From this solution, a spider diagram is drawn that clearly and visually indicates the 'shortcoming' of the sales person. This is then used in the weekly sales and pipeline meeting. From a positive conversation, sales managers and sales representatives look together for possible improvements in the sales process. The role of the manager here is mainly coaching to bring more deals through the sales funnel to a successful closing. When it turns out that at the same data point in the spider diagram, the sales representative has difficulties or makes mistakes, training is provided to address these.

What strikes me in this comparison is that both examples use technology to make processes more efficient, to help the manager in a coaching role and to help the employee with any learning moments. Yet in this organization, data from one system cannot be used because the employees work in a different job category.

The above example shows that stakeholders or pressure groups often have a huge impact on the learning enterprise. As we will see in part 4 of this book, it is therefore also essential to involve them in new initiatives from the outset in order to seek with them the added value that technology can bring to all.

The ethical debate on social media data for corporate use

Another source of data that is being debated internationally with and without trade unions is from social media. People analytics from social media can be linked, for example, to the organization's corporate values. Recruiters can thus use social media background checks of candidate pools to assess them on values and quickly identify the most suitable candidates for the job. That this is not abnormal and is accepted is also known by students who polish their LinkedIn profiles and other social media well before applying to jobs.

Yet, there is also a limit to what is acceptable and what international laws prohibit. For example, employers may not discriminate against a prospective or current employee based on information on the employee's social media regarding race, colour, national origin, gender, age, disability, and immigration or citizenship status. But what about a student or employee who actively participates in climate demonstrations or speaks out politically on certain issues? Internationally, the differences are considerable.

For example, the laws of the State of California provide that they are an at-will state under Labor Code 2922. This means that employment can be terminated with notice to the other party whenever either party wants. In other words, employers can fire employees for anything, including their posts on social media.

Even in US regional differences are very diverse, and sometimes contradictory, as evidenced by Section 7 of the National Labor Relations Act USA (the Act). This act guarantees employees 'the right to self-organize, to form, join, or assist trade unions, to engage in collective bargaining through representatives of their own choosing, and to engage in other concerted activity for the purpose of collective bargaining. This law also provides that if a group of employees posts information or participates in a 'group chat' on social media about certain topics such as wages, working conditions, workplace safety, or other working conditions, they cannot be disciplined or punished by the employer for that activity.

When we look at the global challenges for uniform regulation of the use of social media data, it is a very difficult balancing act between individual freedoms of expression and association and legitimate business interests. For example, we see that the final assessment in Europe and the UK of what is ethically justified often comes down to a decision by the courts based on the facts that have occurred. This local and personal approach may be the most ethical but it certainly does not make things easier for business leaders.

From the above examples, the data-driven organization has many advantages to support both the organization and the individual employee in their growth. Yet, it still brings challenges. Data specialists have a major role in determining the future strategy of an organization and will therefore be part of the core team that will reflect on the opportunities for the learning ecosystem in part 4 of this book.

References

Harvard University (2022) Multimodal Learning Analytics, lit.gse.harvard.edu/
   multimodal-learning-analytics (archived at https://perma.cc/D85R-WARQ)
National Labor Relations Board (2022) About NLRB, www.nlrb.gov/about-nlrb/
   rights-we-protect/the-law/interfering-with-employee-rights-section-7-8a1
   (archived at https://perma.cc/E8KP-2LFW)

PART TWO

Learning to stay relevant for the future

04

Lifelong learning in a world of change

Earlier in this book, I talked extensively about the speed of innovation, its impact on people and ethical issues related to it. In addition, partly due to expectations of the future workforce, companies will start to organize themselves differently, in a more value- and data-driven way. In this context, I have already referred several times to the breaking down of silos within organizations and to a more cross-functional approach that also involves intelligent cooperation between people and machines.

But people too, as citizens and employees, will have to adapt to the new, increasingly virtual world. Lifelong learning will be necessary in order not to be left behind. However, this learning extends beyond digital skills alone. Competencies that make us human will also distinguish us in an increasingly digital world.

A strategic need for organizations to engage in re-skilling now

In the current economic climate, with globalization and rapid innovative developments, many jobs as we know them today will soon no longer exist. Add to that the impact of the COVID-19 pandemic and we know that we will be moving towards a new normal where the pressure to re-skill, by acquiring new skills and competencies, will increase. Adapting to the new expectations will be a necessity in order to maintain or win a competitive position in the war for talent.

This need is endorsed in the Future of Jobs Survey (2020) mentioned before where 94 per cent of business leaders say they expect employees to acquire new skills on the job. They see a sharp increase from 65 per cent in 2018. Moreover, the same report found that on average only 62 per cent of their employees have access to this necessary retraining. Alarmingly, the report also indicates that by 2025, this will increase to 11 per cent of their workforce.

Another finding is even more striking: only 42 per cent of employees make use of the opportunities for retraining offered by their employer. Therefore, motivating and guiding employees towards a personal growth mindset, which makes them want to make use of the opportunities for retraining, should be the first priority of organizations. If organizations do not now include a motivational learning strategy in their mission, they will soon be saddled with employees who cannot keep up in the future. We already saw this in Belgium in 2019 at telecom giant Proximus. The announcement that 1,900 people would be laid off shocked the business world and what was even more striking was that the same organization had 1,200 vacancies open at the same time.

Situations like this are unfortunately no exception, but a harsh reality in many organizations, and there are various reasons for this. On the one hand, I see organizations that do not have a value-driven vision of the future with regard to keeping their staff deployable. Replacing them is easier and sometimes cheaper.

Some organizations do have this vision, but do not know how to convince their employees of the need to unlearn habits and behaviour. A holistic approach that makes learning part of the culture of the organization is essential to motivate employees and to get them to take up craftsmanship.

Lifelong learning: a tantalizing torment or a gift to support craftsmanship?

What I have described so far points to the need to invest in learning as an employee, as a manager and as a human being. However, it is not easy to find the motivation and the will to learn when the perception is that it is primarily a 'must'. I know very few people around me who get up in the morning and shout: 'Yay, I can learn again today'. In fact, they see it as a torture that never seems to end. For them, lifelong learning feels like a lifelong punishment. Just as it is for children when you say that school is just a training ground for learning.

I like to compare it to the torment of Tantalus, a Greek myth that I remember from high school. In this myth, Tantalus is said to be chained to a tree with ripe fruit above him and standing in a lake of drinkable water. Every time he thinks the water is high enough or the branches are close enough, they get a little further away and are again unreachable. Many of us seem to have that feeling when we think about lifelong learning. Just when we think we are there, we have to start all over again.

It's not an easy task for employers to motivate their teams again and again. One of the cases that can provide inspiration here is that of ING. According to Maarten van Beek, self-directed learning – and thus motivation to learn – can only be developed if you know that you can make a difference by pursuing your own goals, both privately and at work.

CASE STUDY
Craftmanship and the ING talent fluidity platform

Maarten van Beek, HR Director ING

ING is fast and ambitious. We demand a lot from our colleagues and COVID-19 made us realize even more that we have to be very flexible. And precisely in order to be flexible and adaptable, we also expect flexibility from our people. That fits in perfectly with our agile way of working and that is why we invest a lot in professionalism supported by what innovation has to offer from a human-centric approach.

This goes beyond following compulsory training or following e-learning on our digital learning platform. It is above all a way of thinking in which you actively look for opportunities to develop yourself. Whether you are an experienced employee or just starting out at ING, continuing education and retraining is important for everyone to remain relevant. In this way, employees not only create added value for ING and our customers, but also build up their own careers.

Developing yourself is an ongoing process, but there are times when you need to stop and think. It is at these key moments that we want to give our employees maximum support. To this end, we have developed a simple framework consisting of three phases:

1 Discovery - How do you want to develop your craftsmanship?

2 Planning - Turn your ideas into concrete plans.

3 Getting started - Turn your plans into actions.

For each phase we offer practical support and tips to get started. For example, we organize Purpose to Impact sessions where a coach – an ING employee themself – helps colleagues to discover what drives them.

These are interactive workshops in which they go in search of their personal purpose. Because at ING we believe that you can only make a difference if you pursue your own purpose, both in your private life and at work. That purpose might be to be captain of the dream team, for example. Discovering your purpose is also the starting point for further work on your craftsmanship. This also offers them inspiration and direction. Of course, they are also supported in this by development interviews with their manager.

Craftsmanship is also part of the 'Big 6' learning programme, which focuses on six competencies we need at ING to stay ahead; customer experience, cyber security, leadership, data skills, non-financial risk management and operational management. Employees can develop themselves on our digital learning platform.

Since 2022, ING wants to take this a step further by developing what we call 'talent fluidity'. This is a platform-based way of matching the skills of our talent with the jobs to be done. This means moving away from old-fashioned job descriptions and focusing on what needs to be done, and creating a marketplace where our internal talent can apply for tasks/jobs that need to be done. In this way, we support both the development of craftsmanship and respond to the expectations of the 'future of work' with regard to project work.

Learning in the flow of life

Lifelong learning starts at a very young age, even before we enter kindergarten. Yet, when we think of learning, we mainly think of the formal education we received at school. However, today's basic educational knowledge is of little use if we have not learned to transform it into applicable knowledge.

I must admit: I love learning and I seem to be able to memorise well, but I do not remember much relevant and applicable knowledge from my primary, secondary or even university education. What I do remember and use is the knowledge that I acquired with my own 'will' after having struggled compulsorily through my school years. And I am not talking (only) about the executive education courses I took. I am talking about the many conversations and events where I gained knowledge without having to search for it. The books that were introduced to me through social media and which I devoured, after which I often contacted the authors to find out more and talk to them about new applications of their knowledge (many of which I gladly mention in my own book). Learning in the flow of life is much more than work. It is growing as a human being, adapting to the world around us that is changing ever faster.

Unfortunately, not everyone has this drive to learn. Yet it has become a necessity to embrace learning with enthusiasm, not only to keep our jobs but also to be nimble and confident in life.

Besides the urgency from the changing world, and partly under the influence of technological innovations, we also see the impact of COVID-19 and working from home on learning. At home, learning moments often have to squeeze in between attention for housemates and other household tasks. Learning thus literally becomes part of the flow of life. And learning never stops. Learning is therefore much more than gathering knowledge, it is being open to new things, having a growth mindset, experimenting, failing and much more.

Learning and ageing

The brain is like a sponge that absorbs new things, or like a muscle that gets stronger when you use it. It is a myth to think that this muscle loses strength as you get older. According to research by Kegan and Lahey in 2016 (Harvard) that plots mental complexity against age, we get interesting and encouraging insights into the possibility of successful lifelong learning.

Simply put, learning is a process by which we develop new knowledge by making new connections between brain cells. This learning process and the new experiences lead to structural and functional changes in the brain, also known as neuroplasticity. As long as there is no pathological condition, this process continues. Moreover, according to Kegan and Lahey's research, mental complexity increases with age. The myth that older employees can no longer keep up can therefore be dispelled. With the right motivation and guidance, they will be able to use their accumulated expertise and knowledge all the more for the growth of their teams and the organization as a whole.

Another observation that needs to be made regarding lifelong learning is described by Professor Nick van Dam in his book *Learning & Development in the Digital Age* as the M-profile or serial mastery of the knowledge worker (Figure 4.1). In today's world, and even more so in that of tomorrow, building intellectual capital is the basis for value creation, according to Van Dam. The traditional T-profile, where you develop deep expertize in one field early in your career, no longer seems tenable, even if you supplement it with new skills during the course of your career.

The workforce is getting older, and the retirement age is being raised accordingly. Jobs or areas of expertise that were once relevant, will soon no longer be. Nick van Dam therefore argues that we are shifting from that T-profile to an M-profile, in which we train ourselves in multiple areas of expertise over the course of our lives. We then complement these with targeted development on the job and informal knowledge that we acquire in life itself.

The M-profile that Van Dam mentions is also very relevant when we provide guidance in study choices or when finding a job. That this should no longer be a choice for the rest of our lives became already clear when we discussed the future of work in the first part. From the future of work and the M-profile, we also learn that multiple expertizes contribute to employability and possibly also to wellbeing. In the next part, it is therefore relevant to reflect on a few (digital) skills that are highly promoted (rightly or wrongly) and the added value of competences and a mindset that support life-long learning.

FIGURE 4.1   From a T-profile to an M-profile for serial mastery

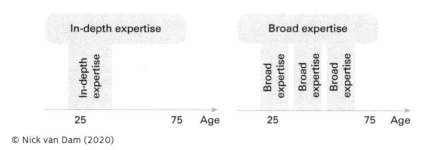

© Nick van Dam (2020)

Digital skills

If we look at the world around us, continuously influenced by new innovations, it has consequences for the skills and competences we need to keep up. Not only to take our place in the labour market, but even more so to be able to exercise our rights as digital citizens.

As digital citizens, we must have the knowledge and skills to use digital technologies effectively to communicate with others, participate in society and create and consume digital content. Moreover, digital citizenship is about confident and positive use of digital technologies, which means more than just skills to use the technology. It is also about competencies and a mindset that allows us to learn, grow and make positive use of the added value that intelligent technologies have to offer us. We often see competences and skills mentioned together, but it should be acknowledged that they often have a completely different meaning.

In this book, I distinguish between them in the following way, to describe what makes us unique as human beings in a world that is becoming increasingly digital:

- **Skill:** a particular task or activity in which a person is highly proficient. It is developed and perfected through practice and experience. Skills can be very relevant to performing a particular task, but can also quickly become useless in today's world.

- **Competence:** a combination of knowledge, skills, attitude and personal characteristics observable in behaviour. It especially recognizes the attitudes and character traits that distinguish and characterize a person, as well as their attitude towards the world and others.

- **Mindset:** a set of beliefs that determine how you see the world and yourself. It influences how you think, feel and behave in a given situation. These often determine how you deal with change and influence your attitude towards learning and the habits you adopt.

The importance of correctly interpreting the above concepts is sometimes underestimated Yet, both for your own employability and for the guidance of your employees, teams and the formation of the future learning organization, it is essential to make a distinction.

Relevance of digital skills

It goes without saying that digital skills are essential, and it is therefore only right that initiatives relating to the digital skills gap have been launched all over the world in recent years. Without these basic skills, it has become almost impossible to take an active part in modern society. We are talking about simple things that certain groups take for granted, such as making online payments or finding and/or keeping a job on the labour market.

The figures show that this skills gap is extremely deep, yet there are large regional differences. Take the 'developed' region of Europe, where even before the impact of the COVID-19 pandemic only three in ten EU citizens had more than basic digital skills. Yet overall, the figures are alarming. For example, the Future of Jobs Report 2020 indicates that as much as 40 per cent of the current workforce will need to upgrade their basic skills in the next five years. What's more, by 2025, 50 per cent of the current workforce will need to retrain because their current skills make them unsuitable for the labour market. Impressive figures that naturally create a sense of urgency, with retraining, upskilling and learning initiatives being widely encouraged by organizations and governments worldwide.

The digital skills gap has a direct impact on the individuals themselves, but it also affects labour shortages and the ensuing war for talent. More so, closing the global skills gap would be a positive accelerator that would generate $11.5 trillion in global GDP by 2028. This is obviously a motivation to create learning organizations that support workers in acquiring ever new skills. So why is it so difficult to close the digital divide or motivate people to acquire new digital skills?

From the learner's perspective, digital skills are a great frustration to learn when we know that after a few years, and sometimes months, it turns out that the skill is no longer in line with the current new developments of the innovation. For many, this is like a tantalizing torment that seems to have no end. The motivation to start is therefore often low.

In addition, the question arises whether the digital skills we find in many lists are accurate and give a true picture of what makes us employable in the future. Take the five most important digital skills employers are looking for in candidates in 2021 according to My Careers Future in Singapore.

1 Digital marketing or social marketing.

2 Business data analytics.

3 Coding.

4 Cloud.

5 Artificial Intelligence.

The first in this list, digital marketing, can hardly be called a skill on its own. It is an amalgam of many skills and competences that take several years to master. For example, many training providers indicate that the minimum two-year programme includes Big Data, cyber security, or cloud computing know-how.

The third place, occupied by coding, is certainly striking. Unlike the others on the list, coding is indeed a skill that can be learned like speaking a language. Yet, here too, I would venture to say that it is not the code you want to crack to have job security in the future.

Cracking the code for employment

From my experience as an educational consultant, I have been asked several times whether coding should be given a fixed place in the curriculum. Not a difficult question, because my answer is almost always an absolute no. Not because I don't believe that coding can have an added value, but because coding is often related to programming languages. And, if we look too narrowly at coding alone, it is as useful as choosing a language in a country where the language is not spoken. Why do I dare to be so blunt? Make the comparison with spoken languages.

There are 1739 languages spoken worldwide. Yet almost 40 per cent are almost extinct. On the other hand, of those 1739 languages, some 23 are spoken by more than half of the world's population. If I wanted to learn a new language that could take me 'far', it would therefore be logical that I would choose one of the 23 most widely spoken languages, for example English (1,132 billion speakers) or Mandarin (1,117 billion speakers). Yet we still see huge differences in popularity to learn one of these. English, for example, easily tops the list of popular second languages with 753 million and Chinese only 199 million. Why is this comparison relevant? Which language would you like your child to learn? The most popular or the one with the greatest future?

The same applies to programming languages, and there are many of them. So many that even a Google search cannot give you an unambiguous answer because it changes daily. On the day I write this, Wikipedia lists over 700 languages in alphabetical order. (Not really useful for choosing the language of the future). Other sources, on the other hand, speak of almost 9000 different languages from which to choose the 'coding language' of the future.

Choosing which programming language to use is thus not an easy task. But neither is there any certainty that learning one programming language will make you successful in the future, because depending on the application field, which is sensitive to innovation, you will need to know other languages.

To make the debate on coding even more irrelevant; in the future, coding may not even be necessary anymore because AI is already capable of self-coding. For example, DeepCoder is a machine learning system that can write its own code. It does this using a technique called programme synthesis. Essentially, it creates new programmes by combining existing lines of code from other software, which is what human coders do. So much for coding being a skill unique for human beings.

Computational and algorithmic thinking

These remarks about the usefulness of coding are, of course, written from a future perspective. That is not to say that coding is not very relevant to the labour market now. To fill the gap now, retraining employees is a possible solution. However, I see a more future-proof solution in computational skills or algorithmic thinking.

These skills will allow us to tackle complex problems, understand their causes and develop possible solutions from there. These solutions can then be presented in a way that a computer, a human, or both can understand. For this reason, a coding language like Python used by social organizations like CoderDojo can add value, when used to guide children, young people or even job seekers in understanding algorithmic thinking as a skill.

This insight is useful for recruiters who are looking for talent and fixate on skills from lists, for example a coding language, and do not look at broader employability skills along with competencies that support them. The enhancement through competencies and attention will support us more as humans in a world where the symbiosis between humans and machines must generate added value for humans.

CASE STUDY

Coding or dancing: what does it matter?

Farah Van Bulck, Ballerina

It may sound strange when I say that you might as well prepare your children for the future by sending them to dance classes or code camp. Why do I say that? From experience as a dancer who started dancing when I was four and went to a CoderDojo when I was seven, I know how to make the comparison.

Dancing, like coding, is based on algorithms. Mathematical patterns that logically flow from one movement to the next. But dancing is more than just the skill of creating the algorithms, it requires social and emotional competences. As classical dancers we are not individuals, we have to learn to think as one. Our bodies must move in synchrony, as if we have one body and one mind. As one connected network with one feeling. Not that we are a machine, on the contrary we show emotional expression in our dance. We can be asked to empathize with the feelings of a 17th century character, subdued yet expressive. Empathy with pure human feelings that we do not recognize in our own. We listen to the music and sense it as pure mathematics. Everything can be reduced to eight counts. This algorithmic skill combined with emotional intelligence (and of course a trained body) makes a dancer the unique artist he or she is.

Swan Lake, and more specifically the entrance of the 16 swans in Tchaikovsky's second act, is perhaps the best comparison one can make. To choreograph us as dancers, you need as much knowledge of algorithms as someone who wants to use AI for a drone show. Without good instructions (algorithms), we all crash into each other. I myself learned this when, as a 14-year-old, I was selected for the Royal Ballet's summer school in London. Just before the performance for the parents, our stage turned out to be a meter smaller than the one we had practised on. As a result, we all bumped into each other during the last rehearsal on the new stage. However, for us and the choreographer this was only a small hurdle. With a few drink cans, we marked turning points on the smaller stage. With just one practise, we had already adapted to the new reality. Admittedly, we are trained on more than algorithmic thinking. Problem-solving abilities, collaborative abilities and cognitive flexibility are all relevant to performing a feat.

Another reason why I say dancers are very well prepared for the future of work is also partly related to algorithmic thinking and lifelong learning. We always think of the next step, we don't only have a plan B but also a plan C for the day we can't dance anymore. We know we can't do the same job until we retire; if I'm lucky and don't have too many injuries, I'll be able to dance until I'm 40. After that I will start my second career. I realize that I will have to learn again, but I realize that lifelong learning will be necessary in every job, so I will enjoy my passion as much as possible first. And what about my parents? They once thought that I would become an engineer or do something with robots, who knows, maybe they will be right one day. Or, who knows, I may even study applied psychology to support people in a machine-based society.

With the above, I would like to indicate that digital skills will be necessary as people and as employees. Yet all too often, the assumption is made that this also means that everyone will learn to code.

Farah therefore gives a good example in the above case that it is not coding but algorithmic thinking that can make a difference. And even more so, the competences and growth mindset that drive us.

References

Berlitz (2021) The most spoken languages in the world, www.berlitz.com/blog/most-spoken-languages-world (archived at https://perma.cc/BSB7-PPTK)

BRUZZ (2019) Premier Michel roept Proximus-CEO Leroy bij zich na nieuws over 'kostenoptimalisering', www.bruzz.be/economie/premier-michel-roept-proximus-ceo-leroy-bij-zich-na-nieuws-over-kostenoptimalisering-2019 (archived at https://perma.cc/JHB5-QHA7)

Coderdojo (2022) Coderdojo, coderdojo.com/ (archived at https://perma.cc/L425-X7SK)

Ethnologue (2022) How many languages are there in the world? www.ethnologue.com/guides/how-many-languages (archived at https://perma.cc/NB3D-MN3T)

Futurism (2017) Our Computers Are Learning How to Code Themselves: Human coders beware, futurism.com/4-our-computers-are-learning-how-to-code-themselves (archived at https://perma.cc/N42L-6UY6)

gg (2010) 83 3 Tchaikovsky, Swan Lake 10 Entrance of Swans, 30 October, (online video) www.youtube.com/watch?v=fQ7ztMH_8yk (archived at https://perma.cc/T3AF-Y5PH)

Kegan R, & Lahey, L (2016) An Everyone Culture Cambridge, Harvard business school Publishing

My Career's Future, Top 5 Digital Skills You'll Need in 2021 (and Possibly in 2022 Too), content.mycareersfuture.gov.sg/top-5-digital-skills-need-2021/ (archived at https://perma.cc/UW6U-QT9Y)

Van Dam, N (2020) Leren en ontwikkelen in het digitale tijdperk Alphen aan den Rijn: Vakmedianet

World Economic Forum (2020) The Future of Jobs Report 2020, www.weforum.org/reports/the-future-of-jobs-report-2020 (archived at https://perma.cc/8DHQ-FP3Z)

World Economic Forum (2022) Closing the Skills Gap Accelerators, www3.weforum.org/docs/WEF_Closing_the_Skills_Gap_Accelerator_1pager.pdf (archived at https://perma.cc/CWX6-JQZX)

05

Competences that make us unique as human beings

That employability is not just about skills is already evident from the story of the prima ballerina for whom the future could go either way. Indeed, without competences to back them up, it is often just as useless as having no skills at all. Competencies are the carriers of skills and are expressed in a combination of knowledge, attitude and personality traits that can be observed in behaviour. Ballerina Farah Van Bulck sees that algorithmic thinking is supported by competences such as optimism, creativity and curiosity for translating a complex problem into an opportunity in the future.

Competencies are what enable us to be successful and unique as human beings in an increasingly digital world. What sets us apart are the behaviours that come with those competences that cannot be taught to a robot and are even difficult to teach to a human. Those are:

- curiosity
- openess
- entrepreneurship
- resilience
- optimism
- empathy
- consilience.

These competences are all, in my opinion, equally important, so the fact that they are listed in a certain order does not have a specific intention.

Curiosity

I dare say that curiosity is one of the most beautiful competences we have as human beings. It is the basis for learning and it makes learning fun.

Curiosity will also characterize the LearnScaper or learning strategist who is always enthusiastically looking for new ways to improve. Being a rebel as a result of curiosity is seen as an added value in this search for opportunities. The childlike and contagious hunger for ever new impulses and challenges is something we might recognize from our own childhood. 'Why, why, why' we would ask to probably exasperated parents. We also see that curiosity is the basis for experimenting with new ideas. Curiosity fuels the growth mindset that I will discuss further and is the basis for intrinsic motivation to keep learning.

Unfortunately, we see that curiosity is not always appreciated in education and business. Following what the teacher or HiPPO says is often the norm because they know better. Nipping curiosity in the bud kills the will to learn and grow. Organizations that invest in the future stimulate curious minds to question the policy and strategy. Not from a negative attitude, but from a quest for improvement and renewal.

When due diligence is discussed in the last part of this book, the why question, the search for a future without being supported by curiosity, is essential. It ensures that we do not focus on problems but on opportunities for nimble and sustainable growth.

Openness

Critical thinking is on most lists of competences that will make a difference to us as human beings. However, I think critical thinking does not cover the full scope and I dare say we need to make it more open.

As humans, we have become increasingly polarized in recent years and have very different opinions on different subjects. This is reinforced by the 'intelligent' algorithms of online media that rarely show us information that does not correspond to our already formed opinions. Moreover, these algorithms will increasingly push us to extremes based on data sets that we feed with our likes and reactions. This is a problem because it precludes the possibility of hearing, learning, stretching and growing other opinions (for the critical reader who doesn't believe me, I now recommend The Social Dilemma on Netflix).

Why emphasize openness and not just critical thinking? It is a crucial competence to actively seek other opinions and to learn from other experiences. The future requires that we dare to debate this openly in order to learn from each other. That we are open to compromise on the basis of critical thinking. These compromises and an openness to other viewpoints give us the perspectives to do things differently than we have always done. Our success, that of our organization and our society, comes from the ability to be open, to listen, to share and to learn.

Leaders who encourage openness therefore like to surround themselves with a team with diverse backgrounds and views. They value the different views of employees and thus build a culture of tolerance and inclusion that enables growth. This culture, in turn, supports an increase in innovative and creative ideas. This can have a huge impact on the business as it will contribute to long-term growth. Employees will feel more comfortable sharing their ideas with others and unique ideas will be shared in a diverse environment. This helps a company distinguish itself from companies that still operate with only 'one voice'.

In addition to the impact of openness as a managerial competence, we see that it is often reflected in the values of the organization, which in turn becomes an attractive employer. More than that, openness will also have a positive impact on customers and potential customers because the different backgrounds in the team will allow you to address different groups of customers.

Entrepreneurship

When we look at the future of work, we see gig workers and temporary workers more and more finding their place in today's organizations and society. However, these workers are often not the only ones who are driven by entrepreneurship. In learning organizations, managers are actively looking for internal employees who bring an intrapreneurial spirit or have entrepreneurial competences.

As mentioned, entrepreneurship is therefore more than starting one's own business. In fact, contrary to what some schools aim to achieve with student-entrepreneur projects, entrepreneurship is more than 'being your own boss'. It is about developing the competences that make you take active responsibility for achieving goals. It is about daring to take risks and actively seeking solutions to turn problems into new opportunities.

Learning organizations such as Google have been promoting this form of entrepreneurship among their own employees for years and actively recruit for it. Moreover, they deliberately organize themselves into innovation hubs in order to exchange ideas. For this reason Google gives its employees up to 20 per cent of their free time without allocating hours or days. This encourages them to develop a new project alongside their daily work; for example, Gmail was born out of the entrepreneurship of its own employees.

Intrapreneurship is seen by learning organizations as one of the best ways to stimulate innovation within the company originating from their own employees. Entrepreneurship and openness together produce solutions that are sometimes far removed from the company's origins. This in turn can result in new projects that sometimes break new ground through corporate venturing or spin-offs and thus contribute to the business ecosystem as a whole.

Resilience

This purely human trait is perhaps the one that has shown its added value since 2020, after the outbreak of the COVID-19 pandemic. Resilience is about adapting to new circumstances, embracing them and jumping further than before. It refers to how you effectively deal with experiences in your work and life by literally bouncing back from a difficult situation to one that feels more comfortable. This means being able to regulate your thoughts, your emotions and your behaviour, which as we all know is not easy.

What also makes resilience so special is that you do not see challenging situations as a personal threat, but as an opportunity. For that reason, we see that resilience and entrepreneurship also go hand in hand. With resilience, you always look for information to reinvent yourself or a situation from a positive approach. Resilience as an employee means that you want to innovate and solve problems. That you want to look at what worked and what didn't work. It means actively looking for the best solution and developing a habit of wanting to improve from experiences, both positive and negative. An important factor of resilience is also that it is not just a reactive competence that is called upon when you face a challenge or a problem. It is the positive and proactive approach that distinguishes resilient people from others. This logically oriented approach, focusing not on the problem but on the solution, is often mentioned together with the optimism that I will describe further in the following section.

Resilience, like any other, is a competence that can be learned, even though it sometimes requires a lot of perseverance when you think you have no choice or are alone, with your back against the wall and no way out. In learning organizations, however, you are not alone and a culture of togetherness is built. Still, it takes a lot of practice to dare to be vulnerable and to open up for advice and new experiences.

Therefore, working on resilience is an important pillar for organizations that want to work on employee engagement and a learning culture. Resilience is perhaps one of the most difficult competencies, precisely because it is so close to failure and pain. This is why it could be considered the competency that makes us more human than any other in this list.

Optimism

Optimism is perhaps one of the most important competences for initiators of innovation projects. Together with curiosity and imagination, they help to form an image of a positive future. This positive and value-driven image of a future we cannot yet imagine is the first step in the learning landscapes we build in the last part of this book.

You could say that optimism and resilience are very similar. Yet resilience without optimism is a lot harder. While resilience supports you when you experience (unexpected) setbacks, optimism is the competence that supports you when you want to move forward. It is an attitude of perseverance that we show in our behaviour.

Strong leadership implies optimism to maintain high employee wellbeing and engagement in times of rapid change. We also see that optimism helps prevent conflict and resistance by providing a perspective to problems and setbacks. As an optimist, you know that it is irrelevant to worry about things that are beyond your control.

Teaching optimism seems very difficult, but it is not impossible. The way you look at the world can be changed by breaking through thought patterns and behaviour. This is where leadership plays a very important role. Achieving more together is the starting point of learning organizations that cultivate competencies such as optimism by encouraging employees to share their dreams. This includes sharing dreams and, more importantly, discussing what makes someone anxious. These initiatives help to step out of one's comfort zone and reach a higher level of optimism.

This can be very relevant in transformation projects to encourage persistent pessimists to join the positive story. (Step 2: Burning platform in the last part of this book).

Empathy

Empathy is perhaps the skill that futurists would most like to associate with artificial intelligence. Empathy is what makes us human. It is our ability to relate, to understand situations and feelings of others and to respond with our own feelings.

I will not deny that artificial intelligence is making strides towards what they call artificial empathy (AE) or computational empathy. Just think of the care robots being deployed in schools or nursing homes. They are already able to detect human emotions and respond to them in an empathic way, not from their own feelings but from smart algorithms. In this way, we are already seeing robots being used to help care workers socialize or offer support in emotional detachment.

In the context of this book, I also see empathy as the ability to work together on the basis of trust and understanding for others in their thinking and doing. It will enable us to work together in cross-functional teams whose members sometimes have different values, yet believe that they are going together for a mission that unites them.

Empathy will also enable us to understand and anticipate other stakeholders and their points of view. It helps us to understand circumstances and challenges from a human perspective. Empathy is essential for the LearnScaper or architect of change to motivate others to do things differently based on their own motivations, which may or may not be different from yours.

Consilience

This last competence is perhaps what makes us most unique as human beings in a comparison with artificial intelligence. More than that, I would argue that consilience will be the difference maker in an uncertain future.

But what is it? The essence of consilience can be seen as the ability to bring unlikely things together, based on an enormous amount of imagination, creativity and insight. Or, for example, the ability to 'see similarities in differences', as Lauren Somers, a young entrepreneur, shares in his story below. Consilience is in our genes and has enabled humans to innovate and adapt to the new normal. Consilience is the competence that gives you a head start. Yet we are often unaware of this competence, or at least not aware enough to make it a habit.

I myself borrow Consilience largely from Edward O Wilson, whose 1998 book *Consilience: the Unity of Knowledge* attempts to demonstrate the unifying potential of natural science, especially modern biology, as a general paradigm for the whole of science. His starting point is that all living activities are determined by information in the genes. For example, he argues that our competences are passed on from our genes and thus enable us to survive, evolve by learning and store new data in them. Our social conscience is also fed from these genes. This social conscience enables us to listen to the world around us, to discern the needs of others and to participate in what our own competences and interests prompt us to do.

Wilson argues that scientists, but also artists and others, have a common goal to give direction from deeper convictions that do not always have to be explained scientifically. According to him, consilience is the competence that enables us to step outside the box, to see connections that are not there in the first place, as long as they contribute to growth or a vision of improvement.

Learning about consilience was an eye-opener for me, and even though it initially seemed difficult to apply this consciously, I realized that as children we do this naturally. Children discover the world by searching for the limits of what is possible. Maybe we should embrace the child in ourselves and let it support us to grow as adults.

When we think of consilience in an organizational context, it provides opportunities for cross-functional teams and experts to search for solutions from different disciplines. But what if we go a step further and share those new insights with intelligent technologies in a symbiosis where we form a superbrain? It all sounds very futuristic, but consilience, where we combine human creativity and imagination with AI, may well provide solutions to huge global problems. It would allow us humans to focus on wellbeing and a future for our children.

CASE STUDY
Seeing the similarities in the differences

Lauren Somers, young serial entrepreneur

At the start of the first lockdown in Belgium in March 2020, the future did not look bright for Studer. At the time, we were a young company specializing in trained students and flex workers for the events sector. Needless to say, our order book was empty overnight. Waiting until the initially brief lockdown was over could have been an option, but we had no faith in that. It was just not in our nature to do nothing. We knew that the market for gig workers and flex workers was on the rise and that this created opportunities for companies specializing in trained experts. We then thought of turning the setback into an advantage. If it didn't work out, we would have lost nothing.

At first glance, trained waiters and receptionists for events do not seem easily employable in other sectors. Yet, I knew that with the necessary motivation and guidance, our students would be able to adapt. For me, the first sectors we approached were obvious. The logistics sector was booming because of the strong growth in online purchases. I also noticed that supermarkets were struggling to find extra staff to guide customers safely in and through the shop. The similarities in the differences were quickly found. Our approach was always to recruit based on competences and less on skills for the job. Our approach allowed us to learn these quickly enough.

Our clients understood that a waiter or receptionist can be perfectly deployed to assist a customer in a supermarket. And for the logistics sector, our app for highly flexible recruitment at peak times was also an absolute added value. Finally, our teams supported the setting up of vaccination centres with our trained and motivated students.

I have also learned a lot from this period on a personal level. The itch to be an entrepreneur was always in me, but now I look even more consciously for innovative challenges. I don't know yet what the future will bring, but it will not be boring.

From the above and more specifically from the cases of enthusiastic young people, we know that lifelong learning and growing in multiple areas of expertise can be fun. Farah and Lauren both want to grow from competences and do not believe in a skill set that will make the difference. Learning is a lifelong pleasure for them and they like to be surprised by the uncertain future. It gives them that sense of always discovering new things. And, even more than the right competencies, both understand craftmanship and have a growth mindset which I will describe in the next section.

Growth mindset as a catalyst for change and growth

As a young entrepreneur, Lauren Somers has competences that add value in the rapidly changing world. In addition, he is bursting with ambition and has a growth mindset that makes him grow as a person. This desire to grow is what drives him to learn, to spot opportunities and to adapt to new situations. This growth mindset or way of thinking strengthens the competences that help us evolve in society.

However, growth mindset and ambition are often confused with each other: it is not because someone is ambitious that they also have the ability to grow. On the contrary, ambition is often a hindrance to growth when no growth mindset is present.

Carol Dweck, the American professor at Stanford, describes a growth mindset as the belief that success depends on time and effort. People with a growth mindset have the feeling that their skills and intelligence can be improved with effort and perseverance. More than that, they have the ability to see possibilities and opportunities in situations that are problematic for others. They want to learn by having experiences, good or bad. What distinguishes them from people who only have ambition is that they have learning, in whatever situation, as a key driver. Challenges and failures are not an impediment to growth, they are just that extra push to keep on learning, becoming better and better. Failure is then seen as a springboard for growth to stretch our existing capabilities.

Ambition, also known as honour, is the pursuit of an ever higher position in the organization or of a larger market share. Here, any small setback can become a major obstacle that undermines morale. In ambition, we also see the individual, sometimes selfish, character that asserts that success comes from one's own efforts and knowledge. We often see this in people who do have ambition, but in combination with a fixed mentality. This mentality states that our character, intelligence and creative potential are fixed and cannot be meaningfully changed through experiences and interactions with others. Learning from failure is not easy for people with a fixed mindset. They experience failure as the end rather than a new beginning to do better from the experience gained.

According to Dweck's research, a growth mindset can already be recognized in students. Students with a growth mindset are said to have a greater sense of purpose. They are very good at keeping the big picture in mind. In addition, students have more 'grit' – passion and perseverance. That extra bit of perseverance and character that makes them more inclined to seek approval and appreciation from themselves than from others. Cultivating a growth mindset is not easy, but according to Carol Dweck, it is possible at any time of life with a little guidance and belief in yourself.

Besides selecting on the basis of competences, a growth mindset is also an added value for the company. Selecting employees with a growth mindset, especially when someone has a managerial role, can have a positive influence on the learning culture of the learning organization. This culture of the learning organization is the breeding ground of the LearnScapes I envisage and will describe further.

Organizations that cultivate this learning culture from the growth mindset of their employees often combine it with a value-driven vision. They see other players in the market less as opponents and more as partners in the ecosystem. These organizations have a corporate growth mindset.

The above reflects a world in rapid change that has an impact on the skills and competences that organizations and employees need to keep pace with this acceleration. As an organization, it is essential to use that knowledge of innovation and human motivation to develop a holistic learning strategy that addresses the needs of the future.

In the next part of the book, we will therefore elaborate on learning strategies and technologies that support this new holistic approach. No dogmatic thinking about things that were once relevant, but an open mind that looks at emerging trends that build on what was relevant in the past. That is the basis of a methodology for continuous improvement.

References

Duckworth, A (2017) *Grit: the power of passion and perseverance*, Vermilion, London

Dweck, C (2012) *Mindset: how you can fulfill your potential*, Robinson Publishing, London

Jr Murphy, B (2020) Google Says It Still Uses the '20-Percent Rule' and You Should Totally Copy It, inc.com/bill-murphy-jr/google-says-it-still-uses-20-percent-rule-you-should-totally-copy-it.html (archived at https://perma.cc/AGX4-KJLU)

Orlowski, J (Regisseur) 2020, The Social Dilemma, Netflix, (online video) https://www.thesocialdilemma.com/ (archived at https://perma.cc/AL8N-XSMW)

Wilson, E (1998) *Consilience: The unity of knowledge*, Random House, New York

PART THREE

Learning strategies
and technology

06

Can learning strategies stand the test of time?

As this book is not only for L&D professionals, but for anyone interested in the growth of people and organizations, I think it is useful to be aware of some of the concepts and models related to learning. I would encourage you to look with an open mind at what works for your organization and your employees, and what doesn't. Squeezing everyone into the same model is not realistic. There is no one-fits-all solution when it comes to learning concepts and strategies.

For example, some studies determine that learning preferences, and therefore learning strategies, should match a personal learning style. These concepts have gained strength especially since the 1970s and 1980s. This seems logical and we should not think too deeply about how different learning preferences can be. Take yourself as a reference point. If you have come this far in this book, you probably like to get ideas from books. However, I can well imagine that you know someone who would hate the idea of ever having to read another book when they finally got out of school and struggled through a mandatory list. Who knows, they might prefer short podcasts on the way to work. But then again, the latter doesn't work for me because I listen to the intonation of the voice and often find it very sleep-inducing.

It is therefore not surprising that learning organizations are looking for concepts and methods that claim to provide answers to all individual, personalized and adaptive learning styles in order to roll out a strategy.

Yet, and it is a contradiction to what seems logical, in recent years there is increasing evidence that personal learning preferences have little or no real influence on effective learning outcomes. As a result, many organizations are no longer looking for strategies that are adapted to personal preferences, but are looking at the measurability of the strategy in order to make adjustments that influence effective learning, if necessary and possible. Both concepts are relevant and I am not saying that one is better than the other. What I do want to make clear is that what works for a predominantly blue collar organization, for example, may not be the right strategy for a predominantly knowledge worker team.

In this chapter, I want to nurture your openness to concepts, so that you can select a workable strategy, or strategies, for everyone in your organization. This approach of not forcing everyone into the same strategy is also very relevant in multinational organizations. I cited earlier Santosh Kher of FedEx MEA and the Indian continent who is a great advocate of cross-functional teams and local support for HR and L&D. He knows from the diversity of his international and locally dispersed workforce that a local and sometimes individual approach often gives the best – measurable – results.

CASE STUDY

Glocalization of learning strategies to meet the needs of internationally diverse employees in a nimble and measurable way

Santosh Kher, Managing Director of Human Resources at FedEx Express

As part of FedEx's MEISA (Middle East, Indian Subcontinent and Africa) region and as part of a global company, it is important to balance centralization and localization. This obviously has implications for HR and L&D strategies, which take place at global, regional, and local levels.

However, it's important to meet the local needs of team members. Therefore, we have a combination of global, regional, and local programmes, policies, and practices within the company. For example, we have employee engagement programmes in all countries in the Middle East and Africa. However, the same activity does not work in all countries. Engagement activities in the UAE are often very different from those in Kuwait, and they also differ from initiatives in South Africa to achieve the same goal and level of engagement. Several factors underlie these differences between countries or regions. For example, cultural differences, language barriers, and local processes and people policies that differ from country to country make local application different. In these circumstances, we see that localization is very important.

Another example is the operational response to different training needs based on country requirements. Here the nuances of the country and the expectations of team members must be considered. It's important to also look at learning from the perspective of the audience and not just from the perspective of the facilitator. To this end, we make regional adjustments to both the learning content and the way it is delivered. These adaptations of global programmes support better learning outcomes because our international workforce can better identify with and absorb the content. To do this, we design a framework for the world or a region from central Centre of Excellence functions. Local HR teams are then empowered to further localize the centralized content or program. This 'glocal' approach combines the best of both worlds by taking the broad framework of global programs and localizing them to the needs of local audiences. This works best for effective implementation and longer-term retention of knowledge and application of what has been learned.

From the global approach, we have compulsory trainings that everyone must complete. We cannot deviate from this, and here standardization is important e.g. when it comes to training on safety procedures. In addition to these global programmes, there are non-mandatory learning experiences that often have more individual objectives for the team member. For these, I prefer a learning buffet, so that individuals can choose what they like or what suits them, depending on their current needs. This includes choosing the way they prefer to learn, including written content, videos, live webinars, etc. In doing so, we aim to meet the expectations that everything should be developed in bite-sized learning 'moments' with content as concise and relevant as possible. This is crucial for us, in addition to the Glocal approach which takes location and cultural elements into consideration, to accommodate individual ways of learning.

What's extra challenging for global companies like FedEx is that all learning opportunities must ultimately connect to the global business and HR ecosystem of Talent Management, Retention, Development, and so on. For this, our cross-functional HR teams work together with one goal in mind, in one framework or learning ecosystem where they can make local adjustments. This is a success story that not only promotes learning and its measurability, but also has a positive impact on the culture of FedEx as a global employer. It ensures that from a regional approach, our team members are proud to be a part of the broader global programs.

The above examples show that a one-fit-all approach is not always the solution. Nevertheless, there are many methods that still have added value from their historical background. In the next section, I will discuss them so that you can decide if they still have value in your organization, adapted to technology and the future workforce.

Learning frameworks and their added value

Many of the current frameworks and theories have been around since the last century and are still being applied from a body of thought that is just as old. They have become dogmas that are embedded without regard to the light of innovation. However, it is by no means my intention to contradict these deeply ingrained frameworks and practices, nor to determine in advance whether they are relevant to the learning organization you wish to build. The purpose of including them in this book is to make you think about what learning was and what it will be in the future. A future where human learning can be combined with technological innovations, and how we can learn in a human-machine symbiosis.

Even if you think that the following frameworks such as Bloom's Taxonomy, *Adult Learning Theory*, 70/20/10, *5 Moments of Need* and Kirkpatrick's *4 Levels of Evaluation*, no longer hold any secrets for you, they might turn out differently in the light of the above symbiosis. Taking them as a reference when developing your own strategy(s) will therefore certainly have added value.

Bloom's Taxonomy

Perhaps one of the most well-known foundations of corporate learning is still Bloom's Taxonomy. It goes back to 1965 when Benjamin S. Bloom published his *Taxonomy of Skills* for use in an academic context. However, it was widely recognized that it could be adapted to most learning environments because it provided a hierarchical classification of the six levels of cognitive functioning and learning: 'knowledge, understanding, application, analysis, synthesis and evaluation'.

The purpose of the classification was to help instructional designers classify the learning goals and objectives that form the basis of any curriculum design. These were then divided into three 'domains': cognitive, affective and psychomotor. This would give learning a more holistic approach. By the 1990s, however, the classification was in need of revision and, under the leadership of Lorin W Anderson, a group of psychologists was brought together to update the taxonomy, including the hierarchical system that moves from the most basic conceptual level to progressive levels of complexity. In the new taxonomy this became: remember, understand, apply, analyse, evaluate and create. It is this revised taxonomy that we recognize in most learning organizations. The question that naturally arises now is whether we can still use Bloom's Taxonomy and whether it is sustainable/adaptable to a future-oriented learning strategy?

Objectives (learning goals) are indeed still very important to define so that both the instructional designer of the learning content and the learner understand the purpose of the knowledge transfer and the expectations. More than that, we see that an organized set of objectives helps instructional designers to deliver the right instruction at the right time. Moreover, we see that from the learning objectives also follows the strategy for the assessment and measurability of the knowledge transfer.

However, one criticism of the extensive mapping of learning goals and objectives is that sometimes a lot of time is spent on drawing up the learning goals. However, in most cases this is only done for the cognitive domain related to remembering, understanding, applying, analysing, evaluating, and creating. Yet I see from the expectations of the future workforce that supporting the affective domain of learning (based on emotions) can have many benefits. Affective goals, which generally focus on awareness and growth in attitudes, emotions and feelings, enable us to live in times of rapid change. They are therefore very interesting for supporting competences that do not only focus on cognitive skills. More than that, they distinguish us from machines by describing how people react emotionally and have the ability to feel the pain or joy of other living beings.

The psychomotor domain (action orientation) is also important in the growing manufacturing industry, where skills are becoming less relevant and where machines often already outperform humans in this domain. The expectations for 'workers' are less straightforward to learn in this respect and will often, in combination with the above, require a high degree of adaptive learning.

In the context of lean learning strategies, which I will explain further, we should therefore perhaps pay less attention to developing learning objectives and more to applied learning when it is needed. This more adaptive and technology-supported way of learning is also necessary when the context and learning needs change, or when something goes wrong. Technology and AI make this possible today without long preparation of learning goals and objectives. This raises the question of whether we should still follow Bloom's Taxonomy, from the 1990s, as a strategy

Adult learning theory

Making learning impactful and engaging is a challenge faced by many instructional designers, but also by managers and on-the-job coaches. One learning theory that tries to answer this is adult learning theory also known as andragogy which, like many other theories, has been around since the last century. However, I still like to share it because it highlights the different ways adults respond to learning and it still proves to be very valuable in getting staff members on board with a strategy that supports lifelong learning. Not only is it still applicable, it offers added value to support learning with hyper-modern technologies.

Adult learning theory was developed by Malcolm Knowles in 1968. However, unlike Bloom's Taxonomy that was originally developed for education, adult learning theory emphasises the concept or study of how adults learn and how this differs from children. It helps to identify learning styles that best support lifelong learning and the future of work.

Like Bloom's Taxonomy, this theory has been supplemented and adapted several times over the years. Unlike the previous one, however, it is based on five (some articles and studies mention six) non-scientifically founded assumptions about how adults perceive learning. This supplemented with principles of andragogy support new strategies to engage learners. Let's take a more detailed look at these assumptions that form the theory:

ADULT LEARNERS ARE SELF-DIRECTED

As we get older we often feel the need to be actively involved in the decisions that affect us. At a more mature age, we may be more able to take responsibility. Self-directed learning therefore does not mean that we prefer to learn on our own and are cut off from socializing with others. More than that, it can be recommended that the learning environment is collaborative, welcoming and filled with mutual respect and trust. This is something I will explain later, when discussing the conditions of social learning environments to put the learner at the centre of their learning (chapter 10).

ADULTS BRING EXPERIENCE TO THE LEARNING ENVIRONMENT

Adults have a lot of experience from which they draw knowledge and references that can be an important resource. Not only for themselves, but also for their peers and leaders or coaches who facilitate learning. Shared knowledge and backgrounds would be of great value, which is why social learning platforms, collaborative assignments and team games prove so valuable in many situations. There is, however, a very important note to be made here. The organization and the manager must give the trust to be allowed to fail as we will see in chapter 10. This must be embedded in the culture of the organization to prevent negative experiences and a fixed-mindset from taking over and to cultivate a positive culture of collaborative learning.

ADULTS ENTER THE LEARNING ENVIRONMENT READY TO LEARN

Adults are more willing or eager to learn if there is a reason to do so, for example if it is for growth and development in connection with their work. But also the personal situation, commitment to the employer or prospects for compensation in the future can be a relevant reason for learning. In addition, learning from an enjoyable experience always gives more satisfaction, which explains why we have seen an accelerated rise in gamified social learning in recent years. These not only benefit personal competence development but also teamwork.

ADULT LEARNERS ARE PROBLEM ORIENTED

Few adults see learning as a hobby; they want what they learn to be applicable. They want skills and competences that will help them solve problems and work better. Understanding how learning contributes to this helps to motivate them to let go of already acquired habits and behaviours and learn new ones. When announcing 'compulsory' learning moments, this relevance is often not given enough attention. Yet when learning opportunities are clearly communicated with the relevance for the individual, the added value for the organization and sometimes even for society, it helps to remove obstacles to learning. Regular communication and information about the organization's vision and the associated challenges often prove to be a good trigger for employees to realize the value of learning.

ADULTS ARE MOTIVATED TO LEARN BY INTERNAL FACTORS

Factors such as increased self-esteem, self-actualization or recognition play an important role in learning, as Tariq Chauhan also pointed out in chapter 2. Identifying personal motivators is an important step in a successful learning strategy. These are not self-evident and the role of the manager as coach and mentor is therefore often a crucial element for success. Trying to understand the internal factors of your employees or teams may require that little extra effort, but it will help even the most reluctant learners take ownership of their own future.

For the learning strategist, manager or even team player, knowing these simple assumptions will add value to shaping the organization's learning culture. And even though they remain assumptions because they are not scientifically provable, they make you think about developing learning methods that work for your teams. Therefore, when we talk about low-risk experiments for learning organizations in the last part of this book, they will be useful to look back at.

70-20-10, is that still tenable in the virtual world?

70-20-10 will probably sound familiar to anyone who has ever been involved in workplace learning. Simply put, this concept is about learning in three distinct ways within an organization.

The concept, and more specifically the criticism and dogmatic interpretations attached to it, often undermine the intentions that Charles Jennings himself wanted to give it. Let me be clear, I am not the biggest fan and I also doubt whether 70-20-10 is still tenable in organizations committed to intelligent cooperation between man and machine. Still, with a little openness, there is a lot of good behind the idea.

Before I outline the concept of 70-20-10, I would like to frame the criticism so that it can serve as inspiration. Jennings initially developed 70-20-10 as a reference model, a framework or, as he says, a do-it-yourself toolkit that seeks to answer the challenges of linking workplace learning to business challenges. In other words, not as a dogmatic concept that must always be implemented in the same way.

Nevertheless, his globally implemented framework has been criticized. For example, there was a lack of supporting empirical evidence that his concept works effectively, the figures he used happened to be too perfect to support his story, and his research did not take into account the proper distribution of respondents.

For science-minded readers, there is reason for this criticism. The study is based on only 200 executives (experienced managers) who were asked to report how they thought they learned. And there is the rub, because what works for 200 managers does not work in the same way for, say, a factory worker.

Learning and development usually start with an awareness of a current or future need for skills and competencies and the motivation to do something about it. These experienced managers got their motivation from a goal they wanted to achieve by investing in their own learning. They were also much more open to gaining experience and reflecting on it, which they felt was the most important way to learn.

The 70-20-10 model explained

So with the conclusions of that small study, Charles Jennings arrived at the learning development model he called 70-20-10, proportional to how the 200 managers learned.

- 70% by doing or by challenging assignments
- 20% by collaboration and coaching
- 10% by formal education through courses and training.

According to the model, most learning gains, and the associated KPI (70 per cent), would be achieved by doing things or participating in challenging assignments. However, this requires a rather broad interpretation. For example, learning could come from feedback, from learning from and reflecting on mistakes, watching the reactions of others, or not being able to cope with a task. In other words: from experiences, at work, in life, or who knows, the metaverse. Informal learning has gained many new dimensions since the model was created.

In addition, 20 per cent of the knowledge gained is said to come from collaboration. However, in the time that this model was developed, collaboration was still very much Human-2-Human, in contrast to the learning ecosystems or LearnScapes that we envisage in this book. For example, it is becoming increasingly normal today that intelligent technology coaches us on the job in the moment of need, as I will show in the next chapter.

To take it one step further, I also dare to look at the 10 per cent that we call formal learning. Can we still make that distinction when we think about workplace learning, for example? When the intelligent machine gives instructions, have we learned by doing, or is it coaching, or do we see the machine as an instructor giving us practical lessons?

The above makes me doubt whether 70-20-10 in its current interpretation is still tenable. I do not think we should still dogmatically try to attach KPIs to something from previous times. By doing so, we also risk not looking at innovation simply because it does not fit into one of the pigeonholes. Still, I am not saying that we should give up this methodology completely. If we dare to step outside the known paths, it can still be used flexibly, as Jan Rypers, digital learning project manager at the Belgian Colruyt Group, knows.

From the ecosystem of companies that Colruyt is, Jan Rypers has experience with enormously different working methods and tools. Each department in his organization has its own optimization levers and culture. So what fits one situation or department does not fit another. The rigorous introduction of one concept such as the 70-20-10 model for the entire organization would then not only be very unwise, but also very frustrating.

Rypers therefore knows that for every question he receives from the various departments, he must think of the employees, the leadership, and the ecosystem in which they operate. And, in many cases also the specific culture of that department. Partly for this reason, he could not completely abandon 70-20-10, which was so embedded in some departments, as it was still proving its worth. From an open and holistic perspective, he came up with his own interpretation of linking this to 'learning in the moment of need' described after his example.

CASE STUDY
L&D professionals can also continue to learn

Jan Rypers, project leader digital learning at Colruyt Group

A model such as 70-20-10 can be useful to widen your field of vision. The point is that what has been our core business for years – training, e-learning and other formal learning opportunities – is not the only way people learn. It's just a pity that those '70-20-10' percentages take up all the attention.

I quickly abandoned the term because I noticed that there were more discussions about the validity of those percentages than about how you can look

FIGURE 6.1 5 Moments of Need and 70-20-10 combined

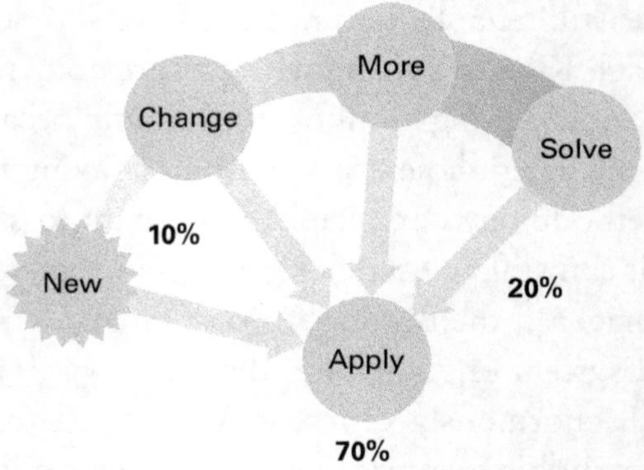

© Apply Synergies

at learning differently. As soon as we let go of the figures, we were able to talk about them and also about the comparison with the 5 Moments of Need (Figure 6.1). Indeed, another model, but it was not as if we had to maintain one model dogmatically. I don't know if those are really the only five moments of need, but that's not what it's about for me. Discussing both methods gave me the language to make clear that when our employees are doing their job and don't know or can't do something, they don't have the luxury of going to a training course or starting up an e-learning. And that we, from L&D, will then look at how we can help them.

The 5 Moments of Need gave me language to explain the importance of L&D always starting from the employee's point of view and the context in which they find themselves. 70-20-10 gave me language to show that our field is broader than our core business. However, the models themselves are never the goal, and if I can I mention them as little as possible. It is not my job to explain models, but to find a common language from which ideas and new insights can emerge, so that we as L&D practitioners can continue to learn.

___

Five moments of need

Another concept that is becoming more and more established is 5 Moments of Need™ by American learning evangelists Bob Mosher and Conrad Gottfredson (Figure 6.2). They relate learning to the moment you want to apply knowledge. I have always been positive

FIGURE 6.2 Learning in 5 Moments of Need by habit of improvement

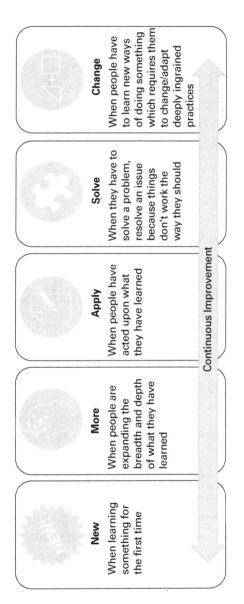

New
When learning something for the first time

More
When people are expanding the breadth and depth of what they have learned

Apply
When people have acted upon what they have learned

Solve
When they have to solve a problem, resolve an issue because things don't work the way they should

Change
When people have to learn new ways of doing something which requires them to change/adapt deeply ingrained practices

Continuous Improvement

about this methodology because it is widely applicable in different organizations for designing and developing learning solutions that support learning in terms of purpose, employability, and applicability.

Another reason why I am a fan of this methodology, which supports initial workplace learning, is because of the benefits it has when you integrate it with informed learning in the flow of life, or learning based on relevant and accurate information when you need it. The latter, as I will explain in more detail, is the basis of lean learning.

You can divide the 5 Moments of Need into two parts with regard to how learning will take place; knowledge gathering and applying knowledge.

One comment that needs to be made here is that this is not about five consecutive moments, an assumption that I experience is often made. It is better to say that all moments have to be designed in order for the knowledge to ever be applied.

KNOWLEDGE GATHERING

'New' and 'More' moments of need could be said to align with traditional approaches to learning. These include classroom training and e-learning (whether or not in a hybrid setting).

- **New** – when you learn something for the first time.
- **More** – you want to know more about something.

In other words, longer courses. In the current context of working from home, this can sometimes be difficult to combine. What I see in nimble organizations that quickly respond to the new normal is that they support the small groups on location and expand them with virtual participants. Zoom offers very interesting possibilities here, so that break-out groups can also work together on a virtual project.

However, a lot of benefits for faster and more relevant knowledge transfer can be found more often in moments that are more focused on application and therefore supported in a very lean way. More information on how to develop lean learning will follow later in the book, but I will outline some initial thoughts here.

APPLYING KNOWLEDGE

The other three *Moments of Need* are directly related to performance support or the correct application of knowledge at work. They are powerful building blocks that transform the way we learn and use knowledge in organizations.

- **Apply** – when you try to apply and/or remember something.
- **Solve** – when something goes wrong.
- **Change** – when something changes.

Tools to support learning will be discussed in more detail in the next chapter, however, I would like to mention the benefits of microlearning apps to apply learning in the moment of need. These apps provide short, relevant information or learning moments via an adaptive algorithm tailored to the learner that they can then apply immediately.

Unlike the longer programmes, the challenge here is applicability, reminding and reinforcing previously acquired knowledge. It is even more important to give the learner the benefits to perform work more efficiently or differently. Measurability, so that action can be taken if the desired effect is not being achieved, is an additional advantage that microlearning applications offer.

As you have already noticed, the fast applicability of knowledge is also very relevant when something goes wrong. At that moment, there is no time to follow longer learning sessions and the employee expects relevant information in order to be able to immediately correct matters and thus avoid accidents or costs. This is an important added value for many companies to invest in technology that supports learning in the moment of need.

The last moment of learning needs, 'change', is perhaps the most challenging to fulfil because it is here that habits often have to be unlearned. Just think of the postman who suddenly no longer has to have a parcel signed for and has to do everything contactlessly as much as possible.

When organizations are faced with change, employees are often uncomfortable giving up what has worked in the past. Unlearning deep-rooted skills is difficult, even if you have a growth mindset.

Nevertheless, I believe that in today's global and economic reality, where we constantly have to adapt to the new normal, learning in times of change is crucial for an organization's survival.

The impact of COVID-19 in March 2020 was immediate. Where other companies could encourage working from home, for many organizations in the hospital sector, this option did not exist. What's more, the workload increased. Not only did co-workers have to deal differently with their employees and patients, these rules also changed very frequently. The most important thing was also to measure whether the knowledge was understood and applied. There was also a need to focus on the staff's wellbeing and involvement in order to provide support during this difficult period.

A good example of an organization in the firing line, which responded with agility to the need for knowledge sharing and the added value of looking outside the box for solutions, was given to me by Alfred Remmits who is an expert on the *5 Moments of Need*.

CASE STUDY
Erasmus MC in Rotterdam

Alfred Remmits, CEO Xprtise

In March 2020, the Board of Governors of Erasmus MC in Rotterdam decided that meetings and physical education could not take place for the time being due to the outbreak of COVID-19. Nevertheless, the very next day Madelon Panman, the manager of the Erasmus MC Academy, was invited to join a meeting about scaling up patient care in the context of the crisis for staff training, especially intensive care staff. Panman immediately set to work with her colleagues at the Academy on a new training plan, taking into account the restrictions imposed by the Board.

The Erasmus MC Academy already had a 5 Moments of Need learning pathway running in which some twenty trainers participate and was thus familiar with the 5 Moments of Need methodology and the performance support platform AskDelphi, in which it immediately saw opportunities for training on the COVID-19 virus.

The first priority was to make content efficiently available to all stakeholders, led by Carla 's-Gravemade, L&O coordinator at Erasmus MC: 'We started a new

FIGURE 6.3 Erasmus MC Rotterdam

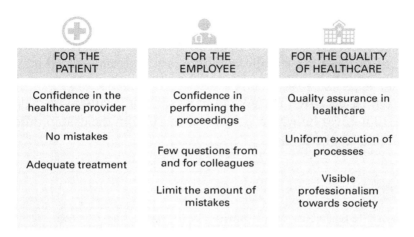

FOR THE PATIENT	FOR THE EMPLOYEE	FOR THE QUALITY OF HEALTHCARE
Confidence in the healthcare provider	Confidence in performing the proceedings	Quality assurance in healthcare
No mistakes		Uniform execution of processes
Adequate treatment	Few questions from and for colleagues	
	Limit the amount of mistakes	Visible professionalism towards society

project group and together with the Xprtise consultants we worked hard to quickly launch the Ask Erasmus MC workplace learning solution for COVID-19. All available content was organized and cut into just-in-time information. Collaboration with other parties helped them to scale the solution quickly.

By deploying performance support according to the 5 Moments of Need methodology with AskDelphi, healthcare professionals have support in the workplace within two clicks or ten seconds when doing their job. This was a particular must-have during COVID-19, not only to prevent major errors, but also to reduce the workload, to make the employees feel secure in the new tasks to be performed and to get continuity in work.

Erasmus MC initially started with a small target group, which is now being continuously expanded. Nine 'roles' have been issued so far, starting with nurse anaesthetists. The following groups are: nurses of non-acute departments, re-entry Intensive Care (IC) Adults, nurses from the IC Children to the IC Adults, re-entry nurses, doctors for IC, doctors for SEH and doctors for Covid-19 Clinic. Erasmus MC receives many thanks and compliments on Ask Erasmus MC from its own colleagues, but also from healthcare professionals from other hospitals. Madelon says: 'Especially because we managed to do this together in such a short time and because we made our study materials available (for free) to other hospitals. From the start, we believed that our investment should benefit everyone and not just our own organization. We are all facing the same tough challenge. Making knowledge, insights, webinars and microlectures available helps all healthcare professionals in the Netherlands and therefore the patients. It also ensures that others want to share materials with us. That's fantastic, isn't it?

Old ways of working in a new guise

In addition to the theories and methodologies already mentioned, there are other concepts that influence learning in the new world. Not all of these are equally revolutionary and often old things are revamped in order to re-launch them as innovative. They are worth mentioning because their adaptability still adds value. Especially in times of innovation where we want to learn from the past in order to be nimble for the future.

Distance learning is not new

Distance learning in combination with work has existed for much longer than one might think. Various sources even go back to the eighteenth century. Students received their weekly lessons by stagecoach and had to complete their assignments and send them back in the same way. This was ideal for people who did not have the means or the time to follow a more formal form of education locally. Learning then literally happened in the flow of life when there was time for it between daily chores and work.

Examples of distance learning in the flow of life using technology are also far from innovative. How did people learn, and still learn, in remote places? Through the internet, the television, even the radio. This is also how the success of one of the first players in the educational technology world (EdTech) began. After Salman Kahn in Louisiana successfully taught his niece maths via the internet using the Yahoo Doodle notebook in 2004, other family members soon came asking for help. Planning all those lessons became quite a problem, so Kahn decided to record videos and post them on the then fledgling YouTube. That way, everyone could learn at their own pace and individual scheduling was no longer an obstacle to helping multiple students. Today, Khan Academy has more than 130 employees and 48 million registered users, in dozens of languages in 190 countries.

Today, we are mainly familiar with MOOC's (massive open online courses) in the field of corporate training, from Degreed, Coursera, edX and LinkedIn, among others. How these tools fit into the picture of a LearnScape or learning organization is explained in the last part where tools and their applicability will be discussed.

Hybrid and blended learning are not the same

I thought I was being original when I wrote an article in 2020 about the opportunities that distance learning brought and used the term 'hybrid' to describe the concept of people learning partly at home and partly in the 'classroom'. It seemed fitting to understand it like the engine of a car that adapts and optimizes itself according to its needs, such as speed.

With this analogy I wanted to offer an answer to the many challenges such as overcrowded classrooms, flexible learning paths, tailored learning content, and the shortage of teachers. This hybrid learning would, in my view, make use of innovative technologies that promote learning for all. For example, AI would drive social networks that could connect students with similar interests, and adaptive and individualized learning would become possible to support classroom and formally driven learning.

A vision where anyone, anywhere, anytime, can learn from content delivered in the most effective way for them. In other words, I hoped we could also transform educational institutions into LearnScapes, where not only the content, but also the connection between learners is supported by technology. It was an idea I had been toying with since 2014 when I developed sCool app with my own children without the possibilities that AI already has to offer.

The fact that hybrid is now used for just about all blended learning forms (digital, together with non-digital moments) is, I think, a pity, because there is a difference in implementation and effectiveness between blended and hybrid. Just because you take a course via a webinar does not mean that you are optimizing the learning itself. On the contrary, the learning gains will in many cases be lower than if you were to follow them in the classroom.

As stated in the introduction, I have learned a lot from observing children and young people in the way they interact with technology and acquire knowledge. Therefore, I would like to share a great example of an educational institution that has done its own thing to support all students, no matter where, when or with whom they are progressing. You will probably notice that the example comes from the world of ballet. The Royal Ballet School may seem far removed from innovation as an education, but it is preparing for the future of work and is very much in tune with the needs of the present and the future in its working methods. It may therefore be an inspiration for many corporate organizations that want to let go of the past and embrace the hybrid in its essence.

CASE STUDY
A lesson in hybrid education

Interview with the mother of a student

Art education, and more specifically the Royal Ballet School (KBA) in Antwerp, must balance time between general subjects and art subjects. As a result, it is sometimes said that little or no attention is paid to general education. But this was absolutely not the case when, as a result of the measures taken during COVID-19, fewer pupils could attend school at the same time. The school decided to switch to half-time education. This meant that the older pupils could only attend classes in the afternoon and the younger ones only in the morning. Still, this was a solution to support all pupils as much as possible in both learning areas.

It goes without saying that dance classes lend themselves least to distance learning. That is why it was decided to continue all those lessons. For the general subjects, a very flexible and hybrid solution was offered.

This meant that pupils who achieved good to very good results received their instructions at home via Zoom. The teacher sat alone at school in his office without a mouthpiece so that he could be understood by pupils with a language barrier. (Many international students attend classes at KBA)

After receiving the instructions for the task, the 'home learners' would work independently. Or, if they wished, they could connect online with other 'home schoolers' to study together.

Students who needed extra support were then helped individually in the large dining hall – where they could sit far away from each other – by the teacher who helped them personally while respecting safety measures. What we saw is that all students very quickly appreciated this way of working and achieved better results. A nice side effect was also that the self-confidence and wellbeing of many pupils received a boost.

This approach also proved to offer opportunities after the obligatory half-time period. For instance, the pupils themselves are asking to continue this method and to adapt lessons to their personal needs and preferences.

Some misconceptions about social learning

Social learning, like hybrid learning, is discussed in many different learning contexts. Yet we often see confusion when social learning in a technological context, on social platforms, is confused with social learning theory. Therefore, in order to avoid misunderstandings, I would like to frame where the theory has its origin, and how it still influences learning strategies. How social learning in turn fits into building learning organizations or LearnScapes is discussed further in part 4 of this book. Here, the link is being made with lean learning and the learning maturity model of organizations that use artificial intelligence for optimal knowledge sharing and learning.

SOCIAL LEARNING TECHNOLOGY

The origins of social learning theory go back to 1941 from the behavioural sciences and psychology based on a series of lectures from professor of psychology at Harvard University, B.F. Skinner. The lectures were on the use of stimulus-response theories to describe language use and development. His basic position was that all verbal behaviour was supported by operant conditioning, a learning process in which behaviour that is positively reinforced is performed more often and behaviour that is negatively reinforced less often, until eventually it no longer occurs.

Skinner's behaviourist theories provided inspiration for Albert Bandura's (1977) redevelopment of the *Social Learning Theory*. This social learning theory is also based on the idea that new behaviour can be acquired through a learning process by observing and imitating others. Social learning would not just take place passively but would need reinforcement. Attention, retention, reproduction and motivation are necessary in order to have real added value in the social learning process. This can be a cognitive process that includes direct instruction as well as rewards and even punishments. In addition, we see that vicarious reinforcement, rewarding someone else for similar behaviour, also has a role in social learning.

The relevance of the social learning theory is therefore to be found in the emphasis it places on the role of various internal processes in the learning individual that also influence motivation to learn. It is also valuable to keep social learning theory in mind when considering the use of social technologies in a learning strategy.

For example, when considering gamification, one can think about what form of reinforcement to apply. This in turn can help to inform the choice of technology from a theoretical perspective. Yet, we also see that some organizations choose social learning platforms that have a different approach without any form of reinforcement. Here, learning comes exclusively from observation driven by intrinsic motivation or vicarious reinforcement. To make this assessment, however, it is essential to also take into account the organization's own learning culture, which will be discussed in part 5 of this book.

RISE OF SOCIAL LEARNING TECHNOLOGIES

When we think of social learning platforms, we often think of innovative technologies that we know today as Learning Experience Platforms (LXP). Yet as early as 2005, with the meteoric rise of Facebook, sharing interests and knowledge became widely popular.

This hyper-connected and algorithm-supported technology was what first inspired me to build LearnScapes in 2014. The challenge I faced was to connect 16,000 employees worldwide to learn and share expertise together. The premise was that many skills could be learned in an easier and more fun way through collaboration and experience with others. I was tasked with developing an Enterprise Social Network (ESN) that was as simple and attractive as Facebook. At the time, my goal was to use simple algorithms – we didn't have Zuckerberg's budgets – to connect employees with the same profiles and interests, i.e. *Human-2-Human*, an idea I borrowed from Bryan Kramer's book of the same name.

Looking for more inspiration to harness the power of social platforms, I came across Mark Fidelman. In his book, he described how social networks contribute to the individual and the organization. He inspired me to look at many existing ESNs, but I was often frustrated to discover that they were mostly repositories of old knowledge where social interactions did not exist.

Not much later, other authors such as Marcia Conner and Harold Jarche would inspire me with their insights into social learning through the use of apps. Yet it was Jane Hart who convinced me that existing public social networks had added value for businesses. As a pioneer, she published the list of Top Tools for Learning since 2011, in which YouTube and Twitter alternated in high places. What fascinated me most was her concept of backchannel learning by following hashtags (#) on Twitter.

My first thought when I heard about backchannel learning was that I was sorry Twitter didn't exist when I was still wasting my time in the university auditorium. I would have much preferred to follow the most important backchannels from my garden in the sun.

As Jane Hart described it, this was a unique tool for sharing knowledge with people who had the same interests, using a hashtag. To optimize this further, I made lists on HootSuite, a marketing tool, of hashtags that interested me and of people who usually shared good content. Finding knowledge suddenly became much easier when technology presented everything to me in neat little lists.

Social technologies that support learning seem well established today. However, there are still many challenges when we want to optimize it. The pillars of social learning platforms and the benefits of implementing this in a lean approach provide for learning ecosystems or Learnscapes. In part 4 of this book, I will go into more detail about this.

Juggling data and performance measurements

Learning strategies and methods are only worth what they effectively contribute to learning in which experience causes a permanent change in knowledge or behaviour. And therein lies the difficulty, because learning can take place in various forms such as formal or informal, conscious or unconscious, correct or incorrect, individual or team-based. Making learning initiatives measurable is therefore a major challenge for many organizations.

Yet, we will see that it is precisely the measurability of learning initiatives that is often necessary even before a project can be started. Even more than the method, the technology and the content of the programme, measurements will be necessary to convince the necessary stakeholders of the relevance of a learning project, and to free up the necessary budgets. However, we should not only focus on data or data-based learning strategies as there is a risk that too much obscures what actually matters, such as learning to apply or change behavior.

Data learning strategies

Data learning strategies seem to be becoming increasingly popular for linking the measurability of learning to business objectives. However, the question must be asked which data is relevant and which is not. When we talk about learning organizations, there are many different data sources coming from applications that are supposed to support learning such as the number of courses produced, learning activities completed, the number of connections, the time spent learning, are just a few. The number of courses produced, though, is not relevant if they have not supported anyone in applying their knowledge. Measuring applied knowledge from these courses to achieve business objectives, on the other hand, is highly relevant. Unfortunately, it is a reality that L&D today measures much that is not relevant to learning.

COVID-19 has shown that even highly educated specialists do not draw the same conclusions from the same data sets. So, the data alone is not useful if we do not interpret it in the right context, or if we manipulate/interpret them, consciously or unconsciously, to endorse a point of view. In relation to learning, all too often a link is sought between the input of learning (e.g. training) and the output of learning (e.g. increased productivity) to justify an investment. In doing so, causality (one event causes another) and correlation (one event influences another) are quickly used interchangeably to support that viewpoint 'based on validated datasets'. It is also important to clearly define in advance which data are KPI (key performance indicators): what do we want to measure as the success of our efforts? If these are not the right indicators, we may create or evaluate learning strategies less effectively.

An example of this is often seen in data-based learning strategies that use gamification to motivate learners. Points are awarded on the basis of learning moments successfully completed within a time span. These points are then used to create a leaderboard and award 'prizes' to the best players. This can be great fun for an ambitious new employee who wants to grow quickly and is also competitive and loves games. Soon the data will show they have the motivation to learn and is a real asset to the team.

But imagine that this new employee who has all the competencies and skills does not see any added value in quickly solving questions from a quiz. In addition, they have a deep-seated aversion to games and even more to leaderboards where names are made public. The very idea that their picture will suddenly be shared with the entire organization is enough to make them not want to score high. Drawing conclusions from these leaderboards is therefore very risky, and even though they seem to say something about a correlation with motivation to learn, they cannot guarantee that the knowledge will actually be applied.

Therefore, when we start an innovative learning project in the last part of this book, determining the right indicators and expected outcomes will be essential for the measurability of success. And, as will be seen later, this exercise is particularly relevant before technology/tools are discussed or chosen.

Kirkpatrick's four levels of evaluation

When we think of the saying 'to measure is to know' and attempts to make causal connections between training and business results, the Kirkpatrick evaluation model, former professor emeritus at the University of Wisconsin, is perhaps the most widely used model worldwide. The idea is simple: measure the effectiveness of training based on what works and what doesn't. Both for the learner and from the perspective of business objectives and business results.

This model was created in 1959. In this next section, I will evaluate it by taking into account the many adjustments that have been made since its creation, specifically by Kirkpatrick's family to ensure that it would still be useful in a current digital context.

The premise of Kirkpatrick's 'simple four-step process' was simple and very relevant in its time. Training (in the classroom for which it was originally developed) in an organization is both a time-consuming and costly affair. The purpose of this model, or process, was therefore to check whether the efforts made corresponded to the expected results.

I will explore its usefulness for other learning contexts as well as those for which it was originally developed and adapted. In doing so, I will look at the advantages and possible shortcomings of this method of making learning measurable.

The 4 pillars of the Kirkpatrick model

1 **Learning is mapped from the participant's experience.** The aim is to evaluate an individual's reaction to the 'training'. This is usually done by questioning the 'trainee' shortly after the training. This already carries an initial risk, as many of the questions are subjective and irrelevant to how the knowledge can be used. Think of questions like: did you find it interesting, what were the strengths, can you apply this in your work environment, etc.

2 **It is subjective because it relates to the motivation the learner had beforehand** and the reason why they participated in the training. Moreover, it is difficult to take into account various cultures that have a different view on assessments. From my own experiences, I know that there are big differences internationally when filling in these questionnaires such as Net promoter Score (NPS). Belgians, for example, rarely give extreme scores and regard a 4/5 as very good and 2/5 as worthless. Our neighbours to the north in the Netherlands like an honest opinion and are more likely to give

maximum scores in their assessment. Drawing conclusions is therefore less easy when this is done anonymously in international groups or mixed groups with a different motivation to participate. In my opinion, therefore, this widely used NPS, from the participants, is not always the most relevant. Without anticipating, I think Pillar 4 offers more opportunities.

3 **Learning is made measurable through post-session evaluation** by managers, peers and others who can help provide relevant analysis of modified performance. The aim is to find out what the trainees have actually learned. It looks at the confidence level of the learner and whether they are motivated enough to changes behaviours, improve skills, etc. Here we see that the challenge are already much greater, as is the cost of identifying this for each learning moment. It also requires the evaluators to have a very good understanding of the participant. Due in part to the different backgrounds and motivations of participants, uniform assessment measures are not straightforward to develop. In a world where learning is supported by AI, it seems to me a huge opportunity to have this done by a non-bias related AI coach like an example I discuss later in this book.

4 **Making behavioural change measurable** is the goal of the third pillar of the Kirkpatrick model. Here, the assessment is done by the participant, managers and HR partners. It goes without saying that this is very time-consuming and difficult to organize. Excluding subjectivity and defining a causal relationship is often a major obstacle here as well as in previous ones. Was performance improved by external factors of the training (new colleague, offer of promotion) or by the training itself? In my opinion, relevant evaluations in this area can be much cheaper, faster, continuous and more insightful by using the latest generation of performance management platforms, as I showed earlier with the case of MassMines provided by Entomo.

5 **The success of the programme** is the last pillar although, in my opinion, it should come first. Here we evaluate tangible results that are defined in advance. 'Why are we doing this?' could then be expressed, for example, as a reduction in costs compared to

another training programme. Other drivers could be a shorter lead time between learning need and course deployment, increased productivity, reduced error rate in production, etc. These indicators, which relate to the lean learning model in chapter 9 of this book, should be the starting point and not the result of a new learning project.

6 **In the Kirkpatrick context, evaluation is very expensive and time-consuming** due to the mostly manual techniques used by HR experts. We also see that a one-time performance review is often not enough, as indicated earlier, and that it is very important to do a baseline measurement beforehand. Determining the right 'measurable' critical success factors is a big challenge and in many situations it is very difficult to adjust once the training has started.

This model has certainly been successful in the past, when time and resources were available. Therefore, in the final part of this book, it is interesting to look at what we can retain and what we can improve.

Confidence based learning

Confidence (or lack of it) in our own ability may also have an effect on how effective learning is. For example, stressful situations can cause us to doubt and second-guess ourselves. It can also be the case that we think we have learned something, yet our performance does not improve. The reason for this is that we often lack confidence in our own abilities or misjudge them.

As early as 1932, the first academic paper was written on the relationship between confidence, propriety, retention and learning. This research stated that measuring confidence and knowledge was a better predictor of performance than measuring knowledge alone, which can be subject to guesswork. More than 70 years of academic, commercial and government research, together with technological development, eventually led to the development of the current theory of confidence-based learning. However, due to the many contributors, it is not clear to whom to give credit, but it is often attributed to Dr James Bruno, a professor of education at UCLA.

Confidence Based Learning (CBL) measures the learner's knowledge level by determining both the correctness of the knowledge and the confidence in the knowledge. This is done by having the learner indicate after each question or task how confident they were in what they answered or did. In addition, the CBL method is also designed to increase retention and minimize the effects of guesswork, which in some cases distorts the results of single-score assessments. The combination of both provides the knowledge base and identifies the difference between what the learner thinks they know and what they actually know. When this is identified, it forms the basis of an adaptive curriculum that can fill in gaps in knowledge and skills.

This process, which is based on continuous improvement and is similar to quality processes such as Six Sigma, will keep repeating a particular skill through different questions until the learner has mastered it. This then becomes confident, correct knowledge that can be applied in practice. What distinguishes it from other assessments is that it is based on four key components. Together they can be used for continuous diagnosis and personal guidance:

- **Diagnosis** – learners answer questions and do exercises to demonstrate any gaps in their knowledge and areas of low confidence.

- **Prescribing** – based on the above gaps, an adaptive personal programme is drawn up that addresses deficiencies and increases self-confidence.

- **Learning** – starting from the personal learning path, the learner works on the different (micro-learning) paths until they feel confident in all content areas.

- **Iterative** – the above learning is repeated from different angles until they master this part.

USING CONFIDENCE BASED LEARNING FOR BETTER PERFORMANCE

Today, with the popularity of microlearning platforms and AI-enabled adaptive learning paths, we are seeing a renewed interest in this theory.

Yet I can imagine that there are also reservations about applying CBL to increase performance. On the one hand, the algorithms are often not what we should expect, which leads to frustration. On the other hand, the repetition and control questions can also be frustrating for the learner and therefore reduce engagement. However, my own studies and interviews with users of such applications showed that this learning method actually reduces the time to mastery. Moreover, the results with regard to efficiency and productivity at work were significantly higher. This is because doubters hesitate or make mistakes when under pressure to perform a task.

Bringing theory together with technology also has advantages in terms of visualising performance data, and customized coaching approaches. This data, which is extracted from the back-end of educational technologies, can be brought together in a convenient block of four, both at individual and team level.

- **Masters** – workers who know the facts and are not afraid to use them.
- **Doubters** – people who know their facts but may not have the confidence to act without hesitation.
- **Misinformed** – people who confidently believe false information.
- **Uninformed** – people who have not yet acquired all the knowledge they need to know.

FIGURE 6.4 The visualization of confidence based learning

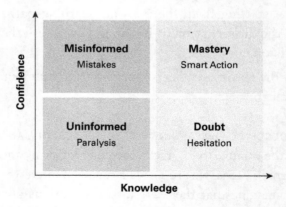

This visualization indicates all learning moments that have been completed and identifies risk areas. These are then the ideal starting points for personal guidance or coaching. The combination of data from the application and the human competences of a coach significantly enhance those learning moments. An example of intelligent cooperation between humans and machine that benefits personal wellbeing.

Managers who make use of data from learning technologies that capture confidence based learning will take actions with regard to the risk zones in the following two quadrants.

The misinformed quadrant is clearly the 'danger zone' where employees are very prone to making mistakes. However, they sincerely believe that they are doing the right thing. If this is not properly addressed during an individual performance review, significant risks can arise. Productivity can drop as a result of mistakes, and products or customer relations can be damaged. Of course, in many cases, someone who makes mistakes will know it, especially with skills such as coding where no output is produced. But in professions such as sales (the example of Etihad follows further on in this book), sales people often do not even realize that they are making mistakes. In this case, it is difficult to know whether the course was poor or whether there are other reasons for the poor results. This also indicates that the CBL method in combination with personal coaching is ideal for making causality in training measurable.

The doubt quadrant indicates when the learner may be very knowledgeable but is hesitant in applying this. These learners would also benefit from personal guidance, yet most methods would not reveal this. Most training programmes aim to eliminate errors by making them visible and giving feedback on them. But what if there are no mistakes, only a lack of confidence? As a result, they do not take the initiative and are certainly not motivated to invest in their own learning.

Intelligent collaboration between smart technologists, together with leadership competences support very positive results in the learning organization. Since this method also focuses on developing confidence and trust, it also supports the learning culture of the organization that cultivates a growth mindset.

The future of learning analytics

The theories and methods already discussed indicate that there is a need for linking business objectives, performance management and learning. Therefore, the last part of this book also explains the continuous improvement method that takes this into account to shape projects. The choice of technology based on the relevant data it can generate is an important aspect. Therein often lies a significant difficulty, because what is relevant for one organization is often not for another.

What we are already seeing is that along with the rise of learning support technologies (EdTech), learning analytics is also developing very rapidly. It seems more than likely that in the future we will be able to measure a lot more, but how far should we go to capture learning in data?

Should we therefore be inspired by eye tracking innovations such as AttentivU, where both brain activity (electroencephalography – EEG) and eye movements (electrooculography – EOG) are used to measure various cognitive processes, such as cognitive load, fatigue, engagement and focus in real time? These so-called Multimodal Learning Analytics are used for passive or active interventions, for example to monitor the condition of the learner. People who are easily distracted will thus be kept focused via soft audio or haptic impulses. This ability to detect cognitive overload therefore seems very interesting when considering solutions that support learning in the workplace and thus anticipate the reduction of risks.

Other examples focus on the added value of automated online dialogue analysis. These would in turn support training in communication skills, or aim to recruit the most suitable candidates. Still, from the ethical point of view in the first part, we may wonder whether we can already trust technology and the data analysis it produces to assess human skills and competences. More to the point, do we risk measuring just to know or is the intention to increase wellbeing?

When thinking about the future of Data Learning strategies, it is important to have a long-term vision and a holistic view of all data that adds value to change and learning. This goes hand in hand with data managed from L&D in LMS systems, performance-based data tracked from the business, HR data tracking personal expectations for the future, data from external (formal or non-formal) learning platforms such as LinkedIn or Coursera, data from social media, etc.

The future of data-driven strategies will therefore not be about data per se, but even more about the exchange of data and the consolidation of data to make intelligent decisions. A learning strategist is expected to have a holistic view of all data, and to be capable of aggregating it to make adjustments to the strategy.

References

702010 Institute (2022) What is the 70:20:10 model? 702010institute. com/702010-model/ (archived at https://perma.cc/MTC6-4YQC)

AECT (2022) *13.2* History of Distance Education, members.aect.org/edtech/ ed1/13/13-02.html (archived at https://perma.cc/7J7D-RX6J)

AttentivU (2022) AttentivU, www.attentivu.com/ (archived at https://perma.cc/ 8PJR-JF8Z)

Bandura, A (1971) *Social Learning Theory*, General Learning Press, New York

Bandura, A (1963) *Social learning and personality development*, Holt, Rinehart, and Winston, New York

Blondy, L C Evaluation and Application of Andragogical Assumptions to the Adult Online Learning Environment, *Journal of Interactive Online Learning*, 6, pp. 116–130, www.ncolr.org/jiol/issues/pdf/6.2.3.pdf (archived at https:// perma.cc/LG3J-7N85)

Bloom's Taxonomy (2022) What is Bloom's Taxonomy, bloomstaxonomy.net/ (archived at https://perma.cc/G45K-LUNF)

BrenchPrep (2022) Why Confidence-Based Learning Improves Performance, blog. benchprep.com/why-confidence-based-learning-improves-performance (archived at https://perma.cc/8AMC-5GJU)

CAPSTAN (2020) 'Distance Education' Is Not A New Concept, It Is Actually Much Older Than Zoom, Google Classroom, Or Even The Internet, www.capstan.be/ distance-education-is-not-a-new-concept-it-is-actually-much-older-than-zoom- google-classroom-or-even-the-internet/ (archived at https://perma.cc/ A5PN-RNS7)

Cloud Watch Hub (2022) Scool, www.cloudwatchhub.eu/scool (archived at https:// perma.cc/MQY5-UN5P)

Gottfredson, C & Mosher, B (2011) Innovative Performance Support, McGraw Hill Education, New York

Hevner, K (1932) 'A method of correcting for guessing in true-false tests and empirical evidence in support of it' *Journal of Social Psychology*, 3, 359–362

InstructionalDesign.org (2022) Operant Conditioning (B.F. Skinner), www.instructionaldesign.org/theories/operant-conditioning/ (archived at https://perma.cc/4SVZ-4BKG)

Kirkpatrick Partners (2022) What is The Kirkpatrick Model? www.kirkpatrickpartners.com/the-kirkpatrick-model/ (archived at https://perma.cc/B3NV-TAWW)

Khan Academy (2022) Khan Academy, www.khanacademy.org/ (archived at https://perma.cc/MMP8-3FP7)

Kramer, B (2017) Human 2 Human: H2H, PureMatter Inc. San Jose

Psychologist World (2022) Operant Conditioning, www.psychologistworld.com/behavior/operant-conditioning (archived at https://perma.cc/U5XV-482S)

Schipperheijn, K (2020) DataNews Knack, Digitaal leren is het onderwijs van de Toekomst, datanews.knack.be/ict/nieuws/digitaal-leren-is-het-onderwijs-van-detoekomst/article-opinion-1596251.html (archived at https://perma.cc/RYE3-M9FM)

Simply Psychology (2016) Albert Bandura's Social Learning Theory, www.simplypsychology.org/bandura.html (archived at https://perma.cc/X8LE-KCYN)

07

Learning technologies

Making learning moments measurable is one of the biggest challenges for organizations that want to implement new learning strategies, as we saw in the previous sections. In what follows in this chapter, I will also try to approach technology from the learner's perspective. To add value for them as an immersive experience or not.

One of the elements I also look at is the possibility it offers to reduce transactional distance and increase learning and learning autonomy.

Optimalization of transactional distance and learning autonomy

When we talk about transactional distance (Figure 7.1) we are referring to the perception of psychological distance between the instructor and the learner and the relationship of this when individualization is intended. Dr Michael Moore (1997) explained this as an inverse relationship between dialogue and structure in any educational transaction. The greater the dialogue, the smaller the structure and vice versa. This can lead to communication problems, misunderstandings, reduced learning, reduced engagement and reduced learning autonomy.

However, learning autonomy is often the driving force in learning organizations for a positive approach to lifelong learning. This means that learners take control and responsibility for their own learning, both in terms of what they learn and how they learn it. This makes them more capable of self-direction and an independent, proactive approach to learning.

FIGURE 7.1 Transactional distance and the relation to learning autonomy

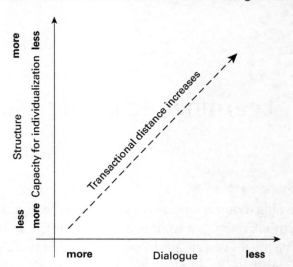

Virtual learning environments and other modern technologies, such as self-organized learning environments, try to reduce the psychological perception of distance by providing structure through dialogue, between the learner and the instructor, with or without an intelligent algorithm. Such systems cater for different types of learners simultaneously and can also adapt minutely to the needs of groups of learners.

Microlearning platforms

Microlearning applications have recently become very popular because of their simplicity and versatility, and the mobile strategy they support. They facilitate learning in the flow of life, which meets the challenges of the future workforce as described in chapter 2 of this book. Whether an employee has five minutes before a meeting or a few minutes at the end of the working day, these moments are the perfect opportunity for mandatory training.

Increasingly, microlearning applications are also called Learning Experience Platforms (LXP) because they are said to focus on improving the learner's experience. However, in my opinion, as I have already mentioned, this is not the only added value. I often see learning, or information, at the moment of need as a much more important aspect that is less cited as a unique selling point (USP). A missed opportunity for many sales people.

Short or micro-content is relative in my experience, however, as they offer average content between 2–10 minutes and vary greatly by application and organization. What the perfect time is, is hard to answer. It often seems to be a goal for content creators to stay within the attention span of online media platforms, which on average is 45 seconds on Instagram and about two minutes on YouTube. My experience is that future generations increasingly need something interesting and relevant from the first second or they will swipe away. Knowing your employees to tailor the duration of relevant content is therefore essential as I also demonstrate in chapter 13 on creating relevant content.

An important observation I make about duration is that too much focus is often given to just that aspect. 'Chunking' or chopping up existing longer content such as e-learnings is not the solution and creates more waste as I will discuss in chapter 9 on lean learning strategies.

Another misconception is that microlearning involves video or creative content made by expensive experts. Many microlearning applications have an authoring tool that makes it as easy for managers, L&D staff and learners alike to share content as it is on Instagram. And this is perhaps one of the most important benefits for corporate learning. If we know that 70 per cent of all knowledge in organizations resides with employees and not with professional teachers or instructional designers, then it is an absolute added value to unlock this knowledge in social and lean learning ecosystems (chapter 10). A comparison with maker platforms such as Roblox is easily made. Here, subject-matter experts create content and share it with everyone in the ecosystem, so that knowledge grows throughout the organization and experts are recognized for their contribution.

A final and measurable example of what makes microlearning so popular today is the ease with which it can be deployed and its ability to increase engagement based on the data it generates. These can be explained as two key pillars: the Spacing Effect and the Retrieval Practice.

The spacing effect and the forgetting curve

The spacing effect shows that people remember information better when it is presented repeatedly over time. Remembering is even better when the time interval between each repetition becomes longer and longer, challenging the brain to remember. This, of course, is at odds with the 'cramming' methods that are still often routinely offered in the form of training or e-learning, where large amounts of data are studied continuously over a short period of time – without reinforcement afterwards.

Studies on the 'spacing effect' are not new and existed before innovative technologies, yet are now being used to extract added value from them. The first publication that refer to this date back to 1985, in the book *A Contribution to Experimental Psychology* by Hermann Ebbinghaus. In it he cited the forgetting curve as linked to the spacing effect. This forgetting curve is also the starting point of very innovative techniques based on neuroscience and Marketing as Anna Tarabasz will explain in chapter 14.

The forgetting curve states that although learning is smooth during training, memory begins to deteriorate almost immediately after training – and this has nothing to do with age as we learned from Kegan and Lahey. On average, more than 90 per cent of the information is forgotten within a month. Of course, there are ways to strengthen retention by applying the knowledge or skills gained shortly after it is gained. This reinforcement creates new pathways in the brain to store and recall information. Microlearning exploits this by moving knowledge from short-term memory to long-term memory. This in turn has a positive correlation with work performance.

Retrieval practice

Retrieval practice, is the oldest, but not the least interesting theory that is being revamped by technology. Dating back to 1909 from research by Edwina E Abbott, this theory is based on the principle that retrieving information reinforces and stimulates learning. This deliberate retrieval of knowledge we have acquired is what is applied in microlearning platforms through the repetition of certain content.

This may or may not be combined with gamified aspects and data tracking that map to trust-based learning. By repeating certain content or skills again, we create a memory trail in our brains that is more resistant to forgetting.

Combined, the spacing effect and retrieval practice are thought to increase recall rates by 78 per cent to 97 per cent according to research by Dr Alice Kim of the Rotman Research Institute of Baycrest and York University.

In other words, microlearning, which draws on the studies mentioned above, has great potential. But, it also has its limitations as for example, its use for blue collar employees who are not digitally connected. It's not a panacea and it's not a one-fit-all, but it does offer many possibilities that, within a nimble strategy, are worth looking at as part of the technological architecture of the learning landscape.

That microlearning and its analytics offer opportunities is something Andrew Stotter-Brooks, Vice President of Learning and Development at Etihad Aviation Group can explain. This example approaches the causal relationship between learning and performance improvement in his sales team, from the perspective of the confidence based learning model, spacing effect and retrieval practice, supported by a micro-learning application.

CASE STUDY

Stuck on the tarmac: the search for the right approach

Andrew Stotter-Brooks, senior VP L&D Etihad

I'm just going to say it: Most professional training is boring. It's often neither engaging nor relevant to employees' everyday tasks. Training is often a check in a box, and any learning is forgotten soon after the training is complete.

If that sounds like your company's approach to employee learning and development (L&D), you're not alone. Some of the biggest and most successful companies in the world treat training as an afterthought—and for our teams at Etihad Airways, we had a long way to go to get our training and development process up to scratch.

Training eModules for our teams have long lived in our internal learning management system (LMS). While the eModules themselves were of good quality, the platform was limited in communication and other features. The modules were also generic. If they weren't relevant to an employee's job, it wasn't worth their time to watch. This was especially true for our salespeople, who are constantly on the move. It was clear that we weren't getting much business benefit from this type of training.

We also had classroom training that was more effective, but limited to sales beginners. Etihad prides itself on having some of the most highly experienced and effective salespeople in the industry, but we didn't help them improve. The classroom training wasn't advanced enough for their needs, and the eModules weren't mobile and didn't fit into their day-to-day routines. They couldn't level up.

When I joined Etihad in 2019 the goal was to build a new approach to training and performance management. Therefore, we looked at different methodologies in a proactive and positive way, changing all of our thinking about the structure of performance measurement. As part of that structure, we looked at microlearning.

In the end, we selected Axonify because it was incredibly simple to understand and use. For me, the real selling point is the concept of daily learning that consists of just three questions. Answering those questions takes a single minute to complete. Everyone finds it frustrating to sit in front of a screen for 30 minutes staring at a training module. But when employees can take a minute to reaffirm their existing knowledge and then get on with their day-to-day activities, it's time well spent. This concept of daily learning merged perfectly with our new straightforward strategy 'Know/Do/Be' L&D strategy.

- **Know:** what the team member must know, including the theory and tools available at a defined career level.

- **Do:** what the team member must do, including the theory, tools and behaviors at a defined career level that they regularly put into practice.

- **Be:** how the employee must behave, including their understanding and embodiment of the behaviors, beliefs, values and knowledge important to the business.

CLEARED FOR TAKEOFF: ACCELERATING A CULTURE SHIFT

This has been a major overhaul to the commercial sales teams. Our head office used to be the driving force behind how our salespeople approach their sales, training, agenda and contracts. But in less than 18 months, we've essentially redesigned the whole sales operating model from scratch, including our methodology. To do this we needed a clear and consistent communication, which is key when overhauling an L&D approach (or any approach, for that matter). We set up daily communications within the implementation team about the new sales and training models that inform everyone of all the new changes, why the changes took place, how they're different and whatever new process exists.

The biggest challenge for our team was in keeping up with the pace of change. We were writing new content nearly in real time. It's difficult for us to think 6–12 months ahead when the bulk of our work is so urgent. But the rapid pace has accelerated adoption, and the sales team sees this new training model as a positive change around learning, performance management and autonomy within their ranks.

Our salespeople feel empowered to proactively take ownership and accountability for how they approach their markets and customers. They know what they should be doing and how to close sales, and now they have the freedom to do it in their own way.

TRAINING ON THE FLY: ENGAGING OUR LEARNERS THROUGH COMPETITION
In the first 18 months since we introduced the new framework, the uptake has been superb. Every month, we see our entire sales staff completing 4,500–5,000 extra training sessions which blows me away because it shows their appetite for learning and professional growth, an ideal quality to cultivate within teams. It demonstrates true engagement, and we can build on that enthusiasm. Our previous history with eModules was never going to deliver that – not in a million years.

A big part of our transformation is to make training fun and engaging by embracing gamification. We created a monthly league table, which shows the top 20 learners of our entire sales staff across the network. If there's anything salespeople love, it's a competition. Everyone wants to get on the leaderboard, and it gets those competitive juices flowing far better than I ever thought it would.

I'm frequently asked how we get those high engagement rates and people think we make participating is mandatory like our previous eModules were, but it's all self-driven learning. People sell it to their peers because it's fun and easy. They just log in, complete their three questions and they're done. The participation rate among all Etihad salespeople is 70%. That's a far cry from our eModules, which have a 60% completion rate across sales teams – despite the fact that it's mandatory.

NONSTOP LEARNING, NONSTOP DATA ANALYSIS

I get an Excel report each week from the eModules, which lets us notify countries of the number of team members that have completed their sessions. But it's nothing compared to the data the platform gives us based on the confidence based learning model. It allows us to see our salespeople's knowledge growth, which is a great metric to share throughout the organization. We can also communicate with individuals or broadcast a message across the business as desired.

Our next step is to engage local managers in leadership development as part of our holistic performance management strategy. We also expect to evaluate a revenue value tied to learning outcomes next year using the impact tool build in the platform

I get a big kick out of seeing other people succeed, and it's been great to see the commercial sales team achieve so much so quickly. It's allowed us to deliver a positive message in a positive way, and that's had a real impact on our company culture. Our teams know that we listen and have delivered the training they asked for in a much more fun and accommodating way. When people start believing that things are going to happen, rather than thinking they never will, that's when you know for sure that the sky's the limit.

Gamification or game-based learning

As indicated, there is often more to an appropriate learning strategy than the choice of technology alone. Depending on the methods and theories on which they are based, they may or may not be a better match for the target group and the culture of an organization. Trying to copy success stories or white papers from other organizations is therefore not advisable.

Measurability, relevance and underlying principles of application can make a big difference and so can another popular selling point of edtech vendors: gamification or gamified learning. Both are on the rise, yet they are often confused, even by vendors of these applications. That is why it is important that you understand the difference when you want to develop your own learning strategy that fits your employees and culture. To summarize:

- **Gamification** is transforming the learning process into a game, or serious gaming.
- **Game-based learning (GBL)** is the use of a game as part of the learning process.

Both goals are relatively similar. Serious games and gamification both try to solve a problem, motivate and promote learning by using game-based thinking and techniques. Yet the subtleties and differences are relevant to understand for a strategy that builds on either a gamified or a game-based learning campaign

Gamification

Here the entire learning process is turned into a game by applying game mechanics and game elements to existing learning courses and content. As with game-based learning, the aim is to better motivate and engage learners. These mechanisms include achievement badges, leaderboards, progress bars, but also different levels in a course and quests.

In theory, just about anything can be gamified, not just learning activities to increase engagement. This can be subtle so that we often don't realize that through gamification we are being encouraged to go further, as for example with LinkedIn. They encourage you to complete your page via a simple progress bar. When you add new relevant information to your profile you can get badges and the highest status 'superstar'.

Game-based learning

Unlike gamification, where game principles are applied to the learning process, GBL uses a game as the starting point for learning. Another distinction we can make is that the starting point of GBL is often the learning of a specific skill or competence, whereas gamification is often applied to the entire learning process within an organization.

Another aspect that contributes to the success of GBL and gamification is the rewards that are awarded. These may seem trivial, but they are part of the success factor when selecting a strategy. You can choose to give rewards for participation and effort, like LinkedIn. On the other hand, you can link them to leaderboards. Both have an added value in some cultures. However, you cannot find this added value by blindly copying someone else's example and then expecting it to be successful. Without a holistic view and vision the results can be the opposite and reduce engagement. This can be avoided by taking into account the individuality of the employees and the company culture. There is a connection with confidence-based learning where some employees score very well – or are very good at guessing – and others score less well because they doubt their own abilities. A public leaderboard is then, as mentioned earlier, often not engagement-enhancing for those who really need it.

For example, I heard from Andrew Stotter-Brooks that one of the rewards offered at Etihad is a temporary parking space closer to the entrance of the office. That may not seem like a nice prize for your organization, but imagine you have to walk for more than five minutes in hot or rainy weather. Stotter-Brooks also knows that within one organization he has to think of other rewards. A department with workers who do not have their own car cannot, of course, be won over with a parking space. Rolling out a learning strategy must therefore be preceded by due-diligence before there can be any talk of GBL or gamification.

Conversational AI is more than just chatbots

A significant evolution that we have recently seen on LMS, and thus also on microlearning platforms, are chatbots that help us with onboarding and often also with finding relevant content.

Chatbots are also increasingly being used with a very human touch that makes us doubt the virtual existence of our conversation partner.

Examples that most appeal to the imagination are these chatbots that we use for role-plays, but also, and increasingly, they are used as support for recruitment purposes and sales training.

This evolution towards state-of-the-art chatbots that use conversational AI and natural language processing (NLP) opens up unprecedented possibilities. Machine learning is used to constantly improve its own algorithm in combination with NLP for modelling and interpreting written or spoken language. Whereas in 1997 we were still impressed by Big Blue beating Garry Kasparov at his own game, today we see that robots are a worthy opponent in several aspects.

This opens new perspectives for intelligent cooperation between humans and machines. Our next recruiter or sales trainer might be a state-of-the-art chatbot, lifelike counterparts that look as realistic as our counterpart in an online role-playing game via Zoom. These virtual Avatar conversational AI chat bots could even fool you into thinking they are real people like Lil Miquela on Instagram. She is 19 years old, perfect skin, works for top brands like Prada and Chanel and has family and relationship problems like you and me. She has 3.1 million Instagram followers (when I wrote this), most of them female, who see her as a role model and aspire to be like her. Similar bots will likely feature in many applications in the future such as adaptive learning programmes where they answer learner questions with personalized feedback. They are also already being used as teaching assistants to help find content or to make appointments for personal coaching when needed.

The line between human and machine with a human touch to gain relevant knowledge is blurring very fast. And who knows, if we are to believe the studies on robots and empathy, these virtual coaches may well respond more humanely than many managers do today.

The rise of VR and AR in adult learning

For many, immersive technologies such as VR and AR conjure up the image of gamers, but there is no denying that these technologies offer many possibilities in the field of learning. They are certainly not new and knowing their origins and broad applicability can be interesting in making them more accessible in multiple learning environments.

VR and AR, like many innovative ideas, probably originated in Science Fiction (SF) stories. For example, Stanley G. Weinbaums already described 'scientific glasses' in the short story 'Pygmalion's Spectacles' from 1935. However, it was not until the end of the 1960s that the first forerunner of the graphical computer interface was built by Ivan Sutherland, Professor of Computer Science at the University of Utah, who was then still a student at MIT. His 'Sword of Damocles' was the first 'head-mounted display', but it was more like two screens that were placed on the head via a sturdy construction on the ceiling.

His giant head-mounted display is often called the first VR, but it was more like AR because you could still see real space next to virtual space. Sutherland was one of the pioneers who would use VR for adult education by simulating the real world. He would eventually develop his prototype into flight simulator products for NASA in the form of huge helmets that created the illusion of 360-degree space. In 1985, Jaron Zepel Lanier founder of VPL Research and sometimes called the founding father of VR, would develop it into the now familiar VR environments and also market the first commercial VR goggles.

To this day, VR in flight simulators are probably the best known application for adult education. As I mentioned in the first chapter, we also see military training relying heavily on new applications with AR and Microsoft Hololens. However, the possibilities of using these XR (extended reality) applications or immersive technologies still have a lot of new potential to offer in supporting people in their development.

In order to understand the added value of these popular technologies, the distinction between VR and AR is important and we see that especially the latter is becoming more and more accessible through the use of quasi-'normal' glasses and accessible hardware.

Virtual reality (VR):

These fully immersive simulations give users the most realistic simulation experience, complete with visuals and sound using VR goggles or head mount display (HMD). These VR headsets provide high-resolution content and a wide field of view by splitting the screen between the user's eyes. This technique creates a stereoscopic 3D effect or 360-degree video completely isolated from the rest of the real world. Combined with input tracking, this creates an immersive, believable experience. This type of VR is often used for gaming and other entertainment purposes, but its use in other sectors, especially education, is now increasing.

Augmented reality (AR)

These semi-immersive virtual experiences provide users with a partially virtual environment. As a result, users still have the perception of being in a different reality when they focus on the digital image. A recognizable example here is the Pokemon Go craze where players chase AR monsters 'in the real world', by walking around in the physical environment. This semi-immersive technology provides realism through 3D graphics, a term known as vertical reality depth. More detailed graphics result in a more immersive feeling. This category of AR is often used for education or training purposes and relies on displays, as opposed to head-sets, with high resolution, powerful computers, projectors or hard simulators that partially mimic the design and functional mechanisms of the real world. This AR opens doors for many applications in corporate learning at the time of need and in combination with coaching in a digital twin environment (see next chapter) opens up possibilities for the future.

XR Supporting humans to be more human

Though technology has multiple benefits, I remain sceptical about it if it does not benefit people as human beings. Of course, ethical consequences and prejudices must be taken into account, but also the consequences for the psychological wellbeing of the user. For example, years ago I worked with a company in the Netherlands that was exploring VR for educational and social purposes that they were doing an experiment to educate people about the poor working conditions in the textile sector. In the middle of Amsterdam, they set up a VR stand where shoppers from one of the targeted shops could sit down if they had no ethical problems with the shop. The goal was to make the immersive experience so real that shoppers would feel like they were working in a sweatshop themselves. It makes you think about the psychological impact of these technologies and even more about how our brain stores this experience in the long run.

This experience made me already sceptical about the use of XR in certain domains. More specifically, I doubted whether, in addition to its unquestionable usefulness in supporting skills, it could be used for purely human competencies. However, as openness is one of the competences for the future of work, I also immersed myself in Jenson8's experience and spoke to founder Jena Davidson about the added value of VR for leadership development with an open mind.

Jena's premise is: 'Making participants comfortable with the uncomfortable leads the way to true self-awareness and to a more efficient, stronger and better performing team'. Thus, learning leadership skills in the real world suddenly takes on a whole new dimension when you find yourself in a stressful situation, in an environment characterized by change. Jena seems to have cracked the code to bring together different innovations and purely human competences.

CASE STUDY
Connect, collaborate and grow... for real using VR and AI

Jena Davidson, Founder at Jenson8

As a psychologist, I wanted to support people and that is also the starting point of Jenson8. As an HR Tech company we put 'the human being' at the centre of technology. The goal, individuals and teams can feel comfortable if they are uncomfortable in an environment that is safe to fail. With this in mind, we offer a VR experience enhanced by AI and human input that reveals authentic, natural and intuitive human behaviours.

LEARNING FROM DISCOMFORT AND FAILURE
Learning requires a certain amount of discomfort before anything is achieved. This is healthy in small doses because it helps you understand that you still have something to learn. Role-play reinforces this feeling of discomfort to the point

where it interferes with the learning process. Many people feel uncomfortable pretending to be someone else, and this can manifest itself in a lack of commitment that is often felt in the workplace where one is expected to play a role that fits in with the team and the culture of the organization.

When this environment changes (for example, due to new colleagues or a new structure), we don't always understand why success is so much harder to achieve and often struggle to make things work as they were before. Amongst these, we tend to retreat deeply into the comfort zone of the behaviour that brought us success in the past. In doing so, we ignore the damage that that behaviour causes and makes success harder to achieve. We do not learn from our failures but reinforce 'wrong' behaviour.

Understanding how our environment affects our behaviour is key to sustainable team effectiveness – and continued career development – but facing the truth can be difficult, uncomfortable and make us vulnerable. We need help to break through those self-created barriers. With this approach, we help bridge the gap between team potential and team performance so it can be used for onboarding cross-functional teams, underperforming teams and individuals alike.

FULL IMMERSIVE VR EXPERIENCE EMPOWERED BY AI

Don't confuse Jenson8 with other VR used for frontline safety and operational training that focuses on skills. With our approach, which can happen 100 per cent cloud based with team members all over the world, we offer an engaging and immersive platform where we as humans cannot hide behind learned behaviours. The combination of the VR game effect and feedback rounds help uncover deeply human behaviours and are the starting point to strengthen competencies for leadership and management development.

Due to the various mundane tests and static learning that we impose on our employees, the data that we get back is not only not contextualized due to the mental state of the participant, but the data points do not provide much more insight than the traditional classification of personality traits and even then, some interpretation is needed to really use the data.

Modern AI techniques and the lower cost of available computing power enable users to provide rich correlations and insights into the true behavioural approaches to a variety of aspects of professional life that traditional methods cannot capture, such as interpersonal communication under stress, immediate responses to ethically ambiguous situations, attention to the key influencing constituents of a task when solving problems, and whether their approaches to team problem solving are dangerously selfish and thoughtless or chronically suffering from paralysis by analysis.

AI allows them to learn things about themselves that no one (including themselves) has looked at, and to learn to see that behaviour in practice, then question it and adjust it. In this try-fail-learning cycle, the necessary understanding is created for change to take place before they go back to the frenzy of daily work.

Jena Davidson shows that innovative technologies as stand-alone often offer added value. When we link them to other systems, or in this case to human thought and action, we see that the symbiosis itself leads to new innovations. This future-oriented thinking outside of the box is also the working method of the habit of improvement discussed at the end of this book.

AR, digital twins and spatial computing to bridge learning and society needs

VR may offer many perspectives and in the eyes of many it seems to be the most immersive experience, but in my opinion AR will offer more and more possibilities for learning and working. Partly because of the simplicity of use through smart glasses such as google glass or the glasses as proposed by AttentivU that I wrote about in the first chapter. These glasses are almost fashionable enough to walk down the street unnoticed. Yet, in reality, they are small lightweight wearable computers with a transparent screen that give the world a new layer.

Another advantage of AR is that it makes it easier for our brains to blend with reality because it provides a unified sensory model of the world. Unlike VR where you are mostly sitting or standing still, your brain will register that you are standing or sitting as opposed to moving in the virtual world. This inconsistency forces your brain to build and maintain two separate models of your world – one for your real environment and one for the virtual world. This perceptual inconsistency is eliminated when you merge the real and virtual worlds into one consistent experience or unified mental model.

Augmented reality already offers these possibilities and opens up new frontiers of applicability for learning and working in the form of 'spatial computing' and/or digital twins. Here, activities of machines, people, objects and environments are digitized to optimize interactions. A simple example is Microsoft Mesh, which will be launched in 2022 within teams to share and manipulate holographic images during meetings and/or learning moments. Spatial computing can go as far as using physical actions, such as head and body movements, gestures and speech as the input of digital systems to control them. In a 3D physical space, feedback is then provided in the form of video, audio and even haptic outputs. This technology already offers optimization opportunities for training and coaching of frontline workers, performance monitoring of factories and warehouses in what are called Digital Twin setups.

In addition to companies that see benefits in AR, spatial computing and digital twins, healthcare institutions are also benefiting from these new innovations. Live streaming of lessons was for many years a common method of making learning accessible to a remote audience. Of course, this was no substitute for being present in a classroom or in the operation room (OR), as Rafael J. Grossmann, MD, a surgeon and educator in New Hampshire, USA, knows. However, it was a good alternative and an addition to surgical training, especially in times when the OR is too busy, or when, as during, one cannot be physically present.

Dr Rafael Grossmann, however, was one of the first to want more than live streaming from fixed positions in the OR that gave spectators a limited view of the operations and the patient. He was also one of the first to go a step further in 2013 by streaming a surgical procedure live with Google Glass. Through this type of headset, it was possible to give all spectators a 'preferred location' in the operating theatre. He facilitated the medical students' experience and allowed them to see his perspective during the operation. In the process, they were able to interact with each other in a virtual, synchronous manner as if they were physically present during the procedure.

Dr Grossmann is a global reference when it comes to innovative techniques that can be used to improve surgical outcomes and training. He also believes that the use of technological innovations will enable healthcare staff to be more ethical and to provide safe, compassionate care. His examples will therefore be applicable not only in the health sector but for all those who wish to embrace innovation for learning with added value for society.

CASE STUDY
Improved surgical outcomes, learning and ethical and safe compassionate care

Rafael J Grossmann, MD, a surgeon and educator

There is ample evidence that surgical outcomes have improved significantly in recent decades. We have to conclude that the smart use of technology has played a key role – from the use of anaesthesia, analgesia and antisepsis to minimally invasive, endoscopic and robotic surgery.

Today's technology is advancing in a somewhat exponential way. I think today's challenge is how to use these technologies to improve education and diagnostics, and to provide equal access to ethical, safe and compassionate care worldwide. I believe the current socio-economic, political and environmental landscape is creating a 'perfect storm' that will exacerbate an already strained healthcare ecosystem. If we look at how the demand for healthcare services is growing in the face of rapidly decreasing availability, and especially access, to safe and affordable healthcare services, we are facing a serious problem.

One of the technologies that can improve education, teaching and learning is immersive media. I have been involved in this field for almost a decade, sharing clinical expertise and futuristic insights to help shape its evolution. For example, in the field of surgical education, we see several platforms using VR as a way to train the next generation of surgeons. I am thinking of platforms like Fundamental Surgery, PrecisionOS, OssoVR and OramaVR that are shaping the future of surgical learning.

Simulation in VR to learn and practise the different steps of a surgical procedure is not new. What is exciting and innovative is the use of haptic feedback to make that experience real in a unique way. This is what Fundamental Surgery has developed: the ability to immerse yourself in real surgery and provide a safe, repeatable environment to learn. Offering repetition and harmless failure through simulation is a major benefit to learning and shows tremendous value in technology for surgical education. But only with the addition of haptics and advanced high-fidelity simulation techniques can the benefits of precision learning be truly understood.

Precision learning is a combination of tracked data points to test a user's sub-millimetric accuracy and the user's interactions with different tissue textures, all within a surgical environment. By combining repetition with not only procedural steps but also individual complex steps, muscle memory is built and skills are transferred by 'feeling' the virtual body, which is a huge step forward from some of the current VR simulation platforms.

With this highly intuitive system, the platform allows surgeons to experience the same sights, sounds and precise physical sensations of the human anatomy, allowing them to hone and practise skills in a safe and measurable environment that perfectly complements cadaveric and assisted/observational learning in the OR, without putting patients at risk. The data from the haptic interactions also creates a personal dashboard to highlight the weaker and stronger areas within each step of the procedure.

Another example is the case of telemedicine. According to a report, it is estimated that around 5 billion people do not have access to safe or affordable surgery (Lancet Glob Health 2015) This is an unacceptable reality and a problem that can be mitigated through the use of these tools.

The global crisis of COVID-19 has shown us the benefits of remote communication and connectivity in every aspect of human endeavour. Healthcare has been no exception, and despite opponents and obstacles, it has made a huge difference. As I see it, telehealth is another means of connecting with patients and colleagues, just like e-mail, telephones, paper and even fax machines. It is a complement, not a replacement, for physical interaction.

We are increasingly seeing reports of how head-mounted display (or HMD) devices such as Vuzix, Realwear, Microsoft Hololens and others have been used to break down geographical and educational barriers to enable remote surgical assistance.

In the field of AR, the ability to conduct teleconsultations with a platform such as Proximie, which uses 'telestration' to bring in the 'hand', skill and knowledge of an expert surgeon to guide a colleague at a distance, is a clear example of the smart use of technology to improve surgical care and provide more equitable and inclusive access to global healthcare.

Thus, I would argue that technology can paradoxically lead to a more empathetic and humane healthcare system. The proper use of these tools can bring us closer to our patients and in a way save the rapidly fading doctor-patient relationship.

In the field of surgical navigation, platforms such as MagicLeap and BrainLab have partnered to enable a 'mixed reality viewer' that visualizes holographic 3D images to facilitate and enhance the performance of a surgical procedure. The images are literally 'liberated from the constraints of flat screens and incorporated into your world'. A surgeon in the OR, wearing a MagicLeap headset with the BrainLab software, can access the diagnostic images of the patient in an unlimited number of axes, making the display much more intuitive and ergonomic.

Are there negative aspects to the use of new technologies in medicine? Certainly there are! Their misuse can make interactions impersonal, less empathetic and less emotional, more mechanical. There is a potential risk of violation of patients' private health information. There are also legal, regulatory and cost barriers to be addressed. These problems are real, but should not be an obstacle to using these tools to improve the way we practise and teach medicine. These problems can be solved if developers, regulators and users take them into account. The problem is not the technology, but the use we make of it.

This example demonstrates the versatility of applications in the healthcare sector. Yet we see that it is not only this sector that benefits enormously from the applicability of new technologies. As many of these technologies become more accessible to the general public, both through hardware and through falling prices for these technologies, I think it is likely we will see exponential growth in all sectors in the coming years.

Blockchain and learning platforms

When we think back to the future of work and the expectations set for lifelong learning as described in the second chapter, we see that a diploma from our early years is often not relevant for long. Even more so, according to Nick van Dam's M-profile, it is necessary to gain more in-depth expertise after our initial education. The question that then arises is how to certify these when they are no longer done in an 'official institution', but through innovative methods such as AR and spatial computing during our careers or with an employer.

The answer is Blockchain. There is still much mystery about what it is and where it can be used. The assumption that it will disrupt the financial sectors in particular has been proved wrong, and we are seeing more and more areas of application where clumsy paper contracts and documentation can be replaced by secure and smart electronic documents that make processes more efficient. When we look at the application within the whole ecosystem around learning, blockchain technology might be the most disruptive. Yet when we discuss the potential, many seem reluctant, partly because of the link made to cryptocurrencies and speculation related to investing in them. Blockchain as a technology, though, is much more than that.

Before I talk about applications that can disrupt the learning ecosystem, it is best to give some background about Blockchain. Cryptographer David Chaum first proposed a blockchain-like protocol in his 1982 dissertation 'Computer Systems Established, Maintained, and Trusted by Mutually Suspicious Groups.' The premise was a cryptographic system that could be used to store and manage data in a secure chain of blocks in a distributed and trusted model. Almost 10 years later in 1991, Stuart Haber and W Scott Stornetta saw the potential in a system where document timestamps could not be tampered with and a year after that Haber, Stornetta, and Dave Bayer added Merkle Trees to the design. This allowed for efficient and secure verification of transactions in a large data structure.

It all sounds rather complicated but the logic is quite easy to grasp. For example, in cryptography and computer science, Merkle Trees or Hash trees are a visual representation of trees of which each 'leaf' is called a node. These are labelled with the cryptographic hash of the data block. This hash is in turn the result of a function that converts data of arbitrary size into a fixed size. To prove that a leaf node is part of a given binary hash tree, calculate a number of hashes proportional to the logarithm of the number of leaf nodes in the tree. Conversely, in a hash list, the number is proportional to the number of leaf nodes themselves. These functions or calculations are defined in protocols that are defined for each type of blockchain.

This Merkle Tree is still the basis of today's blockchains. However, it was only in 2008 that Satoshi Nakamoto (it is not known whether this is a pseudonym or even a reference to a group of people) created the first decentralized blockchain based on the idea of the Merkle Tree. Nakamoto later significantly improved the design by using a Hashcash-like method to time-stamp blocks without having to be signed by a trusted party. This would be the core component of the cryptocurrency bitcoin, which was introduced a year later.

Today's blockchains can be described as databases storing transactions which are encrypted in blocks and stored on a large network of computers. As each block contains information about the previous one, they form a long, immutable and unbreakable chain of information. In summary, a blockchain is characterized by the following characteristics:

- **Near real time** – because several miners worldwide are encouraged to validate a transaction as quickly as possible in order to earn cryptocurrencies.

- **Peer to peer** – which means no trusted partners or middlemen, thus avoiding extra costs and a lot of processing time.

- **Distributed** – because the proof of the transaction is validated and maintained in different places.

- **Immutable** – once the file has been created it cannot be modified, making it very reliable and less risky, and preventing fraud.

How it works and what the jargon is should become clearer with the help of an example. Suppose you are in this story a node or a leaf on the enormous Merkle Tree and you have a file on your computer of transactions on your computer. In the world of blockchain, we call this computer a ledger or a hardware wallet that is the digital vault in which transactions are kept. In addition to you, there are other independent 'bookkeepers' who also have a file of that transaction, so it is distributed. These bookkeepers, who in the world of blockchain are called miners, receive an email each time you make a transaction informing them of this. Once they receive the email, they will validate as quickly as possible whether you are allowed to make this transaction. Why fast? Only the fastest one is paid in cryptocurrency for the calculation time needed and for the right mathematical key to put the block of transactions on the right place in the open ledger. When the first one validates the transaction they send out a message to everyone which not only proves the speed also gives the logic for validating the transaction. This is the proof of work. If the other slower bookkeeper agrees, everyone updates their file and another block of information is added to your file of transactions and the blockchain is made longer.

The above opens up many possibilities beyond the financial sectors, as traditional intermediaries can be eliminated for validating transactions or documents. It can be applied to just about any multi-step verification. This makes it faster, cheaper, better validated, more traceable and much more secure than other transactions due to the collective verification of the ecosystem. As the digital and physical worlds converge, the practical applications of blockchain will only increase.

Blockchain exists mostly in public environments involving global miners and nodes but it can also exist in private environments such as in games like Upland which I discussed in the first part and where transactions are property rights of virtual real estate (NFTs). In the future ecosystem, organizations will be able to collaborate in a secure, controllable and virtual manner. And that, in turn, will open doors for learning organizations that want to focus on lifelong learning.

One of these opportunities that is already being explored is the validation of skills and abilities of employees. Today, we see that these are often only awarded through traditional diplomas issued by recognized (and expensive) training institutes. Knowledge gained 'on the job' or through innovative platforms is not yet recognized because its validation is not recognized. Yet there are also advantages for institutions and trainers to use blockchain, both in terms of certification of the program and in terms of extra income. For example, a training provider could make a course available online. Each time a learner successfully completes it, the ecosystem associated with it is notified and the course is validated. When the learner has completed all parts of that course, the trainer receives crypto coins and the students receive validated credits.

This indicates a huge potential for validation of learning. This could be enhanced when private and public blockchains are connected. For example, credible digital certificates could be issued, the sharing of validated learning resources could be realized, and intellectual property of courses could be protected with data encryption. Consider also the promises of the metaverse and many young 'gamers' currently 'studying' in meta-worlds such as Roblox and Fortnite could graduate at 12 years old as accomplished experts with digital skills.

Is the future of learning in the eduverse?

Immersive experiences, AI, blockchain and many other innovative technologies all have an impact on learning and working in the future. Yet there is one place where all these seem to come together with promise of a new universe, the metaverse. As described in the first chapter, gamers and marketers in particular are already eagerly seeking the opportunities it has to offer. They will also offer new possibilities for learning, which will facilitate learning in the flow of life. However, I would like to address some of the misconceptions surrounding this hype and how this relates to opportunities for learning ecosystems.

The metaverse does not exist

Virtual worlds that we enter with advanced VR or AR glasses or a HoloLens are already opening doors, but these immersive worlds are not – yet – the metaverse that everyone is suddenly talking about.

At the heart of the metaverse is the vision of an immersive internet as a vast, unified, persistent and shared domain. And a vision it is, for the most part. Yet the promise of the metaverse is a new and radically transformative medium, made possible by major innovations in hardware, human-computer interface, network infrastructure, creative tools and digital economies.

The unification of the different worlds, for example Roblox and Fortnite, as a connecting universe is still in its infancy. And that is also the challenge of seeing them as the example of a learning ecosystem. To create a truly connected and attractive universe, or metaverse, we need quantum computing, mature blockchain technology, stable cryptocurrencies and protocols around NFTs that enable the connection of the different worlds. And this is where the shoe pinches, because each of them uses different blockchains and protocols that are not yet aligned. Building a complete, decentralized virtual world, one with its own economic systems, takes time and risks that must be taken into account. Compare it to the internet as we know it today. The different worlds are like sites, but the access to surf from one site to another like on the internet does not yet exist. And it is this connection, or unification, that makes learning ecosystems unique. Wherever you are or with whom you are, you can always find the knowledge you need.

The opportunity for the metaverses to become digital skill universities or eduverses

For the time being, metaverse-worlds mainly live in the world of gamers and many think that a game cannot replace the real world. Yet, that is what they once said about e-commerce and today it seems that e-commerce business is replacing physical shops more and more. All the more reason to think now about how these new worlds will transform learning.

I dare say that the opportunity for closing the digital skill gap lies in the creator worlds of the metaverse. In chapter 1 of this book I already mentioned that Roblox, with 202 million users, is a huge creator ecosystem where mostly very young developers make games for each other. Yet, for the beginning game makers there is a learning curve. The Roblox University was launched to deal with this. Here, 'students' will find video tutorial series and a virtual campus where novice game makers can hang out and test their knowledge (and earn prizes for passing quizzes). Becoming a student at ROBLOX University is also very simple and accessible. You don't have to register. You don't have to pay tuition. You just have to want to learn how to build and script games!

In addition to creator platforms for developing digital skills, there are also massively multiuser online (MMO) problem-solving games that support the challenges of the jobs of the future. World of Warcraft, for example, where learners of all ages and everywhere form guilds that exchange knowledge and skills to solve challenges together. In this peer-to-peer social learning network (SLN), we are all co-learners and do not need classrooms.

A next step towards the real metaverse – or should we say eduverse – as a learning ecosystem seems to be getting closer when we look at the possibilities innovative technologies have to offer. Who knows, maybe soon, when blockchain is mature enough and knowledge gained from games can be valourised, we will no longer send young people to university as they will obtain a master's degree in digital skills while playing in the metaverse. Perhaps now is the time for recruiters to enter those meta-worlds themselves in search of the best candidates.

In this section, we saw that old theories and methods together with innovation are creating new opportunities for learning and knowledge sharing. In particular, we saw that under the influence of gaming, learning is being approached in a much more immersive way to support the applicability of learning at the point of need.

This offers many opportunities, but also requires learning architects to have an increasingly strategic and holistic insight into the organization, its employees and its expanding and often virtual ecosystem. For this purpose, in parts 4 and 5, I will offer tools that help to transform the organization into an innovative, lean and tech-driven learning organization, a LearnScape.

References

1E9 (2019) Lil Miquela – the new 'It-Girl' that received $6m funding, 1e9.community/t/lil-miquela-the-new-it-girl-that-received-6m-funding/280 (archived at https://perma.cc/X8DL-FC3H)

Alice Kim, PHD (2022) Profile, alicekim.ca/about-me/ (archived at https://perma.cc/9VMJ-4KVA)

Axonify (2022) There are three key scientific principles at the core of the Axonify solution, explore.axonify.com/20-gen-1063-performance/20-PRO-1006-how-axonify-incorporates-brain-science (archived at https://perma.cc/K267-HWDN)

Bersin J (2021) A New Category Emerges: the creator platform for corporate learning, joshbersin.com/2021/07/a-new-category-emerges-the-creator-platform-for-corporate-learning/ (archived at https://perma.cc/2JCT-46Q9)

Ebbinghaus, H (1885) Memory: A Contribution to Experimental Psychology, *Über das Gedächtnis*, Dover, New York

Falloon, G (2022) 'Making the Connection: Moore's Theory of Transactional Distance and Its Relevance to the Use of a Virtual Classroom in Postgraduate Online Teacher Education', *JRTE*, 43(3), pp.187–209

Fortune (2015) Who Is Satoshi Nakamoto, Inventor of Bitcoin? It Doesn't Matter, fortune.com/2015/12/09/bitcoin-satoshi-identity/ (archived at https://perma.cc/Z452-TEM4)

Grossman, R. (2022) Rafael Grossman, www.rafaelgrossmann.com/ (archived at https://perma.cc/L8W4-SHUH)

Jenson 8 (2022) Immersive HR Tech Delivering Key Insights, jenson8.com/ (archived at https://perma.cc/V28R-CUXL)

Jeremy Norman's History of Information (2022) 'Pygmalion's Spectacles,' Probably the First Comprehensive and Specific Fictional Model for Virtual Reality, www.historyofinformation.com/detail.php?entryid=4543 (archived at https://perma.cc/MU3F-GAB3)

Kegan, R & Lahey, L (2016) *An Everyone Culture*, Harvard Business School Publishing, Cambridge

Microsoft (2021) Mesh for Microsoft Teams aims to make collaboration in the 'metaverse' personal and fun, news.microsoft.com/innovation-stories/mesh-for-microsoft-teams/ (archived at https://perma.cc/627D-VW82)

National Library of Medicine (2014) Retrieval practice enhances new learning: the forward effect of testing, www.ncbi.nlm.nih.gov/pmc/articles/PMC3983480/ (archived at https://perma.cc/BA4V-XA6K)

New Scientist (2013) Virtual Reality: Meet founding father Jaron Lanier, www.newscientist.com/article/mg21829226-000-virtual-reality-meet-founding-father-jaron-lanier/ (archived at https://perma.cc/5W44-RV66)

Roblox (2014) ROBLOX University Launches Alongside Game Creation Challenge, blog.roblox.com/2014/09/roblox-university-launches-alongside-game-creation-challenge/ (archived at https://perma.cc/SVH6-XL5Z)

Sherman, A T et al (2019) 'On the Origins and Variations of Blockchain Technologies', IEEE Security Privacy, 17 (1), pp. 72–77. doi:10.1109/MSEC.2019.2893730 (archived at https://perma.cc/MCY8-JKR2)

Teacher Tool Kit (2022) The Earliest Study on Retrieval Practice, www.
    teachertoolkit.co.uk/2020/11/01/retrieval-practice/ (archived at https://perma.
    cc/69YH-FB4Q)
van Krevelen, R and Poelman, R (2010) 'A Survey of Augmented Reality
    Technologies, Applications and Limitations' International Journal of Virtual
    Reality, 9 (2), pp. 1–20. doi: 10.20870/IJVR.2010.9.2.2767 (archived at
    https://perma.cc/7W5E-TXTJ)

PART FOUR

Lean learning ecosystems and LearnScapes

From the previous chapters we have learned that technology has a great impact on the 'future of work' and learning. Learning at the point of need seems to be gaining popularity and to be increasingly feasible through smart symbiosis with intelligent technologies.

Making learning its use for the individual, the organization and society measurable provides more and more insights. But above all, in a world increasingly driven by innovation, wellbeing and being human seem to be paramount. However, being human also implies looking for connections and added value between people, and this too can be enhanced by technology.

These are also the principles of the learning economy in which lean learning ecosystems or, as I call them, LearnScapes, are deployed in a nimble manner. In this chapter, this organizational form is discussed from lean principles translated into learning ecosystems and the social context in which they are strengthened. In these LearnScapes, the symbiosis between man and machine is established, which generates added value for society as a whole.

Building a learning ecosystem or LearnScape does not happen overnight and requires a method of continuous improvement, as will be described in the final section of this book. It requires a strategic and holistic plan that is rolled out in several phases. Each time, it looks at what can be learned from the previous phase in order to improve further. This method of short sprints can be compared to the scrum method of software developers, as it allows for continuous adjustment based on progressive insight. This also means that we start from the now, the current strategy, in order to grow nimble into the future.

In the next part, we will take a closer look at the drivers that make a LearnScape what it is. A nimble lean social learning ecosystem. This system that grows from the current organizational form is made visible in the learning maturity model which provides insight and allows you to situate your own organization in the steps it needs to take to become a nimble LearnScape.

08

The learning maturity model: from data repositories to LearnScapes

A learning ecosystem does not come into existence in a few simple steps; it requires vision and the need to involve all stakeholders in the process. However, we can already be inspired by some of the organizational drivers for unlocking knowledge.

The learning maturity model for organizations that I developed in 2014 makes it apparent from a simple analysis how far organizations are from the ultimate social lean learning ecosystem. A LearnScape that grows from the individual to support the ecosystem. To do this, I divided them into five symbolic types of organizations with characteristics and drivers that you can compare your own organization with (Figure 8.1).

- Data repository organization
- Broadcaster of news
- Interactive communicator
- Social collaborators
- LearnScapes

I would like to emphasize explicitly that no organization will fit 100 per cent into one of the types I describe here, nor is it a scientifically tested model. Often, organizations will recognize themselves in one or more representations. However, holding this schematic model in the light of one's own organization provides a basis for finding opportunities for improvement.

FIGURE 8.1 The learning maturity model

© Katja Schipperheijn

The five drivers of the learning maturity model, as shown in figure 8.2, are:

- **Emphasis:** starting point of the technology-supported strategy.
- **Owned by:** owner, manager or facilitator of the knowledge flows and/or about data.
- **Style:** manner in which knowledge is shared.
- **Technology:** systems that add value to knowledge sharing.
- **Success:** measurability of the shared knowledge.

The above-mentioned drivers of the organization with regard to the knowledge flows all have their own dimension in the different maturity levels that characterize the organization. In addition, the culture of the organization that wants to make the transition to LearnScapes is of great importance. However, it is deliberately not included as a driver because confusion between culture and learning culture should be avoided as will be described in the last part of this book in step 3 of the model for continuous improvement.

Though this scheme was developed in 2014 it is still more than relevant. More so from my experience, I dare say that it will remain relevant for many years to come.

Furthermore, in 2014, the idea of a LearnScape was often still a futuristic vision of the future. Motivating business leaders was then often a bridge too far, but as the past chapters demonstrate, that future has now caught up with us and procrastination is no longer an excuse. Contrary to what we may think, those organizations that are furthest away from LearnScapes often make the transition the easiest. Yet, this is not so illogical.

FIGURE 8.2 The learning maturity model

	Emphasis	Owned by	Style	Tech	Success
Data Repository	Collecting rather than sharing	IT Dept.	Static	Database	Number of docs
Broadcast of News	Spread the word	Communi-cation Dept.	One - 2 - Many	Broadcast Site	View ratings
Interactive Communication	Comment, discuss and rate	Company wide	Two-way	Apps and services mish mash	Rates, likes and comments
Social Collaboration	Internal collaboration networks	Company wide know-ledge centers	Human - 2 - Human	Collabo-ration hub	Performance increase
Learning Eco-System	Bridging the know-ledge gap	Interest wide	Interested - 2 - Interested	Learning eco-system	Lean performance measurement

© Katja Schipperheijn

For them, it is often more urgent to adapt legacy systems and practices with a future-oriented strategy. The opportunity cost related to replacing legacy systems is often much higher for them as well, as I describe in the last part of the book.

Let's now look at each of the components of the maturity model in turn.

Data repository organizations

The learning organization in its most simple form is recognizable in technology that is still used in most organizations. Databases or knowledge banks that continue to be filled. Protected by firewalls, large collections of documents are made accessible by the knowledge managers, who in these organizations often turn out to be employees of the IT department. Success depends on the number of documents they can secure. The first priority is to protect the knowledge stored on their own company servers from outsiders and other unauthorized persons.

Another consideration is that because the knowledge is stored in a static way, its relevance is often not measurable. So, you get old dead systems that may grow in volume, but contribute little to the growth of the organization and the necessary knowledge of employees.

An observation that can be made about data repository organizations has to do with securing knowledge or, in other words, influence and decision-making power. The complex structure, which often characterizes databases, is also reflected in leadership organization charts. Top-down decisions are made by the HiPPOs and the motivation for their decisions and choices is rarely explicitly shared with the lower echelons or the external stakeholders of the organization. Of course, there will be data repository organizations where knowledge sharing and decision making happens in a more engaged way. These organizations already have an advantage in working from a collaborative culture on systems that support these knowledge flows. What can be a challenge here is that IT departments are not so keen on seeing their legacy systems disappear; they are a threat to maintaining their own working methods and possibly jobs. Retraining many administrators of old technologies is then often the only solution to prevent them from being written off along with the legacy systems themselves. As a stakeholder in the discovery phase and the search for opportunities for improvement, they are therefore essential to be involved as early as possible. If they come into the project later, they are often the people who delay implementation and in some cases even block it completely.

Finding an example of such a data repository organization is not difficult – many I know of are still deeply rooted in this form of organization. However, I did not find anyone who wanted to tell their story here. As a business leader, you can of course see this in a positive light; there is plenty of room for improvement and quick-wins are easy to find.

Broadcaster of news

Another type of organization, the broadcaster of news, seems to be very far removed from the first. Yet, they often go hand in hand. As mentioned, the model is not an indication of the number of steps an organization takes, but a representation of how far they are from a LearnScape. The technology and the measurability are possible quick-wins for improvement in this aspect.

Broadcasters of news are often full of good intentions from a leadership point of view. Communicating a lot about relevant strategy and changes in working conditions had added value during the COVID-19 pandemic period. Often, though, the method and technology they used was vastly outdated. In addition, responsibility was often placed entirely with the internal communications teams whose approach lacked HR's knowledge of engagement. The one-2-many approach was therefore often a failure, although that is not certain as effective measurability of communication in these organizations is often non-existent.

When we look back at the advantages of information that has to be applied 'at the moment of need', these 'distributors of news' often miss their target. They are not yet able to reach their target group accurately enough. Nor are they able to measure the change or effect of their information broadcast. If the success of the communication could be measured in any way, it would be by the number of 'likes' they receive or the number of times the message is read. However, a response that the message has been read does not mean that it has been understood and even less that it has been acted upon.

Although the starting point in the previous section was not so much knowledge sharing but more the objective of informing employees, this is indeed an aspect of a learning organization. For instance, we saw in the second part of this book that informing about strategy and the added value of learning have a positive impact on learning and behavioural change. Therefore, when we look for quick-win projects in the discovery phase in the last part of this book, it may be necessary to look at communication and learning together in a holistic way. In this way, bringing together learning and communication technology can often pay off quickly.

Interactive communicator

The previous two types of organizations had clear owners of knowledge sharing, such as the IT department and internal communication staff. On the other hand, we also see organizations where everyone in the organization feels called upon from their silo to share massively unstructured knowledge with everyone else.

In contrast to the way data repository organizations and broadcasters of news spread knowledge in a very structured way through fixed channels, we see here an abundance of different overlapping channels. I don't think I have to explain too much about how annoying this can be. Admit it, even you don't read all the internal notes that are fired at you daily via mail, intranet, WhatsApp and who knows what other channels. Not only are they disturbing for the recipients, but it is nearly impossible to measure the 'success' of such knowledge and information overload.

Making these flows controllable is therefore a crucial step for companies that really want to engage and support employees. No more IT departments or communication services deciding what you should or should not be able to access or receive. You can take the wheel in your own hands and can participate in knowledge flows that are relevant to you, whether or not supported by smart technology. This is a necessary first step in cultivating a culture of knowledge sharing.

Still, the interactive communicator has taken the first step towards the collaborative and value-driven organization where employee knowledge and opinions make the difference. Platform-wise, we see content management systems like those in the data repository, but also learning management systems and other knowledge databases, relevant or not, are linked to other tools that support communication and knowledge sharing. Silos and hierarchies are beginning to fade and the freedom to share knowledge, to anticipate and to have a different opinion is spreading.

It is also the first time that we see legacy systems and new niche applications overlapping and sometimes already reinforcing each other. Yet, here comes the danger that, with all good intentions, we may again miss the boat. As a data analyst, making measurable data from the many channels becomes a hassle that is very difficult to manage. Not only from the point of view of the abundance of data but even more from the point of view of the relevance of the many likes, rates, comments, downloads and number of clicks.

Interactive communicators are interesting when they share knowledge that is relevant to the employees and they also deliver knowledge about employees and strategy to the organization.

Motivating everyone to participate in the conversations is the challenge of organizations based on the idea of interactive communicators. This exercise is a first step towards social collaborators who also put the learner at the centre as explained further in this chapter. They look for opportunities for experts with specific professional knowledge or skills to support others. The challenge is to allow knowledge to flow effectively and efficiently between employees (and managers) and across silos using technology.

Social collaborator

Social collaboration, the almost LearnScapes, is what many organizations have been striving for and what is becoming more and more feasible through technology. Yet since the outbreak of the COVID-19 pandemic, we see that the systems of many organizations claiming to be social collaborators have been tested.

Social collaborators are used to working together on often very diverse projects. Employees no longer work for the organization, but are part of cross-functional teams. These social organizations are almost entirely adapted to the future workforce that works on a project basis and where gig workers are equal colleagues.

Can you imagine that in these organizations there would still be databases where you, as a (temporary) newcomer, have to find your way through the many folders and documents (if IT has already given you access as an outsider)? Or that you have to memorize all the expertise of team members because your mailbox does not work with an expert locator that not only searches by name, but also allows you to search someone by knowledge or skills.

In social collaborator organizations, technology ensures that through linked data from different systems and simple algorithms, you are connected to the person or knowledge you need, when you need them. Here, technology works for the people and not the other way around. No more wasting time looking for information. Connected applications not only make content easy to find, they also provide the Human-2-Human (H2H) knowledge sharing that Bryan Kramer described. This H2H knowledge sharing is valuable, especially in fast changing circumstances, to get and keep people involved. It supports a culture where collaboration adds value for the employee and the organization. With social collaborators, both connected employees and connected applications increase performance.

The LearnScape

As mentioned, organizations do not have to go through all the steps to create a LearnScape. Often, they have characteristics and identify with multiple organization types. For example, I mentioned earlier that organizations can be both data repositories and news broadcasters. The one does not preclude the other. Both types also have in common that they are still stuck in silos and the data and knowledge do not yet flow to the right place in the organization when it is needed. A combination of these two also misses all the benefits of a social collaborator where, regardless of hierarchy, cross-functional teams share knowledge to realize personal growth and to boost the company's results.

The latter is the ultimate goal of a LearnScape where intelligent technology supports this knowledge sharing. Not only does it lead to a learning culture in which Human-2-Human knowledge exchange takes place, but through this intelligent collaboration between people and machines, knowledge provision is co-designed at the moment of need. It should be a priority for business executives, especially now that technology makes it possible. And yet only 7 per cent of executives focus on building portfolios of humans and machines working together intelligently, according to Deloitte's 2021 *Global Human Capital Trends Report* I cited earlier.

When I survey executives about their reasons for not looking at this integration, I often hear valid but troubling motives. These often seem to be motivated by pressure groups such as trade unions who believe that jobs will be lost because of this new collaboration of humans and machines together. This seems to contradict other research that suggests that AI and the intelligent cooperation between humans and machines will actually create jobs. However, there will be a major shift from jobs that can be automated to jobs that require a higher degree of expertise, such as training AI algorithms and many other AI-related skills.

There is more that makes a LearnScape unique, especially the mindset of the executives at the helm of these organizations. Learn-Scapes build on all the successes and failures of previous organizational forms. They use the principle of perpetual improvement. These executives build their organizations – and the technology – like Lego blocks that are easily put together. But, whose parts can just as easily be replaced or changed if they no longer add value.

The latter is something that many organizations have not been able to do in the past, partly due to a lack of innovative technologies. AI solutions were not yet intelligent enough and many legacy systems simply could not be connected to allow knowledge and data to flow through the organization.

Finally, and perhaps the greatest value of LearnScapes is that they don't just thrive from within the internal ecosystem. They also share their knowledge with external stakeholders, enabling them to learn faster and grow more nimble. This is collaboration in the ecosystem economy, as internationally renowned author and keynote speaker Rik Vera states in his book *The Guide to the Ecosystem Economy: sketchbook for your organization's future*.

The LearnScapes model also introduces the concept of lean learning and lean performance management as a prerequisite for success. This was often the biggest challenge in 2014 as technology that could support this was then far from up to date, more so intelligent AI that supports us to reduce the 'waste' I discuss in the next section was then non-existent.

References

Beyond Limits (2022) why artificial intelligence is poised to create more jobs, www.beyond.ai/news/artificial-intelligence-creates-more-jobs/ (archived at https://perma.cc/KL4T-VG4J)

Deloitte (2021) Deloitte 2021 Global Human Capital Trends Report, www2.deloitte.com/ua/en/pages/about-deloitte/press-releases/gx-2021-global-human-capital-trends-report.html (archived at https://perma.cc/R4ET-34SU)

Kramer, B (2022) There is no more B2B or B2C: It's Human to Human, H2H, bryankramer.com/there-is-no-more-b2b-or-b2c-its-human-to-human-h2h/ (archived at https://perma.cc/U4WL-NA2W)

RIK VERA (2022) The Guide to the Ecosystem Economy, www.rikvera.com/keynotes/the-guide-to-the-ecosystem-economy/ (archived at https://perma.cc/3876-5BBD)

World Economic Forum (2020) The Future of jobs Report 2020, www.weforum.org/reports/the-future-of-jobs-report-2020 (archived at https://perma.cc/ZKE4-CJ7P)

09

Lean learning

Nimble organizations are also looking for ways to cut costs and simultaneously improve their business results. Yet, the L&D department is still often seen as a cost centre rather than a necessary investment that can positively impact business results.

This department, which in these organizations is often in a closed silo, remains under constant pressure to find more cost-cutting ways. L&D is challenged by the pressure of accelerating digitalisation requirements, the impact of the pandemic, the Future of Work with gig workers, learning in the flow of life and cross-functional project-driven teams. In addition, they are expected to provide relevant knowledge at the point of need to increase productivity and engagement in learning. To do this, they must develop a framework in which less is sometimes more.

During a conversation with Flemish expert on human capital development, Christine Verhasselt, which also goes back to 2014, we came across the idea of lean learning and how this, together with social learning (discussed in the next chapter), are the most important drivers for LearnScapes.

Initially, lean was a systematic approach developed by Toyota and mainly applied in production organizations and in software development. An important starting point was to identify and eliminate everything that did not add value directly. Nowadays, we see that organizations also apply lean to leadership and the organization as a whole.

It was a small step to develop this further in relation to learning development and the benefits this has for LearnScapes. The starting point here is that when we look for opportunities for the future of learning, this method often delivers quick-win projects. This for both the learner and the ecosystem on more aspects than just costs.

It was a small step to develop this further in relation to learning development and the benefits this has for LearnScapes. The added value of applying lean to learning is that it quickly makes opportunities and quick win projects visible. Both the learner, the organization and by extension the ecosystem, will gain benefits from this that go beyond cost savings.

The first step in applying this approach to learning was to define waste from a lean perspective. Waste would be any learning activity that does not directly help a learner to perform better at work or supports wellbeing.

From the approach I take, I offer a framework, Figure 9.1, in which we can classify waste into eight categories. This is in contrast to some lean experts in other application areas who base themselves on seven

FIGURE 9.1 Waste in lean learning development

Time	**Inventory**	**Motion**	**Over-Production**
Loss of time collecting or waiting for learning	Excess of content and knowledge not used or found	Useless deformation of material to fit all	Production before needed or more than needed

Transport	**Defects**	**Skills**	**Over-Processing**
Unnecessary movement of people or material	Outcome of learning does not achieve the requirements	Underutilizing peoples, talent, skills and knowledge	More work or higher quality than is required by the learner

© Katja Schipperheijn

forms of waste. In the context of learning, however, I prefer to separate 'inventory' from 'unused skills'.

Therefore, by identifying waste in a lean learning development approach, we focus only on those activities that add immediate value to learning and its effective and efficient application. From my experience in a world of accelerating change and technological innovation, I would estimate that 70 to 90 per cent of current learning and development activities can be considered wasteful.

If you look at the descriptions of learning waste in the following paragraphs with an open mind, they will help you to find drivers and urgencies for change in your organization. These are often quick-win projects that are easy to defend to all stakeholders on the 'burning platform' discussed in the last section of this book.

Overproduction

Too much content is perhaps one of the most common wastes we see, especially in linear training or onboarding models. All employees, regardless of their background, must follow the same curriculum to become certified. As a result, many of them have to learn more than what is required to perform their jobs. Providing only the relevant content when employees need it and can apply it would significantly improve learning outcomes.

Another common example of overproduction relates to popular LXP platforms and apps such as LinkedIn. So much content is produced and shared that it is simply no longer feasible for the learner to find what adds value. If smart AI is not used, these applications sometimes look like data repositories that become redundant because nobody bothers to search for knowledge anymore.

If we want to make learning lean, technology adds value to applications that propose adaptive and personalised pathways. A good example of this was discussed earlier with Etihad Airlines in part 2. Here, the learner receives only tailored knowledge supported by AI and models such as confidence based learning that also make this measurable.

Overprocessing

Nobody likes to do too much work, especially useless work, and yet in my experience of L&D, over-processing is quite common. Knowing that this is not a popular statement, I would like to explain how over-processing relates to learning.

From the lean principle, all steps or non-essential learning activities are redundant if they do not add value to the applicability of the learning. The most imaginative example here is probably a training course where 100s of complex slides serve as supporting material. Many attendees may not remember the first slides immediately after the training, and sometimes not even the last one, due to the challenges of paying attention to a long slide show. However, what we often see is that to increase retention, the slide decks are printed out so that learners can review them again later. But this is just as much waste, because not only does the course quickly disappear into a deep drawer, it also does not contribute to the applicability of learning in the moment of need. Not to mention the sustainability and the impact on the environment.

A somewhat less obvious example, according to Christiene Verhasselt, are the before and after assessments. These extra steps, which are prompted by models such as Kirkpatrick, often contribute nothing if they are not carried out very meticulously – and, as mentioned, very time-consumingly and costly. Measuring learning is not a useful step for anyone if it does not lead to change in training, better learning or better business results.

Time

Reducing 'time' is also a common opportunity for lean learning. Here we can distinguish several shortening factors related to 'time'. The most obvious, however, is what we call waiting time. This is the time between needing to know something and actually being able to apply it. It is the time between the business stating a learning need and L&D being able to roll out a solution. Not only is this time often a huge waste for the learner, it can also do direct damage to the organization and the ecosystem.

If an employee needs to learn or is unsure about something in order to perform a task, they will search for that knowledge or assume they have mastered the task. However, uncontrolled knowledge seeking and assumptions create risks of making mistakes. These mistakes can have a negative impact on costs, safety, customers and everyone in the ecosystem.

When we think of time, we also think of the time it takes to acquire knowledge. When we are learning in the flow of life, it is often not feasible to take two days of training, or even one hour off. Micro-learning and applications ensure that learning takes place at the moment it is needed, possibly mobile, therefore offer much added value.

Time has an enormous influence on the organization's results in more ways than one. Viewing time as a waste from a lean perspective is therefore a necessary step that delivers quick results for improvement.

Inventories

Many organizations use only a fraction of the data and knowledge they have. The unused data and knowledge do not contribute to the learning process of the employees and the organization. It is useless content that, moreover, is often very expensive to maintain.

An excessive inventory makes it difficult for learners to find relevant information. Not only are old systems such as the knowledge databases discussed in data repository organizations often repositories of unused knowledge, but many so-called learning experience platforms that offer Netflix-like experience content also fall into this category. It is often no longer possible to find anything in the overload of content on these platforms or to see the relevance of it. There is therefore a risk of learners dropping out because they cannot find what is relevant to them quickly enough. Inventories are thus closely linked to wasted time.

When organizations look for opportunities for improvement, it is an added value to link data about effectively used content to business results. In other words, is certain content very successful and do we see a correlation in improved skill or even business results of the organization. This is not easy for many organizations because these data points are not available to them. However, innovative technologies such as performance management platforms linked to learning platforms already offer this solution.

Skills

The fact that competences and skills in an organization can be defined as waste may seem strange at first glance. Yet this form of waste is hugely present in many organizations.

When there is insufficient collaboration or when expertise (knowledge) is insufficiently shared with others who can benefit from it, it becomes an underutilized resource and can therefore be considered as waste. This knowledge, which does not live on servers but within team members, is therefore similar to underutilized knowledge databases (inventories).

Reliable systems that can detect underutilized skills and competences are a first step here. Then, for example, pathways can be established on a social learning platform where everyone in the ecosystem is linked based on expertise and interest. A gamification aspect can then be developed that encourages members of this community to help others. Examples are mentors in onboarding programmes and also open chat boxes that support learning at the point of need. We also see that more and more organizations are using their own employees in the maker economy for corporate learning. A good example here are salespeople in fashion retail who upload videos showing the products they display together, which helps them sell better. A causal link with business results is not hard to find here.

Making expertise and competencies measurable should not be a challenge in this day and age. However, motivating people to share this knowledge is often less obvious. A learning organization therefore not only focuses on learning but also on a value-driven culture that embraces knowledge sharing.

Transport

In the post-pandemic era, transporting people and/or material to a location is probably one of the first types of waste to be found. Yet today we see that sustainable solutions that also take into account wellbeing have not always been implemented.

During the pandemic, many organizations looked for solutions, temporary or otherwise, to bring people together virtually. This resulted in often frustrating solutions where participants would spend days watching a webinar given by an instructor with a slide deck as if he or she were standing in front of a live group; yet we all know that the spirit is often out of the presentation, the transactional distance becomes too great and interaction comes to a virtual standstill. For these situations and some organizations, waiting for the return to 'normal' was slow.

On the other hand, we see organizations that did not take temporary measures but used the pandemic to accelerate innovation by several years. These organizations that have embraced other forms of learning often see no need to return to on-site learning. Some took advantage of the opportunities that immersive platforms had to offer, as described in the case of Dr. Rafael J. Grossmann or Jena Davidson in part 2 of this book. In these examples, eliminating waste also goes hand in hand with increasing wellbeing and a positive impact on society.

However, it does not always have to be the most innovative technologies that add value to learning without travel and time away from work. Often, well-organized LXP and social microlearning platforms add just as much value to learning with and from colleagues. At Etihad, for example, a large proportion of skill- and competency-related workshops were successfully transferred to a new platform, with all the added value in measurability and personal coaching.

Defects

Defects in training or learning content are often less easy to measure, partly because they are often subjective from the learner's point of view. The factors that also determine whether the training has contributed in terms of content and design are therefore less easy to reflect in a causal relationship.

When we want to measure effectiveness, we often look for data in the required outcomes such as, for example, performance improvement, behavioural change or customer satisfaction. In addition, we see that models such as Kirkpatrick are still widely used despite the many resources that are often required for this. Technology, however, allows many digital courses to be measured in real time. A simple example goes back to the number of times a training course was taken and recommended to others. Think also of smart algorithms that can very quickly recognize good content and make it go viral.

Yet measuring is not always knowing. If the right requirements are not set, defects are difficult to detect. From a future-oriented strategy, it is therefore necessary to determine in advance what the success factors are, how they can be measured and how this data collection can be adjusted if necessary. This step, which is discussed in the last section, is a dimension that is included in the selection of technology (OODAP model).

Movement

Movement has a connection with transport, but this type of waste is rather similar to defects. Where it differs from the latter is that it is very specific and easy to avoid.

In a good strategy, content is made for a specific target group or application. However, when we distort it for wider use, usually to save costs, it is often a poor copy of the original and does not meet the specific learning needs of the target group or added value of the platform. A common example here is the cutting of content from live training courses or webinars for use on micro-learning platforms.

Instead of saving money by reusing content, we lose our main goal, which is to add value to the employee with the right individual learning content that he or she can apply to better perform a task or support wellbeing.

Another assumption is that reusing content is cheaper, but as we see in the last part of this book where we talk about relevant content, these unnecessary moves are often very time consuming and therefore expensive. Starting from a white canvas is the only method that is truly lean and supports employees to do an excellent job.

Mapping all the above wastes for a new strategy, or to evaluate an old one, often pays off very quickly so it is worth including them as standard in discussions. If this is a structural part of the organization with qualifiable indicators, lean frees up time, money and resources.

References

Bersin, J (2021) A New Category Emerges: the creator platform for corporate learning, joshbersin.com/2021/07/a-new-category-emerges-the-creator-platform-for-corporate-learning/ (archived at https://perma.cc/3754-F9J4)

McKinsey & Company (2022) How COVID-19 has pushed companies over the technology tipping point—and transformed business forever, www.mckinsey.com/business-functions/strategy-and-corporate-finance/our-insights/how-covid-19-has-pushed-companies-over-the-technology-tipping-point-and-transformed-business-forever (archived at https://perma.cc/6X85-NRM8)

10

The six drivers of LearnScapes to make learning central

I said earlier that this is not a book for L&D professionals alone, and that it can be useful to turn to your colleagues in other teams to discuss certain concepts with them. The next part is relevant for anyone who is interested in moving their organization towards a nimble LearnScape that benefits both the employees and the organization. What I want to describe in this part is also interesting for the learner to understand what your added value is in a learning ecosystem.

To design or manage such LearnScapes, it is useful to understand some of the drivers, as shown in Figure 10.1, from the point of view of the learner that are central to their experience. In the LearnScapes I envision, each employee is a stakeholder in the ecosystem. Together they have an impact on the growth of the LearnScape and together they are also the centre of the ecosystem around them.

The six drivers aren't intended as rules to be implemented and followed in all learning organization strategies: they are observations from my experience and discussions with ecosystem thinking experts. Neither these principles nor any other concept or theory is the key to success.

The following elaboration of the six pillars provides support when rolling out a new social strategy. They help to anticipate certain obstacles and support the use of untapped knowledge and skills that may otherwise go to waste.

FIGURE 10.1 The six drivers of LearnScapes

Learner at the centre

Everyone participates differently

Teamwork and peer coaching

Social learning and lean learning

System security

Bridging the knowledge gap

© Katja Schipperheijn

Social networks put the learner at the centre

I mentioned in the previous section that social networks have much in common with LearnScapes. What is more, in social networks the learner navigates independently and determines what is relevant to them. When social networks make use of algorithms that take these preferences into account, the experience becomes even more personal. At least, this should be the starting point of smart algorithms as described earlier.

When someone navigates through these social networks, extra knowledge is often gathered informally, fuelling the interest in new knowledge. This is also the starting point of good algorithms to motivate someone to absorb more and more relevant knowledge.

We also see that it is often not only the primary content that provides added value, but above all the interaction of others. We see, for example, that on enterprise social network (ESN) in particular we sometimes share and absorb more vital knowledge about the organization by reading comments on content than by organizing a formal learning event for this purpose. In this way, the culture of the organization is also brought more into focus and drives engagement.

Social networks put the learner at the centre of their co-workers, the knowledge and the tools needed to contribute to personal growth and thereby that of the organization.

Teamwork and peer coaching

In the future of work, optimizing teamwork and peer coaching will have even greater added value. Think of project work, cross-functional teams and gig-workers in the platform economy who often only work together virtually.

If we develop LearnScapes for them as social communities where they are encouraged to create their own content, this has many advantages. They get to know each other based on their interests and this strengthens the collaboration. We also see that expertise is strengthened by the collaboration and support they receive from others.

On top of that, we see that in some organizations, well-founded gamification can contribute to a culture for knowledge sharing and peer coaching, so that everyone in the LearnScape grows together faster (though not every organization can benefit from gamification).

Nielsen's 1-9-90 rule and how everyone participates differently

Nielsen's rule is not scientifically based but as with Jennings' 70-20-10 rule, there is a logical reasoning behind it that is interesting to keep in mind.

- **Lurkers:** 90 per cent do not actively engage in the conversation however they read or observe.
- **Intermittent Contributors:** 9 per cent of users contribute from time to time.
- **Heavy Contributors:** 1 per cent of users participate a lot and account for most contributions.

The above states that 90 per cent of the participants in a community do not seem to contribute to the success of the community. This is true both in formal social networks such as ESN and in a community of practice (COP) on LinkedIn, for example. This is surprising to some because connections are already being made between this group of people who share a common concern, problem or interest in a topic.

An estimated 9 per cent actively respond to existing discussions or content they encounter while walking through the virtual community. And, even more remarkably, only 1 per cent of participants would create content and feed the community. From this starting point, one might wonder what the point of rolling out a social learning network is if only 1 per cent contribute knowledge.

The question we should therefore ask ourselves first is who gains the most from learning in online communities. All too often, it is assumed that only the 1 per cent who visibly contribute is measured as a 'success factor'. However, that is a false assumption; it is often the lurkers or the peeps that make up 90 per cent of the group, that achieve greater learning gains. These lurkers are often very critical, but still want to be informed. However, they simply do not feel the urge to participate, in contrast to the often virtual shouters (1 per cent) who sometimes mainly want to be seen and do not learn much themselves.

When we talk about the 9 per cent who participate in response to others, we see that they often generate the most learning gain, both personally and for the group. This is often based on critical responses, which in turn provoke other responses. From this conversation, new ideas can emerge for all other members of the community, especially if we embrace openness as a competency in a value-driven organization. What is striking is that this group often responds actively online, but not in live meetings. This may have to do with their perceived anonymity or the virtual wall behind which they hide.

Why is this relevant to know? All too often, KPIs on social learning platforms are set in relation to interactions. Yet these interactions do not measure the learning gains, either for the individual or for the group. We also see that if we want social learning platforms to be about all learners, we need to look for added value to motivate more and more people to join the conversation. Via Gamification or from an attractive learning culture. But both take time.

Bridging the knowledge gap

LearnScapes, unlike data repository organizations, offer access to knowledge to employees and stakeholders inside and outside the organization. They have already adapted to the future of work and gig workers and cross-functional teams are part of the strategy to grow nimble and project-based.

Organizations stuck in silos or a top-down hierarchy often face knowledge gaps, i.e. doors that remain closed so that knowledge is not shared between certain departments. These gaps are often the cause of problems that surface when it is actually almost too late. They are also often a blind spot that leaves opportunities untapped. I recently had a project where a sales director asked me to build an app to give his employees more access to knowledge. Without anticipating too much on the steps you can take to build a LearnScape, by applying the Five Why method it became clear that the app was not the solution. Much more urgent was the need to collaborate with other departments that were already much more advanced. Both in sharing knowledge and in the technology they used.

LearnScapes are unique as social and lean learning ecosystems because they go beyond what is possible in social collaborator organizations through the symbiosis with AI. They consciously aim to bridge knowledge gaps between teams and outside the organization. For example, what sales and marketing learn from the ecosystem is integrated into the organization's learning strategy. They consciously use data and the benefits of smart technologies to prevent knowledge gaps and fuel innovation.

Social learning and lean learning go hand in hand

Social learning leads to people becoming better informed through the shared knowledge and expertise that exists within an organization (and beyond). Interaction with others gives employees a broader perspective and enables them to make better decisions. It recognizes that learning happens with and through other people, who bring them into contact with relevant content, learning resources and expert information.

Lean knowledge transfer and the use of social learning platforms with intelligent technologies push learning professionals and organizations outside their comfort zone by challenging old ways of thinking and learning. The combination of user-generated content, accessibility and the social network stimulates lean learning. Not only by acquiring knowledge but also by stimulating motivation and involvement.

Learning and development here is less about organizing training courses and more about facilitating knowledge sharing among like-minded people. To this end, they look for methods to make as much relevant information as possible accessible as quickly as possible through collaboration. Only in this way will knowledge flow through the ecosystem so that all those involved can grow together faster.

By applying lean reinforcement with social learning platforms, user-generated knowledge is shared, through optimal and intelligent collaboration between human and machine, with those who benefit most from it at that moment. This in turn sparks new ideas, creates a culture for sharing and learning, and maximises the return on investment in learning.

System security is key to the LearnScape's success

A good system protects knowledge leaks and sensitive information. And, it supports employees in easily finding, creating and sharing knowledge, learning resources and expertise with their colleagues. The IT people with a data repository mentality are naturally happy about this. Securing data is a priority for them, but that's not what security means when we talk about LearnScapes.

Technical security is of course very important. Nobody wants sensitive information to end up as public knowledge. In addition, as mentioned before, we also have to be very careful with the possibilities and shortcomings that intelligence technology has to offer. Believing that technology contributes to personal added value and wellbeing cannot always be guaranteed. Therefore, in addition to technology, we also need specialists who understand and/or can use the algorithms, taking into account possible shortcomings such as ethics or bias.

However, what I would like to endorse as a prerequisite for the success of a LearnScape is more than trust in the security of the system and the design of ethical AI algorithms. It's about human connections and links. In a LearnScape, everyone must be able to participate free of fear. Trust is a key concept between participants in a learning ecosystem. When someone is afraid to share knowledge and/or participate, the principle that everyone should be able to be central is not met.

Trust, however, is not only the most essential condition for participating in a social network. It is also the most difficult for the architects of these LearnScapes to achieve. This is essentially a part of the culture that supports a growth mindset. Everyone needs to trust that failure is not punished, that making mistakes by one individual contributes to learning by all.

Trust and a culture that supports a growth mindset are not built in a day. It is a recurring process that is paid attention to during the various steps that are taken to achieve continuous improvement.

Taking into account the drivers that have an impact on social learning ecosystems will help you to better assess the chances of success and KPI of projects. You can also use them to analyse current social learning strategies. For example, you can investigate how you can motivate more than 1 per cent of the users of your platform to share knowledge, whether or not by adding gamification to the strategy. Important with these drivers, as with all the other models I mention, is that you place them in the context of your own organization and that from there they are a starting point for continuous improvement.

CASE STUDY
How an IT consulting firm had to move from a social collaborator to a lean
learning ecosystem to support its continued growth

Matthias Feys, Q at ML6 | GDE for ML & GCP

Consulting is one of the most difficult business models to scale. At its core, the
expertise of the team is the product. To make this scalable, you need to
efficiently share expertise throughout the organization. This is what ML6, a high
tech AI consultancy, was also up against, especially in a period of strong growth
and labour shortage. With insufficiently graduated experts, they recruited young
talents with potential and trained them with a relentless focus on knowledge
sharing. The entire company structure was built around cross-functional teams.
They introduced the 'squads' and the 'chapters' organizational design, made
famous by Spotify. The recruitment process was structured to truly gauge
learning capabilities and emphasize the importance of knowledge sharing as a
cultural value of the company from the outset. The company quickly grew to
over 50 people in three countries.

When the company reached 100 highly specialized knowledge workers in
five different countries, things started to change. Manual approaches to
knowledge sharing started to buckle. Google drive folders were exploding with
information, making it difficult for people to find the information they needed.
Traditional initiatives were started, such as building an intranet and updating
excel sheets with reference cases and internal experts. These approaches were
still siloed and slow. They still required much manual effort and messages on
who did what, when and where were still frequent little disturbances on
the general chat channel.

The solution was not to add more tools or processes, but to add intelligence
to the existing systems. To use AI to connect the various collaboration tools and
make expertise accessible, reusable and measurable across the organization.
For this ML6 looked at Uman, a new start-up that was working on a solution
specifically designed for the professional services sector. Their three-step
approach was to use knowledge graphs and a powerful technology to transform
the fragmented information from different collaboration tools into a collective
brain, accessible to everyone in the organization. Being AI experts themselves,
ML6 understood as no other the power of the underlying technology.

1 The scattered information on CRM system, Google Drive and Slack was
  connected in real-time, while keeping the permission scopes intact to prevent
  data leakage.

2   AI automatically tagged the raw information on the relevant axis with respect to their areas of expertise, industries and customers they worked for, etc. In addition, it identified internal experts based on the documents they worked on and the insights they shared in shared chat channels. All this information was made accessible through an intuitive search interface and in the workflow. Finally, they can also close the expertise gap. If the team is looking for domain or industry knowledge but crucial assets are missing, they can activate internal experts to build the necessary assets so the whole team can benefit.

3   Finally, Uman's AI continuously measures how expertise evolves so that strategic decisions can be made based on facts. Data reveals in which areas new expertise is being developed, where opportunities for growth lie and where customers are being lost and efforts need to be stepped up.

From the cooperation between humans and AI, a truly scalable expertise-driven organization was created. In the process, intelligent technology also added value to a collaborative culture by breaking down silos and automating manual efforts for a frictionless, direct and connected experience.

Reference

Nielsen Norman Group (2006) The 90-9-1 Rule for Participation Inequality in Social Media and Online Communities, www.nngroup.com/articles/participation-inequality/ (archived at https://perma.cc/QE6F-WC84)

PART FIVE

Building LearnScapes

In the first parts of this book, I shared the need to have a positive attitude towards nimble learning strategies that evolve in a world of accelerating change. The consequences of the COVID-19 pandemic are still having an unprecedented impact on employees. In addition, we saw in the first part of this book that younger generations have different expectations when it comes to the future of work.

Moreover, the increasingly rapid innovations and developments in artificial intelligence have a hard-to-predict influence. Strategies that do not take the volatile future into account will sooner or later reach their limits. Therefore, it is essential that organizations - no matter how disrupted, digitized or even virtualized they are - commit to a nimble strategy that supports a growth mindset. This growth mindset should be the first priority of forward-thinking leaders who understand that intelligent collaboration between people and machines will not only drive the bottom line of the business. If properly implemented, it will also support the wellbeing of employees.

In this context, learning is much more than what has so far been entrusted primarily to HR or the L&D department. Learning is the responsibility of everyone in the organization and fostering this learning environment is therefore a strategic initiative supported by all. Learning is also more than just 'training' in skills and knowledge. It is ensuring that employees are informed about the purpose of learning and are therefore motivated to shape their own learning paths. Moreover, these engaged employees value not only their own learning, but also the sharing of knowledge, collaboration and supporting others in their growth.

Finally, and I can't repeat it enough, you should know that a LearnScape is not built in a day. It takes time and dedication to cultivate a new culture where learning supports everyone in the ecosystem.

Habit of improvement: five steps to nimble LearnScapes

For all these reasons, it is necessary to draw up a nimble learning strategy that involves your organization, its employees and stakeholders in growth. To this end, in this final part of the book, we will work pragmatically with a five-step method for continuous improvement.

- **Discovery:** analysing current learning needs for future success.
- **Burning platform:** create a trusted case for engaged learning with all stakeholders.
- **Path to improvement:** where technology, content and the learning culture come together.
- **Joint execution:** no success will ever be achieved without collaboration.
- **Future growth and improvement:** never stop learning.

All steps are equally important and linked, so each will follow from the previous one, although they may not take up the same amount of time and resources.

This easy-to-apply method requires that we always look at the previous steps to achieve continuous improvement. Yet, this is not a blueprint that will work out the same for every organization or project. That is why, within the different steps, I will provide various methods and tips that can inspire you in your own projects.

It is important that these five steps are repeated with every new opportunity that presents itself. This also implies that different projects

FIGURE A.1 Five continuous steps to a LearnScape

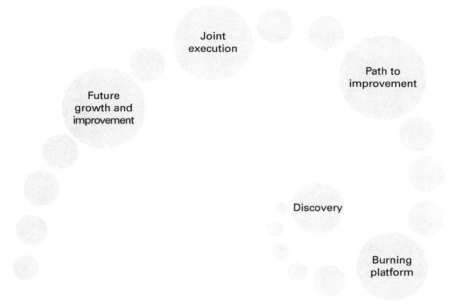

© Katja Schipperheijn

can be in a different step and be worked out next to each other. However, it is the role of the learning architect or LearnScaper of the nimble organization to assess them together from a holistic approach. This further increases the learning effect through cross-fertilization and knowledge sharing between the different project teams.

As you can see in the visual representation in Figure A.1, this methodology is grafted onto the Fibonacci. This means that, in principle, a project grows endlessly, learning from the past. However, this is also the biggest pitfall for many organizations that just keep on building without re-evaluating the previous step each time as in the Kaizen principle. Why do we do this, what worked well, what worked less well and where do we want to go in the next step?

Finally, I want to emphasize the added value of the LearnScaper as a connector. Knowing why we do something and what the goal is, is totally irrelevant if the stakeholders are not on board. Even more so if certain stakeholders or pressure groups see in the new strategy a possible threat, either to themselves or to others.

11

Step 1: Discovery: analysing the current learning needs for future success

This first step largely determines whether a project will be successful. Yet it is often done too quickly so the real opportunity does not come to light.

Whether or not a project is approached with sufficient thoughtfulness is often predictable in advance. Where or by whom it is initiated is a major determining factor in this, as the following examples indicate.

- From a strategic thinking exercise on lean or organizational optimization.
- From an existing project that is being evaluated, which may lead to improvement projects or new projects.
- From a training need from business or HR.

The first two require a holistic and strategic approach. Methods like lean learning development, the learning maturity model or drivers for social learning can help to find improvement opportunities.

The last example is often prompted by a current, urgent need or problem. This time pressure is the most common reason for assuming the solution too quickly. Although quick is relative, these projects might take two months to two years to implement. In this fast-changing world, the problem might have already disappeared by then.

A good discovery phase is preferably not done as a reaction to a problem but as a strategic exercise to prepare for the unknown future. The initial approach seems longer, but is more effective in the long run. Paying attention to the distinction between problems and opportunities is essential here. Opportunities are worked out in a flexible way, in contrast to problems that can be a sticking plaster on a wound, as we saw all too often at the beginning of the COVID-19 pandemic. Quick fixes were sought that were often not aimed at improving work and learning or supporting wellbeing. However, identifying problems is certainly a very good starting point, such as mapping waste. This can often be a very good motivation for stakeholders, especially from a cost perspective.

To support this discovery, I would like to share with you some methods I use that may not be widely known or that I adapt from existing sources.

This discovery phase falls into two categories:

- **Starting from a problem:** on the basis of Wh-questions and algorithmic business thinking to define the underlying problem or root cause analyses.

- **Starting from opportunities:** projection of the future and the way of thinking with regard to innovation.

Wh-questions

Why as the most important LearnScaper's tool to start any project

The ability to apply the 'why?' described in this section is therefore a competence that we must relearn or at least nurture. A competence that often seems very simple, but apparently is very difficult for seasoned executives who have learned to make quick decisions, or not to be questioned! My tip is therefore: don't try to think like a professional, but let the child in you free. Don't rush, don't assume you already know the answer after just one question.

The first tool I offer is *Five Whys*, a very simple iterative questioning technique used to determine the cause-and-effect relationships underlying a problem in order to arrive at an opportunity. This technique was originally developed by Sakichi Toyota and used at the Toyota Motor Corporation during the evolution of its production methods, so, the link with lean is not far off.

To use *Five Whys*: the basic competences that add value are curiosity and openness, complemented by the other competences that will be important for everyone in the future. Below I give the five sequential steps you go through with a case to illustrate.

ASSEMBLE A TEAM TO COLLECT PROBLEMS

When I do a workshop, I always try to put together a team with all stakeholders that can have a positive or negative influence on the course of the project. In other words, not only the stakeholders who are already familiar with the problem, but also those who are perfectly happy with the situation as it is. These include the administrators of legacy systems, but in some countries also pressure groups such as trade unions.

As a facilitator, always be open-minded and positive. The more problems, the more opportunities for improvement that may result in a quick-win project. These first small successes will also convince less convinced stakeholders of the added value of the transition that you as an organization and the ecosystem want to achieve.

> **Tip:** Let each participant independently write down a possible problem that has an impact on the way knowledge is shared in the organization and with the ecosystem. These can be individual problems such as access to certain knowledge, but also more complex problems such as the re-boarding of employees who may no longer have job security due to automation.

SELECT PROBLEMS

Once a selection has been made from the problems presented, it is interesting to look at the future and at possibilities for quick wins. These quick wins will be important later on to start the transformation process with small steps and low risk. It can be interesting to look at problems that only have an impact on a slightly smaller group that is open to change. This group can then later act as ambassadors for the transformation.

Examples: The scheduled training cannot take place because of COVID-19 or employees are not committed to the transformation. Of course, I have been hearing both of these quite often lately. The first is a possible quick-win as you can decide to do a virtual training, however, on short term, this may be a good temporary solution, but it is often not a lean solution that also contributes to more efficient learning. The second will be less easy to tackle on short term, but it will be essential to address for future success of the organization.

THE FIRST 'WHY'

This is where it gets fun, although as a moderator you will often have a challenge with the more introverted participants. However, an opportunity arises here if you need to hold the session virtually. As a moderator, you can then give everyone a turn and ask for their input.

Start with the first question and probe for the causes that might underlie the problem. Try not to forget openness; the opinion of others can be very valuable to gain insight into perceptions and what moves people. Try to get to the root of the problem together.

Asking *'why?'* sounds simple, but it is not. Avoid guessing at the causes and rely on facts if they are available.

Example: *'Why* are employees not involved in the strategy?' might be very difficult question that can yield many answers and where you will have to abstract from what is essential and what is not. If abstraction is not evident I suggest to use the approach of algorithmic business thinking explained further in this chapter.

ANOTHER FOUR TIMES 'WHY?'

For each of the answers you generated in Step 3, ask *'why?'* four more times in a row, referring to the answer to the previous question. Try not to reason too long at times, but move quickly to the next *'why?'* until you have a complete understanding and only then draw conclusions.

In the example case that follows, a single root cause cannot be identified in a single track of 'why' questions. In that example, there are several relevant causes and a double track may be better placed. The causes in both columns can then be related to each other. From this relevance, we then look further to see if there are any recurring patterns at the root of it.

> **Tip:** When should you stop asking 'why'? It sounds simple: when the original problem no longer provides any useful answers. As I have already indicated in many examples, numbers are often an inventor's guide. Dare to be creative!

SELECT THE ROOT CAUSE THAT CREATES AN OPPORTUNITY TO WORK ON

If there is consensus on the root cause that needs to be addressed, it is important that it is supported by everyone who participated in the (virtual) workshop. If the core group does not agree, this will manifest itself later when we want to convince other stakeholders to take the leap into an uncertain future. This leap or transformation project starts with the burning platform that I will explain later.

Determining the root cause is an essential step that is often taken too quickly and where assumptions often lead to the wrong decision.

CASE STUDY
When a problem is not the problem, and an opportunity arises

Face-to-face training is totally out of the question in several scenarios, and can be taken care of, and improved, by innovative technology. Still, I restrained myself from commenting or directing, and rigorously went over the Five Whys with the one company. I should add that in the back of my mind, I was already abstracting what was essential and what was not. For example, I did not want to focus initially on the question: 'why do you still want to apply 'training' in these times? What does training have to do with learning if it is not underpinned by a growth mindset and learning in the right moment of need? I didn't say that and sometimes not saying anything is better in this first phase. Let your teams come up with the answers themselves. Later, in the transformation phase, they will defend their idea as ambassadors.

I wanted to let them discover for themselves what was at stake using the Five Whys method. In Figure 11.1, I share the outline of our conversation. As you can see, the cause of the question could not be reduced to a single track. However, the track we chose was the one where the urgency was the highest and the quick-wins the biggest in order to start the transformation at a later stage. So, building a new app to book face-to-face training was not the problem we choose to address. However, it would have been much easier to fix on short term. In addition to showing potential paths towards resolving the issue, this exercise also revealed a lot about the organization's journey to becoming a LearnScape. I would particularly like to highlight the following: *Because I work for the business and not for HR.* So, the fact that the two departments were not working together was the reason why the business side thought they needed a new app. In short, I did not develop a new app or search for an existing one. Neither would contribute in many aspects to lean learning and certainly not fit into the long-term vision of learning.

FIGURE 11.1 Example Five Why model

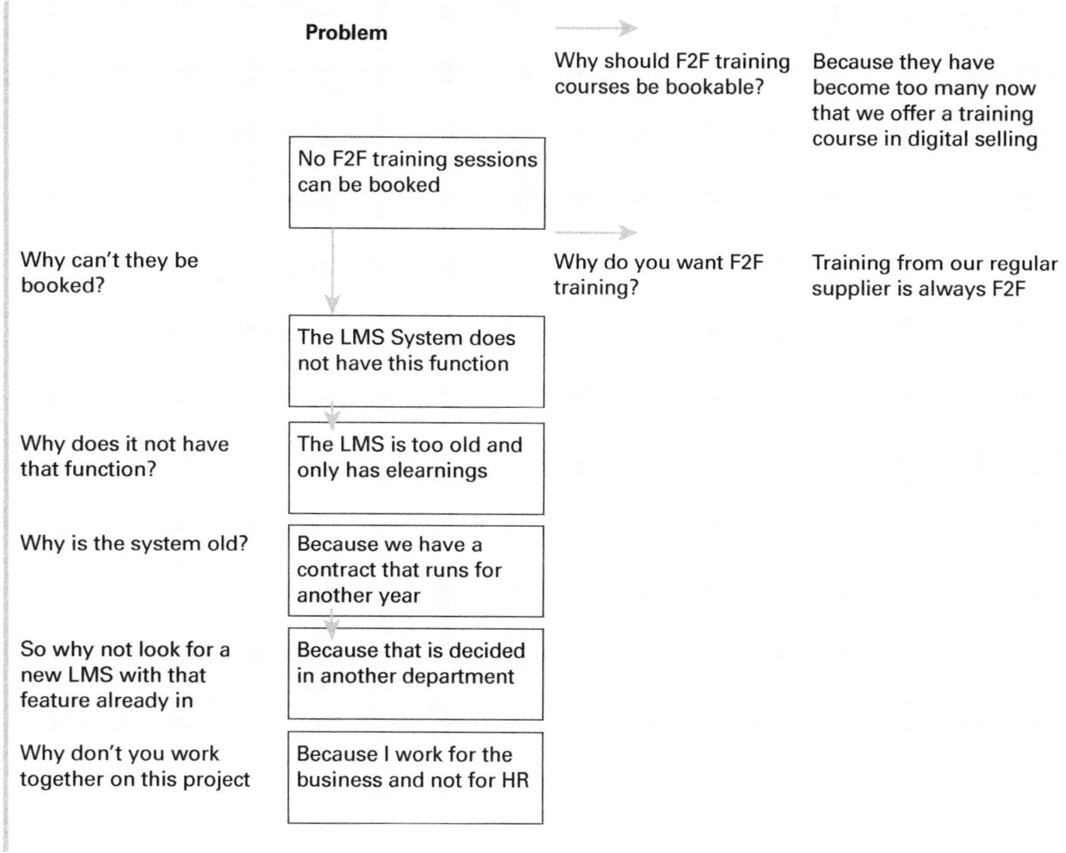

	Problem		
		Why should F2F training courses be bookable?	Because they have become too many now that we offer a training course in digital selling
	No F2F training sessions can be booked		
Why can't they be booked?		Why do you want F2F training?	Training from our regular supplier is always F2F
	The LMS System does not have this function		
Why does it not have that function?	The LMS is too old and only has elearnings		
Why is the system old?	Because we have a contract that runs for another year		
So why not look for a new LMS with that feature already in	Because that is decided in another department		
Why don't you work together on this project	Because I work for the business and not for HR		

Five Whys is a very simple approach, yet sometimes a problem cannot be reduced to a single cause. When it turns out that there are in fact more causes for the problem, it is often useful to do a further cause-and-effect analysis which I will discuss later or to apply the basic principles of algorithmic business thinking, which is also discussed later in the chapter.

Five Whys may not be the most appropriate tool for tackling a complex problem, but it can identify quick wins that can be addressed quickly. Something that will prove to be a huge added value when building LearnScapes to get stakeholders on board.

More Wh-questions: what, who, when

A useful follow-up to the why-approach involves even more questions that clarify the big picture to be worked out as a project at a later stage. For this purpose, we will focus only on the essential problems that we have defined from the above, where we have a possibility for improvement.

More Wh-questions help us build a business case that we can present in the next phase about the burning platform we are going to create. As with the Five Whys, it seems simpler than it is. Assumptions often result in misinterpretations, delayed implementation and even possible blocking of the further roll-out of the project.

What and why

Once the root cause of a problem or problems has been identified based on the Wh-question, it is important to set priorities. These priorities can have different motivations, such as;

- Reducing waste and cost, therefore improving efficiency and effectiveness and making it attractive to some stakeholders.
- Increasing staff wellbeing and commitment.
- An urgent need to teach new skills or competences to a target group. This in turn can be prioritized by including parameters

such as risk to the organization, new ways of working, or a new organizational strategy, etc. (in 2020, this was one of the most common drivers for change).

- Increasing attractiveness as an employer by training potential candidates who do not have the right skills, but the right competences and growth mindset.

From the example of the training booking application, we can also see that multiple opportunities can be launched in a similar way in different processes, possibly with different stakeholders. This makes it very easy to open the door between the business and HR. A conversation and the win-win to work together soon pays off. From this cross-functional cooperation, opportunities can then be sought where they reinforce each other. This can therefore result in two projects running simultaneously side by side. Nevertheless, it is not advisable to have too many projects next to each other. Looking for similarities in the differences to find overlaps can make the learning organization even more lean.

From the perspective of 'why', it is also an added value at this stage to question the measurability of a project. If there is a direct causal link that can be made with a KPI (e.g. reduced employee absence days), this can be an added value when presenting the project on the *burning platform* to convince even the most reluctant stakeholders.

Who

Now that we know what the problem is and why we are solving it, it is important that someone takes ownership. Not to blame afterwards, but to ensure that the focus remains on the problem and the associated opportunities. This role involves more than just project management. It is the role of learning architect (LearnScaper) who stands in the world of tomorrow, but can translate it to the present.

Unfortunately, in many cases LearnScaper in charge of the project is not a member of the management team. Therefore, it can be an added value at this stage to get sponsorship from the management team, so that the LearnScaper can exercise sufficient influence and control. Mapping the span of control can certainly be an added value. I say in many cases, because there are clearly more and more organizations that see the added value of including this strategic architect of tomorrow's organization, in the executive team.

With whom

A transition project for a learning organization is rarely a one-person job. They are best surrounded by a cross-functional team with specific knowledge of the drivers and the obstacles that can influence the project. Defining the 'who' already in this step will have added value when moving to a *joint implementation phase*.

In LearnScapes we look for added value through collaboration between humans and machines. In this phase, we look ahead to the measurability of the project, the success factors and how we can use (data from) intelligent systems for this.

The case described earlier concerning a training app had a lot of data on net promoter scores (NPS) of the many training courses they offered. However, this data was not being collected and tracked using technology nor was it being brought together with other data systems to make intelligent predictions.

The 'parties' with whom we are running the project therefore consist of more than a project team of people. Where machines can add value can already be identified in this step.

When

When are we going to adopt this project? As you can imagine, in many cases that answer should have been yesterday. In many data repository organizations, the transition has been years behind, so a quick catch-up is necessary to reduce a potential competitive disadvantage.

Moreover, we note that even the smallest adjustments can bring about a 'butterfly effect'. In other words, innovation processes are sensitively dependent on the initial conditions. As a result, it is almost impossible to predict the future and there are always unforeseen circumstances. For the most reluctant stakeholders, this is often a reason to do nothing. However, the choice has to be considered here: what if we do nothing. What impact will doing nothing have on our employees, the organization and the ecosystem in the short and long term? This also determines the urgency, but often more importantly, it is an essential question that will need to be answered on the burning platform.

'When' is also very important in the sequence of steps to the LearnScape. Think about the order of priorities that will have an impact on the organization in terms of quick wins that do not require too much risk and time investment. These quick wins will later be interesting in convincing even the most reluctant to change.

Algorithmic business thinking

When I mentioned earlier *'searching for the problem behind the problem'* using Five Whys methodology, I was inspired by the principles of algorithmic business thinking (ABT). This way of thinking was developed by Paul McDonagh-Smith to create value through intelligent systems of human-and-machine portfolios.

The four basic elements of ABT are:

- **Decomposition:** break down into several challenges to make it more manageable and assign priorities.
- **Abstraction:** make sure you address what is relevant and what not.
- **Pattern recognition:** can you find similarities in different challenges that can be tackled together?
- **Algorithm:** describe the change process.

Algorithmic business thinking has great value when you are dealing with very complex problems where the cause is not easily identifiable. Add to that the fact that you sometimes work with very diverse teams and leaders, with different experience in technology for knowledge sharing and data analysis, then it can sometimes be a challenge to keep uniformity and structure in your way of working. The basic elements of ABT provide the necessary guidance and often support complex problems with a methodology that facilitates implementation at later stages.

Another situation where ABT adds value is when we derive different possibilities. Here pattern recognition and consistency will help to find the similarities in the differences. All steps in this method are equally important and follow a fixed path. Not only can you not change the order, you can't skip a step either.

When tackling silo thinking (for example, the application for F2F training), we create the vision of structured and spontaneous collaboration between HR and stakeholders from the business departments. This is a complex problem as opposed to building an app. A hierarchical and silo-based structure is not something we can tackle all at once. Here, the four steps of the ABT fundamentals offer more guidance to reach a solution, or as Paul McDonagh-Smith calls this solution the algorithm. It's important to note that a solution must therefore not be a digital solution within an organizational context.

A complex problem can often be broken down into several challenges to make it more manageable and assign priorities. Some examples are the leadership style, the way the organization is structured – either formally through processes or informally in its culture – the IT systems and so on. We must first dissect and decompose these challenges until we find the essence of what we want to address as an opportunity.

Having made the challenges manageable, the next step is to abstract the relevant. Abstracting is often a difficult step because it takes us out of our comfort zone. However, this step will later be of great value when implementing a new strategy. 'Who are we doing this for?', 'Why are we doing this?' and 'What do we want to achieve with this?' need to be understood and agreed!

What also makes algorithmic business thinking different is that we compare different problems, or opportunities, side by side to look for patterns. Are there things that seem different, but are actually similar in origin or consequence? Can we address two or more causes with one solution? When we have separated the essential from the non-essential and recognized possible patterns in them, only then can we start thinking about the algorithms of the change process.

These algorithms, are rarely really about code or even artificial intelligence. They are the description of the change process, the steps to improvement. The link here is a structured methodology for getting from A to B, just as artificial intelligence does. This method is very useful when in later phases the symbiosis between man and machine is actually envisaged. By learning to think like a code developer in this phase, the project will become more efficient and possible obstacles or challenges will emerge more quickly.

The above methods all contribute when we want to adapt our organization or way of working with regard to learning and knowledge sharing in a flexible and future-oriented way. In none of the methods is an end point the ultimate goal, but finding possibilities that are a first step towards improvement.

When we have made a choice based on the above, we know who we want in our team. We have mapped out a possible timeframe and the intention is to develop a business plan. However, this plan will only succeed if we have all stakeholders on board. In the next section, therefore, I will look more closely at the role of the project initiator or owner and why this does not always have to be the person who discovered the problem, saw the opportunity or led previous workshops.

Looking to the future

We know from 'when' that most projects have already passed their expiration date. Daring to leap into the future to anticipate problems is not everyone's cup of tea and could be seen as like playing the lottery. Nevertheless, there are methods that support experimentation and 'thinking in the future'.

It is impossible to give an overview of all the methods, so I have selected a few that had a significant effect on me. Innovation coach and MIT Sloan Certified Design Thinker Marc Mekki has given my understanding of design thinking another dimension. This method, which is more like a software upgrade for the mind, makes confidently approaching an uncertain and volatile future a lot more tolerable.

I am also very honoured that Dr Stephen Shepard wanted to share his reverse engineering with me. This approach looks at the future not from the point of view of technology and innovation, but from a value-driven vision. Something that I believe is the approach that fully fits future generations, and benefits everyone in the ecosystem.

However, neither method is future-proof, and there is always that element of uncertainty. That is why all the projects we start are essentially an experiment, even though you will never be able to sell it to the management team under that name! When it comes to a transition that also affects people especially, unnecessary risk and experimentation are something we prefer to avoid.

Design thinking

Experimentation through trial and error is deeply human, allowing us to adapt to challenges. Innovation should therefore not always be about technology, but about adapting to the unknown future from a human-centric perspective starting from a point of uncertainty and ambiguity. We may not be able to predict the events ahead but we can make sure our reaction to them always places the wellbeing and prosperity of people at the centre.

A method that offers structured support for this is design thinking. It teaches us to tap into our inner resources to come up with smart solutions, the essence of innovation. A design thinker thrives on uncertainty as long as they are allowed to study, interview and observe the target audience. In doing so they are given the leeway to freely ideate and prototype before having to commit to a fixed course of action.

Design thinking is taught worldwide, at renowned schools such as MIT, Harvard, London Business School and so on. Yet, as I learned from Marc Mekki, the methodology can diverge considerably depending on the sector, case and practitioners. According to him, it is not a linear step-by-step process guaranteed to produce a winning outcome; design thinking is not a script. What it does involve is reprogramming the brain to enable us to solve problems not on the basis of knowledge, but on the basis of imagination and creativity. It is rooted in a sincere desire to understand the spoken and unspoken needs of the people we create for. This approach fits in very well with today's times when we think in human-centric terms.

Design thinking typically breaks down into five main stages that may initially seem similar in their entirety to the five steps of the habit of improvement method. The big difference is that this method is not about innovation and technology and therefore focuses less on continuous improvement. The first three steps, however, can be an added value to look at opportunities for improvement from a human value perspective. That is why I like to share a case of Marc Mekki who situates design thinking in the culture sector, namely the San Francisco Opera (SFO).

EMPATHISE

Never surmise that ideas have merit without first observing and interviewing the presumed end users of a proposed solution. At the outset, eliminate all assumptions and suspend any conceptualization of potential products or services. Design thinkers aspire to start projects as blank canvases, free of presumption or bias. They understand that only a deeper understanding of the expressed and latent needs of people can lead to the genesis of successful solutions.

DEFINE

Analyse the observed and expressed needs for the purpose of uncovering patterns and overlap. Filter, categorize and rank with the aim of retaining a shortlist of common denominator needs used as the catalyst for the ideation stage. A successfully constructed needs list informs design thinkers about desirability.

IDEATE

A multi-disciplinary team engages in successive conceptualization sessions. Typically ideation sessions are preceded by 'ice-breaking' activities to build the trust and rapport necessary to allow for unrepressed creative thinking. It is crucial that every member of the ideation team feels comfortable and that no idea can be considered taboo or crazy. Ideally, ideation sessions involve stakeholders from all levels of an organization as well as its customers. Resulting concepts are ranked and filtered with the aim of retaining one or several concepts to take to the prototyping stage.

PROTOTYPE

Using affordable and readily available off-the-shelf components (be that hardware, software or a combination) the team mocks up a prototype of the product or service. Prototypes are typically non-functional representations of the envisioned solution, a stage that precedes the 'minimum viable product' (MVP) stage. Prototypes allow design thinkers to coalesce abstract ideas into a more concrete representation. This makes it easier to debate the merits and pitfalls of a potential full deployment. A successfully constructed prototype informs design thinkers about feasibility.

TEST

First exposure of the concept and associated prototype to outsiders for the purpose of gathering feedback, critiques and suggestions. Prototypes are ideally exposed to a cross-section of stakeholders, customers and even competitors. For commercial solutions, this is the time when sales and marketing teams get involved to advise on challenges and opportunities that may arise were the solution to be released commercially. Very often, this stage represents the most significant stress test of á new concept. Depending on the outcome, concepts may return to any of the previous stages of design thinking, or may be abandoned entirely. A successfully completed testing stage informs design thinkers about viability.

The following case was shared with me by Marc Mekki and international expert in innovation and design thinking, which situates design thinking in the cultural sector, namely the San Francisco Opera (SFO), provides an overview of this widely used method.

CASE STUDY
San Francisco opera labs

Marc Mekki, Innovation coach and Corporate trainer, MIT Sloan Certified Design Thinking

Convincing young audiences to spend a night at the opera isn't an easy sell. However, as a team assembled by the San Francisco Opera (SFO) discovered, the reason why may come as a surprise.

By empathizing with their target audience – the first pillar of design thinking – through street-side interviews with a cross-section of youthful San Franciscans the team discovered that a lack of enthusiasm typically wasn't due to a resistance to musical theatre per se but rather an expression of timidity towards the perceived complexity of the etiquette and cultural norms associated with opera.

Simply put, youngsters were intimidated by the idea of committing an unspeakable cultural faux-pas; no one wants to pay good money to end up mortified and embarrassed in front of their peers. The problem, it turns out, wasn't opera music itself.

Thus, sanctioned by the SFO, an innovation project was culminating in a series of pop-up performances dubbed 'Barely Opera'. Having picked a casual music venue – a far cry from the ornate features of the Opera House – the multidisciplinary team designed an experimental program filled with non-traditional elements like casual dress, projection screens, a photo booth and a 'wheel of songs'. Within hours a website and logo were produced and the event announced across social media and online forums.

When the doors opened on March 2, 2015, a line of nearly 400 people stretched around the block. The success of the experiment led directly to the creation of a SFO-sanctioned production arm called 'SF Opera Labs' that was responsible for a series of successful avant-garde pop-up events across the city which led to a much deeper understanding about the needs and wants of a previously impenetrable demographic and, crucially, a deeper appreciation for the power of experimentation, rapid prototyping and iteration, also pillars of design thinking.

What had previously held back innovation at the San Francisco Opera was the same trait that holds back most organizations from becoming perennial innovators equipped to face the volatility of the 21st century: perfectionism. Do it right or don't do it at all. Sounds familiar?

While this spirit is highly commendable on an individual level it wreaks havoc on an organization's ability to innovate and pivot. The world is a distracted and distracting place. Grabbing and holding the attention of audiences in this era will hinge on your ability to truly understand their needs and to innovate continually at every level of the organization.

Further holding back innovation is the misconception that it is causally linked with modern digital technology and that those less technologically adept aren't suited to innovation. But innovation isn't about digital technology. Humans have been innovating for tens of thousands of years, often coming up with creations that would stand the test of time far better than the passing fads of recent decades. Arrowheads, for example, in continuous use for more than sixty millennia, were created through relentless trial and error by humans closely observing and understanding the needs of fellow humans.

Social innovation, political innovation, personal innovation... At some stage technology will likely factor into each transformational process, but it is not itself the purpose. Innovation is first and foremost about upgrading our mental processes. Think of it as a software update for the mind, removing the outdated ideas of the 20th century and replacing them with mental processes tailored to the realities of the 21st century.

Reverse engineering

Predicting the future is impossible, even for the most experienced futurists like Allen Kay. Yet, he too claims that the best way to predict the future is to invent it. This statement is not only a well-known adage from the tech world, but has also been proven true on numerous occasions.

Besides the method of design thinking, there are others that, despite the high degree of uncertainty about the future, work with a pragmatic structure. Reverse engineering is one such structure that is very useful when we want to map out a transition path. I was taught this method by my friend Dr Steven Shepard and have used it before in developing learning applications and in helping organizations to reinvent themselves in a LearnScape.

Instead of starting in the present and marching forward, reverse engineering starts in the future by developing a desired vision that we want to achieve. It then lets us walk backwards, identifying and eliminating any obstacles that would otherwise prevent us from reaching that future state.

I believe that the vast majority of our companies would benefit from improving processes by reinventing, repositioning and redirecting them towards a more sustainable and productive future. Yet I find that starting is the hardest part of creating the future. Faced with an abundance of data, we run the risk of being paralyzed by over-analysis, which leaves us stuck for a long time. We try too hard to hold on to what seems 'normal' to us. We need to understand the uncertain future and want to be able to predict and record everything based on past knowledge. And even if we manage to free ourselves from this need to understand everything, we risk getting stuck again. We over plan and work out too many possible future scenarios. We filter out truths using Bayesian interpretations (an interpretation of chance as a reasonable expectation) and in the end, we are often no closer to understanding where the future will take us than when we started.

The methodology of reverse engineering itself is based on the assumption of a desired and achievable outcome where we choose a point in the future that is far enough away. This allows us to let go of the present and the past and make assumptions that are free of their grip. The goal of the reverse engineered future is to achieve a vision that all stakeholders can endorse. To move the organization forward in the best possible way.

Reverse engineering may sound complex, but it is quite easy to implement. Not only is it simple, it is also fun to do when you are working with a team that consists of a cross-section of all stakeholders in the ecosystem. These diverse stakeholders all have their own backgrounds and goals that often don't seem to align in the short term. When we look far enough into the future with a value-driven approach, we still come together in a better future for all. Therefore, finding a project is not just about the goal that needs to be achieved. The process itself often provides interesting insights into what drives the organization and how culture affects it.

For the reverse engineering of the future, we consider three components that are each different, yet all interconnected.

VISION

Vision is the projection of the desired end state that you are striving for with your organization. Crucial in creating this vision is the willingness to let go of how things are done today. As with unlearning skills and behaviours from employees, this is often the biggest challenge. The competences I described earlier will therefore be of great value for the LearnScaper moderating this.

Tip: a good approach here is to imagine that your organization is still in a start-up phase, where you are actually setting up your organization or department for the very first time.

In this phase of the reverse engineering workshop, participants have the freedom to design the future organization, free from past and present adversaries and distractions. What you will often observe – as in traditional scenario planning exercises – are objections like, 'that is not how we do things here'. As a moderator, it is best to put the brakes on such thoughts. What you should not inhibit, however, is the content of the vision itself. The vision can be as radical and drastic as the participants want it to be, as long as it is feasible and can be realized within the agreed time frame.

As for an achievable vision, I like to give the example of my own start-up and the sCool app for primary school children that I created with my own daughters in 2015. Equal opportunities for all children in primary school, regardless of where, when and with whom they learn. So, they will all develop those skills to exercise their citizenship rights in the virtual world.

The vision was set over a period of 12 years so that we could introduce the app and its teaching packages to all primary school pupils twice. We had also thought of the older generations that we would not be able to reach as a result. From initiatives that stimulate (grand) parent involvement, we wanted to reach these generations through young children. I admit, it was a challenging vision, but not unachievable. We had to take into account the cumbersome nature of education, for example. As a result, lobbying to get all stakeholders on board was more difficult than developing the app itself. But now, many years later, similar initiatives have been launched around the world. The vision was achieved not only by developing an app, but even more so by spreading it in the ecosystem.

VALUES

Values are the most critical components in the reverse engineered future. They define how the LearnScape wants to be seen by its employees, customers, partners and competitors. These values emanate from the core of the organization and define how the company should behave in the larger ecosystem. LearnScapes with a powerful and compelling vision of their own future, based on a set of strong and equally compelling values, will not thrive alone. They will find that external forces slowly, inexorably align with the company because of this vision and underlying values.

This is the starting point we want to achieve when designing our LearnScape. So, when we want to reverse engineer the future, we already take into account the impact of the project on the values of our future LearnScape. The values I am referring to are linked to the symbiosis of human and artificial intelligence we are striving for. This symbiosis should primarily support the wellbeing of people, taking into account concerns such as ethics or the risk of bias, lack of tolerance and even discrimination.

In the case of sCool, our vision was also shaped by values, with inclusion and equal opportunities for all prevailing.

MISSION

Unlike the vision and values, the organization's mission is somewhat more tangible. Most organizations have a mission statement that they share widely with the world. While the vision makes us passionate about life, the mission makes us passionate about our work. Both are needed in a healthy, sustainable LearnScape.

Another important difference with the vision is that the mission has an end date attached to it, which is worked out through the strategy. This strategy can have different phases, each building on the previous one and containing clear objectives. This is the basis for the action plan. Since in the structure of reverse engineering the process starts with the future, the rest of the process is based on identifying all the obstacles, challenges and problems that the company encounters along the way. The strategy we outline is to foresee these obstacles and provide a nimble solution for them.

Returning to the sCool app, the vision was: 'equal opportunities for all children in primary school, regardless of where, when and with whom they learn'. Our values were clearly defined and all had to do with equal opportunities. Our mission was to give everyone access to learning through a social app for education. We had added several objectives when developing our application, such as accessibility, inclusion of non-native speakers and access for children from disadvantaged backgrounds who had less or no support at home.

In designing the strategy, we did not look at what the students already had, but what they would like to have in the future. For example, we believed that artificial intelligence could predict when pupils would struggle in a particular subject, and we wanted to use AI to positively steer pupil behaviour towards a growth mindset. This approach also meant that we would not look at what technology can do now, but what might be possible one day. The idea was that we would use technological components that were always replaceable if they no longer met the requirements of innovation at that time. We built, as it were, an application from Lego bricks that we did not yet have available.

Doing nothing is the biggest experiment

I would like to emphasize that in some cases, doing nothing is also an experiment. An experiment in which we also do not know what will happen in the uncertain future. Again, I would like to take the example of the app to book trainings. What if we did not build it or buy it? What if we did nothing? What is the risk for the teams who cannot book these training sessions? Is it a limited risk, does it affect one regional team, when does it affect the company's results? In this example, the risk of doing nothing was obviously very low, because the old manual way worked, although it may not have been very efficient. In the longer term, however, there was added value in putting the problem into a larger framework from a holistic point of view.

Understanding the consequences of inaction is as important as understanding the problem. This analysis is made far too infrequently, yet it is of great added value in defending a project, as I will explain when calculating the opportunity cost in the next section.

What not to do in the discovery workshop

A final but important note about the discovery workshop is about the people who initiate or lead the conversation.

Often, this discovery phase is driven by white papers offered by sales people from companies that want to sell technology. In itself, there is nothing wrong with white papers that add value. They can be a very good starting point for a discovery phase of possible added value of a technological innovation. 'We are doing it because other successful companies have done it,' is still better than, 'we are not doing it because we have always done it that way.'

However, to go to the next step, the burning platform, we risk nothing more than showing a presentation by a vendor that naturally puts forward their technology as the best.

References

Leadership, Executive Crash Course Press, Williston

Management is a Journey (2022) Five Whys – act like a child and improve problem solving, managementisajourney.com/five-whys-act-like-a-child-and-improve-problem-solving/ (archived at https://perma.cc/LL6A-MBWZ)

MIT Management (2021) Boost digital transformation with algorithmic business thinking, mitsloan.mit.edu/ideas-made-to-matter/boost-digital-transformation-algorithmic-business-thinking (archived at https://perma.cc/U2UC-CZ5A)

Research Gate (2017) The Five Whys Technique, www.researchgate.net/publication/318013490_The_Five_Whys_Technique (archived at https://perma.cc/A7TS-QKMX)

Schipperheijn, K (2022) Reverse Engineering for the Value Driven Learning Organization, habitofimprovement.com/2021/10/09/reverse-engineering-for-the-value-driven-learning-organisation/ (archived at https://perma.cc/4VAD-Y6VC)

Shepard, S (2009) Reverse Engineering the Future: A Prescription for Change

Serrat, O (2017) Knowledge Solutions. Tools, Methods, and Approaches to Drive

SoundCloud (2021) Algoritmic Business Thinking and Learning Strategies for Corporate Growth by Katja Schipperheijn, soundcloud.com/katja-schipperheijn/abt-and-learning-stratgies (archived at https://perma.cc/XP42-WUWC)

The Investors Book (2021) Span of Control in Management, theinvestorsbook.com/span-of-control-in-management.html (archived at https://perma.cc/DLV2-5RXZ)

12

Step 2: Burning platform:
a supported choice for change

In the discovery step we looked at problems and opportunities. Once the problem and opportunity has been identified, the next step is to translate this opportunity into an effective business case. Or an algorithm when following the ABT method. However before we can start on the business case, all stakeholders should be aligned on the urgency and need for change.

The name burning platform expresses this urgency that is essential for change to take place. More than that, it emphasises that doing nothing, as I indicated in the previous section, can sometimes have even more disastrous consequences. It also emphasises positive thinking, even in the most challenging moments.

Daryl Conner, who is believed to have introduced the concept first in his book *Managing at the Speed of Change*, referred to the analogy with the disaster that took place in 1988 on the Piper Alpha drilling platform in which 167 people lost their lives. A disaster involving human error that could have been avoided.

How this story, which I often give as an introduction to a workshop, is a motivating story to engage stakeholders is twofold. On the one hand, many people died, but two of them showed that the uncertain future sometimes offers more perspectives than the old situation. They were faced with the terrible choice of dying a certain death by the flames at their back or having a minimal chance of survival by jumping into the pounding ice-cold waves.

On the other hand, it gives us a clear example of where intelligent technology supports us as humans. If Piper Alpha had had the predictive analytics AI software developed by the Belgian startup Trendminer at the time, which would have detected the need for maintenance, this disaster could have been avoided. We expect the same predictability from lean learning in the moment of need.

Another well-known writer and strategist I like to use at the start of a project to hold a mirror up to all stakeholders is John Kotter. In his fictional story 'Our iceberg is melting', he compares penguins with people who want to cooperate in a transition project or not.

> **Tip:** When I show a short video and ask the participants to name each other with the names of the penguins, we see that this often breaks the ice and people take a slightly more open attitude to change.

As a LearnScaper, understanding that many of us have an aversion to change, and even more so, understanding where it comes from, helps to get the project carried and launched from all stakeholders. For example, in the introduction to this book, I mentioned that 93 per cent of executives do not yet prioritize the added value of intelligent collaboration with machines. A reluctance that, from my experience, is often fed by their own fear of change or that of stakeholders influencing their strategy.

When the burning platform workshop is preceded by an introduction that frames the added value and urgency for change from a human and technological perspective, we can start working pragmatically with facts and figures that seek solutions for the problems or opportunities we discovered in the discovery step.

The OODAP-model to make the opportunity for improvement visible

From the techniques I gave earlier for identifying opportunities for improvement, an interesting project can be created. But that is not enough to start a project and make it run as smoothly as possible with all those involved.

For this purpose, an additional method can help to make the options that provide the answer possible. Since many methods have already been described in our field's literature, I would like to offer you a relatively unknown method that you can make your own.

I first encountered the OODAP framework of Professor Malone and Chris Macomber during my studies at MIT Sloan and have since integrated an interpretation of it into many of my workshops. For me, the visual representation and method of working together are a great added value of this framework. It is also widely applicable for analysing business issues related to information technology, transformation technology and many other types of business decisions. The acronym stands for the five elements to be identified in a given situation: objective, options, dimensions, analysis and proposal.

The OODAP framework I use is easiest to explain with an example. I will use a fictitious organization with a manufacturing environment where skilled labour is hard to find in the tight labour market. As a result, production cannot be scaled up and there is also the risk that some employees will (temporarily) drop out due to illness or other reasons. The opportunity is found in 'quick training' of new employees so that they can be deployed in the high-tech production environment. Finally, we see that through continuous training and performance-related data, learning and the factory can become leaner.

Objectives

Defining the objectives seems simple, but formulating it in such a way that all stakeholders are involved from the first moment is less easy. Thereby we want to assure that we are as an organization value driven and human-centric.

Suppose in the discovery phase we define a goal where one project addresses multiple opportunities for improvement. Without strategic insight into the organization and empathy, it is often difficult to assess why certain stakeholders still put the brakes on. Motivations to participate in the change process differ depending on one's background, but also on one's ability to assess the impact on one's own work and that of the organization. Fear of the unknown is often a decisive factor for a stakeholder to hold back a project. Translating the goals for the organization into the impact of the different stakeholders may take extra time and empathy, but it will contribute to success at a later stage.

Example: From our fictitious case, we see that the goal is initially very obvious, which is to train new employees or to redeploy current employees at a maximum of six months in order to scale up production. The goal can be translated to different stakeholders:

- Quick to implement and more production in up to six months from the market and the company's demand.
- On-the-job learning: there are already too few employees, so taking employees away from production will create an even bigger backlog.
- Sharing expertise that is already present in the organization: A few very experienced employees have a lot of knowledge that can optimize production.
- Avoid technical downtown by detecting errors in the processes.
- Preventing staff turnover: Due to the high work pressure, more and more staff members drop out.
- Reducing the cost of vacancies by fast onboarding and reboarding (internal flow to production manager or external flow to easy jobs).

In this, we see that stakeholders from the business (meeting increased demand), HR (welfare and recruitment), L&D (more efficient training) and production see added value in the goal by translating it into opportunities for them.

Options

From the objective that offers opportunities to all stakeholders, a selection of solutions is made that responds to this. This requires insight and a thorough market study. And, as said, that is more than just reading a few white papers or worse, getting advice from consultants/vendors who benefit from a certain option.

When we relate options to the benefits for certain stakeholders and map them to the most common solutions, we often see that alternatives that initially did not offer much added value, suddenly seem interesting. In our example of the *Five Whys*, it may be interesting to develop the app for the business and then add it to the ecosystem of apps and platforms that HR has yet to determine. The urgency for the business, and the loss of revenue, may outweigh the additional cost of building an app.

Therefore, we need to look at our options, i.e. a set of alternative actions or choices that we can take or make in the given situation. These options are not exclusive. Often, additional options emerge when we analyse dimensions that reveal a new option a little later in the process. Openness and the will to adjust choices made is important throughout the process and analysis.

Example: From the objectives we see that an innovative solution supporting workplace learning would add value for the different stakeholders. To this end, the following options were considered:

- Customized e-learning on LMS (Legacy) with onboarding video.
- Existing content on a new LXP platform.
- Use of our own specialists to learn during production.
- A microlearning application with an authoring tool to quickly create content according to needs.
- An AI application on a microlearning tool that supports learning when it is needed.

These options are still vague and require a deeper analysis in the next step where dimensions are added. This still takes into account the urgency support and the specific needs of the organization's stakeholders.

Dimensions

The dimensions that will enable us to give scores to the different options will be discussed in this third phase. The evaluation criteria will influence the decision without letting emotions or personal motivations of stakeholders on the burning platform take over.

When we think about technology-related decisions that improve cooperation and knowledge sharing in an organization, many factors can be of influence, for example: the time for development or the processing speed of the data that the new application supports. As mentioned, the link with the business is often a decisive factor in connecting time and urgency. However, as I mentioned, we must always remember that technology should support human wellbeing.

Along with time, costs will of course also be relevant, even if the application's price tag is not the indicator for costs. Sometimes hidden costs are just a little harder to detect, for example the cost of not implementing or implementing too late. Cost mapping is no easy task and requires a thorough exercise of everything that can influence costs. For example, user costs related to hardware, software, training or implementation may also be related to risks such as downtime, *disaster recovery* or security risks.

The quality or added value of the solution for all stakeholders is another dimension that influences our decision-making process here and requires due consideration without bias and with respect to all stakeholders. If we think about different qualities that may have an impact, there are in fact many capabilities that we could consider. For example, usability or ease of use, or perhaps compatibility with regard to interoperability with existing hardware, software or industrial or regulatory standards.

Flexibility is another essential added value. On the one hand, we quickly see the relevance of scalability, regarding the possibility of accommodating large numbers of users or transactions after an experimental phase of the project or when the organization grows fruitfully in the future. On the other hand, we need to think about future technological innovations. Investments made now must be flexibly integrated with future expectations or improvements that are difficult to estimate now.

Finally, in today's society we also have to consider sustainability and the impact on society. Solutions that score poorly with regard to the environment or the wellbeing of employees would score exponentially worse, so that price becomes less relevant and cannot be the decisive factor. Something that, unfortunately, is still the norm in public companies.

Know that in this phase of the exercise, new options sometimes emerge as we look open-mindedly at the impact of our intentions on all stakeholders and society. Dare to go back to the sketch board every now and then, but don't let every new possible option stop you.

> **Tip:** Dimensions are specific to the organization. However, you can take inspiration from the following commonly used dimensions in IT-related decisions with a human focus:

Time

– Development time of the solution (here max six months)
– Speed of work and efficiency with a human focus
– Urgency or learning in the moment of need

Costs

– Development costs (buy or build)
– Implementation costs (training users, testing, downtime, etc.)
– Operating costs (hardware, software, etc.)
– Risks (downtime, disaster recovery, security risks, etc.)

Quality

– Usability (ease of use)
– Compatibility (integration with existing hardware, software, or standard)
– Flexibility (easy to adapt to future needs)
– Scalability (ability to handle a large number of users or transactions)

- Reusability (usable for other potential purposes)
- Sustainability
- Maintainability
- Safety
- Correctness (free from bugs)
- Ethical
- Measurable

Analysis

For the analysis phase, it is not necessary to hire expensive consultants. Sometimes very simple assessment matrices are the best way to evaluate visually the defined options and dimensions with all stakeholders.

A weighing matrix can easily be done in Excel, but is just as interesting with post-its on a wall to support team spirit. The end goal is more important than the approach: making a supported decision that has added value for the organization and the stakeholders in the ecosystem.

You could opt to work with high, medium and low (H, M and L) to indicate the added value of the dimension. Post-its in different colours could also be used to map out the considerations visually.

An example will be given in Figure 12.1 which is a simplified representation of a weighing matrix where we take all the options and weigh them with some dimensions that have added value for the different stakeholders.

From this, the efficiency of on-the-job learning and the possibility of obtaining measurable data for improvement processes are decisive criteria. This means that we give the large category of micro-learning platforms with simple authoring tools and the AI applications on-the-job the highest scores.

A refined OODAP methodology can be used, for example, on the basis of possible technology providers, where we include them as options and the functionalists who offer them as dimensions.

FIGURE 12.1 OODAP-model visual example

	DIMENSIONS					
OPTIONS	Speed of implementation	Efficiency on the job	Measurable learning	Scalable	Reusable	Cost
Customized e-learning on LMS (Legacy) with onboarding video	M	L	H	H	H	M
Purchased content hosted on LXP external provider	H	L	M	H	H	M
Specialists train new employees (no tech involved)	H	M	L	L	M	L
Customized microlearning with authoring tool	M	H	H	H	H	M
Lean workplace learning application with AI that serves as a specialist	L	H	H	H	H	L

Proposal

When we have considered all the options and their dimensions, a final step is to come up with a proposal that offers the most added value and that eliminates the critical uncertainties.

We translate this proposal to the various stakeholders. In other words, the burning platform brings everyone together and clearly articulates the opportunities that the new way of working offers for everyone. Only when everyone is aware of the why and of the added value can we work on an implementation that is supported.

Often, the analysis will help you choose the best options to propose. If not, the analysis should at least help you identify the critical uncertainties that still need to be resolved.

When we bring our plan for a new learning strategy to the burning platform, it is enough to know the options. Discussions with suppliers can take place at a later stage. By splitting this into an initial analysis followed by a detailing of the suppliers, a lot of time is often saved and the focus remains on the own opportunities.

Only when we come to an agreement after the concept has been approved on the burning platform is this exercise repeated with effective providers in order to arrive at requests for offers that correspond to the desired proposal.

Calculating the cost of opportunity or missed opportunity

These opportunity costs or missed opportunity costs are an important factor in the calculation of total costs yet they are often overlooked. They are the costs of the economic choice we make expressed in terms of the best missed opportunity. It sounds complicated, but what they reflect is the valuation of the unrealised return of the best possible alternative against the decision finally taken.

It often sounds more complicated than it is, but fortunately templates and examples for calculating this are easily found online. What's more, the preparation of the burning platform normally involves your organization's finance department. This cross-functional collaboration will enable the correct analysis of the costs.

Two different methods are often used for this purpose:

- **The labour cost method:** in situations where temporary staff are taking the place of employees who are undergoing training. Here, the cost of missed opportunities can be calculated based on the information about the daily wage. This method also applies to situations where you have employees work part of an extra shift to cover the time needed by another employee to attend training. Also take into account the inefficiency factor in this calculation if the staff you replace do not have the same skills.

- **The value contribution method:** the amount that each employee contributes to the organization's gross income. Here we do not assume temporary replacement but a reduced contribution to the value creation or production of the organization. This usually has an even greater impact.

When, from the previous example of the OODAP methodology, we make the choice between formal training, whereby the employee is taken out of production, or a smart technology that supports learning at the point of need, we see that the calculation often wins over financial stakeholders. Often, these innovative technologies pay off quicker than initially thought, especially when they are almost plug and play. This is what makes lean learning at the point of need for workplaces so interesting.

The above indicates again that good preparation is needed to convince all stakeholders of the added value that innovative technology has to offer. This exercise requires insight into the organization beyond what white papers from other organizations promise.

> **Tip:** In many production environments, there is no staff to replace employees in training. This implies unplanned downtime of a production line which often adds to the total cost of training. Make sure you factor this into the motivation to implement learning at the point of need, supported by smart technology.

References

Connor, D (1993) *Managing at the speed of change*, Random House, New York

Kotter, J (2016) Our Iceberg is Melting: *Changing and Succeeding Under Any Conditions*, Pan Macmillan, London

OODAP Model Copyright © 2006 Thomas W Malone and Chris Macomber

Learning Solutions (2015) Tip: Include Lost Opportunity in the Total Cost of Training, learningsolutionsmag.com/articles/1849/tip-include-lost-opportunity-in-the-total-cost-of-training (archived at https://perma.cc/4YV8-AM7D)

TrendMiner (2022) Advanced Analytics for the Process Manufacturing Industry, www.trendminer.com/ (archived at https://perma.cc/28AN-YL96)

13

Step 3: Path to improvement: where technology, content and the learning culture come together

Once we have accepted the benefits and possible solutions from the previous steps, only then do we look for suppliers or partners to integrate them into our organization. As I said before, we do not start from a solution provided by vendors or consultants, but from an opportunity to create human added value through technology.

From the preparation steps for the burning platform, we know which options and dimensions will determine the choice of technology. However, this does not mean that the choice has already been made. When we explore the market in this phase, we quickly come to the conclusion that many providers promise all sorts of things. Overlaps make it almost impossible. In addition, many white papers and salesmen try to make us believe that they have the perfect 'one-fits-all' solution.

At this stage of the project, it becomes even clearer that not only technology is an important aspect when we lay the foundation for a new programme. The desired knowledge we want to share, with whom we want to share knowledge, what data we want to use to measure success and possibly adjust learning are all relevant to the choice we make. Moreover, even if we find a whitepaper describing exactly those requirements, we must not forget that each organization has its own individuality. Employee mentality, commitment and, more broadly, the culture of the ecosystem are often the key factors that make the project succeed or fail. If technology, content and culture are not aligned, we see that many good ideas often do not land in the organization and that frustration among stakeholders is often all that remains.

It would be premature to think that if promising innovation is introduced, the learning culture in an organization will follow. Or that super cool expensive immersive experiences in VR are an added value if the content is not relevant to the target group. There are plenty of examples of promising projects that fizzle out after a while and everyone goes back to how they used to do things. As I mentioned in the introduction, I myself thought that COVID-19 would be that Black Swan that would uncover the added value for digitally supported learning and working. However, less than a year after the start of the pandemic, I saw that frustration and even despair made many staff long for the 'old normal'. The hastily implemented tools did not work in the old culture and way of thinking. Moreover, managers themselves did not believe in the added value of intelligent cooperation between man and machine. As a result, the temporary solution would never get off the ground. Only when learning content and technology are aligned and supported by all stakeholders can innovation succeed.

Example: From the burning platform is an agreement to start one project. In this step, we therefore repeat the previous table (Figure 13.1), where we list the options by potential providers that seem to match the expectations from a first market survey. However, as in the previous step, these are not yet a definitive shortlist and can still be adjusted depending on the dimensions or even a demo.

Note that we only include those providers that meet the options from the previous selection. So, returning to a provider that only offers existing content without the possibility of having their own employees create content via an authoring tool does not qualify. Likewise, providers that do not offer adaptive AI-supported learning paths do not qualify in this example.

FIGURE 13.1 Simplified matrix with optional providers following the OODAP-methodology

OPTIONS	DIMENSIONS						
	Speed of implementation	Cost	Adaptive learning	KPI learning	Mobile solution	Gamification	Integration
Supplier 1	M	L	H	H	H	L	H
Supplier 2	H	M	H	H	H	M	H
Supplier 3	M	H	H	H	L	L	H
Supplier 4	H	L	L	M	M	M	H
Supplier 5	L	H	H	H	L	H	M

From the example I am deliberately including different dimensions and weights than in the preparation of the burning platform. This is to show that stakeholders have added other dimensions based on the common agreement. For this reason, the price may be given greater weight than the integration with existing technology. Whether this is the most nimble and effective solution for the future I will leave open for now.

Analyses from the options and dimensions:

- **Implementation:** time should meet the high need to train the first group of employees on the job in six months at the most.

- **The cost:** of one solution may seem higher than the other, but when we calculate the opportunity cost of a delayed start-up and possible loss of production due to other suppliers in this competitive market, speed is important.

- **Adaptive learning paths:** providers who do not offer this are often seen as dead knowledge databases after a while. Content may be beautiful and interesting, but if the learner does not find knowledge at the moment of need, efficiency will suffer. A low score in this respect is therefore an exclusion.

- **KPI of learning:** to learn from and adjust initiatives in the future, data is essential. This means that we want more than some data of who has attended a training course or an NPS of this training. When we look at intelligent support for learning through technology, adaptive learning pathways ensure effective change in the workplace. It is also advisable to possibly make a further breakdown of measurability from the tool but also from the production environment.

- **Mobile solutions:** from a future point of view, we want a solution that is scalable to other departments. Non-mobile solutions therefore receive a lower score. However, it may be that by integrating tools, parts of the solution can be mobile and others cannot. Far-reaching analysis is required.

- **Gamification:** this depends very much on the company culture and the way individuals and teams are assessed. Far-reaching analysis by HR can certainly offer added value here.

- **Integration:** any solution that cannot be integrated is not future-proof. However, in this example, the cost of integration with the current legacy system must be considered. Can the solutions coexist for the time being and still show an overall KPI of learning. This implies extra work for HR and therefore needs to be taken into account in the cost of implementation and success of sustainable development.

What you can see from this is that Supplier 3 has a very good score everywhere, but their solution is only available at the workplace itself. Scalability to employees who are not learning at the production facility is therefore not possible. Think, for example, of the installers who will install products at customers' premises. They cannot learn at the moment of need. When in the future they are also included in projects of the learning organization, this can be a game changer. Future-oriented thinking is therefore one of the most important steps when choosing learning strategies and, more specifically, technology. Supplier 2 seems to come very close to meeting expectations for a partner that can grow with them. Now is the time to invite this provider for a demo.

Technology and tools

Perhaps one of the best known attempts to classify EdTech is by Josh Bersin, the leading author and L&D expert. But he is certainly not the only one. Many are trying to classify platforms based on the way knowledge is shared, or stored. At their core, most platforms are still content management systems (CMS) or content libraries, and a name doesn't change that, even if we call them microlearning app or LXP. This is not surprising when storing content is still a main requirement of organizations (beyond data repository organizations which I discussed in chapter 8). The CMS is still the backbone of many L&D departments.

Partly because of these commercial and often confusing designations, selecting the right tool for your organization is often a difficult task. Add to that the fact that large vendors offer more and more functionalities, it is difficult to understand what makes them unique and what their strengths are. For example, the core learning management system (LMS) sometimes offer an authoring tool, or they have algorithms for pre-setting adaptive learning paths. Yet both are not the solution we were looking for when we wanted to let employees create content or use technology to support us in the moment of need. For the success of the project we are using as an example, it may be more useful to choose a niche player that integrates with any existing legacy CMS is the organization.

The ultimate all-in-one and one-fits-all solution may be a dream of many an EdTech provider, but the future seems to lie in integrated tools.

The future of integrated tools

For years there has been a paradigm shift from the stand-alone app to a greater focus on connected ecosystems, driven by ultimate agility that grows along with expectations. Connectivity and integration are key in a human-centric approach.

This integration between different technologies makes it possible to share a lot of information and this opens up new possibilities that seem endless. As a result, the shared knowledge which increasingly supports lean learning, and the data we obtain from the systems have both expanded enormously.

The future of LearnScapes is therefore to be found in connected and integrated systems. Old systems that do not integrate or that are only maintained 'because we always did it that way' do not belong in a LearnScape that wants to grow. We don't just look at technology that supports learning from an LMS-like approach, but we also dare to look at the possibilities that innovations in immersive technologies, robotics and even the metaverse we discussed in part 2 of this book have to offer. This future view will become increasingly important in the final step that drives continuous improvement.

The fast growing EdTech landscape

For organizations that want to invest in their employees and thereby support growth in the ecosystem, the ever faster growing EdTech market offers many opportunities. This in turn is fuelling an unprecedented growth in new EdTech startups and associated investments. For example, after the huge increase in investments in 2020, 2021 saw even more growth.

In 2021 startups raised US $20 billion in VC funding worldwide, more than 1.3x the 2020 total. This growth was mainly driven by megarounds, which accounted for 62 per cent. Not only are $100 million-plus rounds becoming more common, but also more and more global. This trend does not seem to be reversing any time soon in the coming years.

All these innovations offer perspectives for the learning economy, but they do not make it any easier to make a selection. For EdTech entrepreneurs, too, it is not easy to find a niche where they can stand out. Nick Van Neck knows that too, his startup MobieTrain from Belgium was able to raise no less than 4 million euros from international investors in 2021. Their success story was partly due to their vision with regard to integration and cooperation, which makes them see competition as partners in the ecosystem. This has been Guy Van Neck's starting point since MobieTrain's early days with international clients.

CASE STUDY

Integration and cooperation as a starting point for innovation

Guy Van Neck, CEO and Founder MobieTrain

Through exciting collaborations with other leading HR-Tech platforms, Mobietrain 'workplaces' offer a full range of learning tools. It combines existing microlearning and mobile expertise with social learning and communication, to enable employees to learn within their own flow of life. For Guy Van Neck, the future lies in collaboration, co-creation and integration with other successful software tools in order to market sustainable technology that ultimately has only one goal: empowering employees and organizations.

The very first integration that Guy Van Neck successfully accomplished with the Mobietrain platform was with retail giant Azadea. With a network of more than 600 shops and 35 international retail markets, they have a huge apparatus of 10,000 frontline employees operating in the Middle East and Africa. The main objective is to continuously motivate, inspire and trigger these employees from their overarching learning management system, of which the Mobietrain microlearning app is a part.

Through collaboration with others, MobieTrain joined forces to boost the Azadea L&D culture. To do this, they integrated the MobieTrain microlearning platform with their existing mobile app. This partnership enabled them to accelerate the launch, onboarding and communication to their employees – the 'Azadeans' – and ultimately increase the engagement of their workforce. At Azadea, they already knew how best to reach their employees. So why reinvent a successful, existing channel? 'Long live the LMS,' says Guy Van Neck. That may seem a strange statement for a microlearning company, but with MobieTrain they want to complement traditional LMS, LXP or e-learning systems instead of replacing them. Reinforcing existing knowledge taught by both learning management systems and classroom training is the goal.

From this intrinsic learning culture, they make targeted data-driven decisions at Azadea, based on the MobieTrain learning content. As a result, they respond to frequent questions from the frontline, which they incorporate into learnings and onboarding processes where the focus is mainly on sales scenarios, customer loyalty programmes, the customer journey and KPIs.

Every day Azadea uploads a CSV file with user information to their SFTP server. These files are processed daily to maintain the user database. In this way, the circle is complete and Azadea uses their L&D toolkit in an efficient way, allowing their custom content, learning culture and their employees to work together intelligently.

The ethical impact of integration

When choosing tools to integrate, we need to think about the data we want to measure, why we want to measure it and whether it adds value to people's wellbeing and is ethically justifiable. For this we would need an application that connects all other systems. This tool would take actions that suggest improvements or proactively detect problems; like a 'central brain' that knows and controls everything.

Thinking back to the first chapters, the question arises whether we want to put this in the hands of a machine. How far are we as human beings prepared to go to let a machine judge what I need to know, when I need to know it, with whom I need to make connections and so on.

I don't expect strong artificial intelligence, or singularity where the machine will dominate humans in knowledge to be for the foreseeable future. This central brain that will control us will therefore only live in science fiction books for the time being. Nevertheless, it makes us think if we want to translate our vision of the distant future into the present. How far do we want to go with integration and whether we want to put our future in the hands of a robot?

In many situations, the selection of instruments seems to be the most important step towards improvement. But without evaluating them together from a human centric approach with taking into account relevant content and learning cultures I describe further, it is nothing more than a potentially premature failed project.

Content

Tools are important in LearnScapes, but it is the knowledge, or content, that will make the difference. Not just the content itself, but who creates the content and how learners are enabled to interact with it as it flows through the ecosystem. The more alive the LearnScape is, the more interactions and knowledge will get to the right place at the right time.

When we talk about knowledge flows, the comparison can be made with popular streaming services like Netflix. These systems strive to provide the learner with an optimal experience with content that is relevant to them. However, even Netflix has relatively simple algorithms that often fail to provide relevant content. EdTech platforms face the same challenge. Sometimes, however, we suddenly see providers from unexpected quarters that surprise everyone.

Perhaps one of the most notable 'new providers' is Chinese multinational internet giant ByteDance, the company behind the popular social media platform TikTok. The exponential growth forecast of the EdTech market inspired them and in June 2020 they announced their new market strategy for the online learning market. Already, hundreds of experts and institutions are producing educational content on their behalf for the #LearnOnTikTok platform. Apparently, it was a small step from a platform with influencers and crazy dance moves to the online education market. As I mentioned in part 2 of the book, TikTok has the best algorithms when it comes to driving users and making content go viral, alongside the resources to invest in ever better AI.

We also know from them that content has to be relevant, fun and unique to keep inspiring the audience. How to make sure content still inspires in this abundance is therefore the challenge for many. The way content is created, also called instructional design, is one of the key drivers. And, as I will demonstrate in the fifth step of this model, L&D can in this respect still learn a lot from marketers.

User generated content in the learning economy

As mentioned earlier, there is an abundance of knowledge in every organization. Yet most of this knowledge is held by the employees themselves and is underutilised. In other words, from the lean approach, this is waste. Activating this knowledge has enormous potential for organizations that want to grow from their employees as demonstrated by the Uman case.

Everyone can possess relevant knowledge, even without being aware of it. For example, an experienced salesperson often knows very well how to stimulate a latent need in customers. But if we do not encourage them to share this knowledge with less experienced sales people, it often does not happen automatically. For many organizations, it is therefore a challenge to stimulate this and make it measurable. In part 2, for example, I mentioned that sales staff in a department of a sportswear chain had created their own content with sales tips that were used on the microlearning platform.

In another project I once worked on, anyone in the organization could make short videos to solve small frustrations, such as the toner of a departmental printer needing to be replaced just when that urgent file needed to be printed. On the ESN, you would soon find a very nice video made by an employee about how to replace a printer toner. In this project, you could then like the share and gamification was added to thank the employee of the month. User generated content is invaluable in LearnScapes that believe in sharing knowledge. Add intelligent tools and you have a wealth of data and can get the knowledge to the right employee before they get frustrated. An employee engagement booster par excellence.

The above is an example of the creator economy finding its way into organizational learning. This is a trend we have known for some time in the meta-worlds such as Roblox, which shows that the creator economy and the learning economy are increasingly overlapping.

Returning to the earlier example of the production environment, we see that the importance of a simple but high-performance authoring tool was essential for the choice of technology. It would not only enable L&D professionals within the organization to create relevant content faster; it would add even more value if it could also be used to share knowledge of the more experienced employees.

How to make good content

Anyone can be a content creator and add value to the LearnScape by sharing knowledge. Lieselot Declercq of d-teach developed a pedagogical quality framework for online training and learning. Her starting point is the vision of the world, followed by the learning vision within the organization, to which the appropriate didactics and instruction are aligned. With her Belgium based start-up d-teach she wants to help learners and organizations that invest in transformation processes to grow into a *future proof* organization of online learning and training. Based on her belief in the added value of knowledge sharing, she shares some tips.

CASE STUDY
The basic rules for good content creation

Lieselot Declercq, Founder d-teach

Content creation may seem child's play for children on social media platforms like TikTok. Even there, going viral is not everyone's cup of tea. Nevertheless, there are a few basic rules and tips that will get you a long way as a content creator, professional or otherwise.

#PEOPLEABOVETECHNOLOGY (VISION)
The basic principle is to put 'the human being' at the centre. Human connection and teaching people how to use technology are essential in our vision and pedagogical approach. The structure of the lessons or courses always starts with determining the objective of each lesson or course. The lessons are built up from guided instruction. There is a strong focus on practice through applied exercises or practical experiments, supported by interim feedback. d-teach allows each learner to develop self-reliance so that they can apply the material independently and no longer need the guidance of a trainer. This approach results in a transformation of the course member as shown in Figure 13.2.

#NOONESIZEFITSALL (INSTRUCTION)
The learner is the starting point. There is no one-size-fits-all approach. It is important to adapt the didactic structure of training to the learner. There are

FIGURE 13.2 Pedagogical framework d-Teach

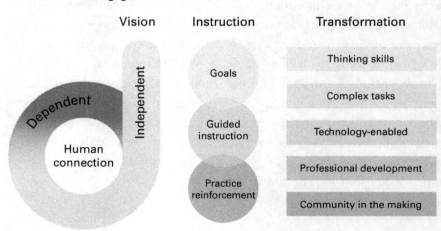

© d-teach 2020

different forms of distance learning and blended learning. This should be discussed at different levels: macro (policy), meso (coordinators) and micro (trainers).

#FUTUREPROOF (TRANSFORMATION)
Online learning strengthens lifelong learning. Learning should be as flexible as the world we live in, learning where and when you want to. Online learning has all the assets for learning in combination with work and private life.

TIPS FOR ONLINE TRAINING

1 Online training is not a copy-paste of offline and physical training. It requires a different didactic approach to what you do online and offline in blended learning.
2 It requires thinking differently; it is important to make a distinction between 'need-to-know' and 'nice-to-know'. What is really essential in the message and what is peripheral information?
3 Provide interim feedback and exercises. This can be done through online feedback, independent practice or by asking good questions.
4 Moderate your activity with 'think time – let them think'. Allow time for the learner to think and build this in deliberately.
5 Don't push, but pull – don't overload with information and text, but ask specific critical thinking questions.
6 Importance of real-time instruction is essential in successful and motivating online training.
7 Not 'high tech' but 'high touch'. Technology is necessary, but the interaction and the human touch make the difference in effective online education.
8 It's all about connections and the network. Online connections and sharing good practices through online communities and learning networks make all the difference. The feeling of being close together despite the distance is the foundation for personal resilience.

Lieselot Declercq explains in her contribution how you can create engaging and relevant content together with your employees. Still, we see that many companies, even with the most experienced L&D staff and instructional designers, do not know how to create content in a Lean way via the right channels at the right time.

Aligned content and tools for learner engagement

Content is often very dependent on the manner, channel or technology in which it is shared. For example, it seems obvious that in some situations microlearning is much more suitable than an hour-long webinar. Or to make the comparison with a burning platform; if the building is on fire, you don't have time to watch a long video about how fire extinguishers work. You want the knowledge you need to extinguish the fire immediately, as briefly and as relevantly as possible.

Content itself can also take different shapes depending on the objective and measurability can be an important factor in that. In this regard, content and technology can be as innovative as they are, but if the target audience does not see the relevance, and therefore does not see the need to adapt or learn, the initiative is of no use.

When creating content, it is therefore interesting to take into account three important pillars as shown in Figure 13.3; job-related knowledge, accurate and verified knowledge and information sharing, understanding of the learning culture and the involvement of employees.

To enable this, a bridge can be built between the L&D and internal communications departments and possibly the online marketing team because of their expertise with data and influencing as Dr Anna Tarabasz will explain in the next step of this model.

The three pillars seem obvious yet we see that to apply it consistently, we need to move away from the former idea of 'training'. Learning engagement becomes a strategic pillar that requires cooperation across organizational silos. We see that organizations

FIGURE 13.3 Learning engagement based in information and knowledge

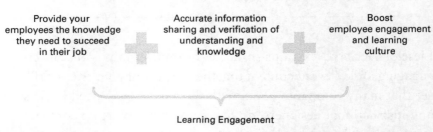

Provide your employees the knowledge they need to succeed in their job

Accurate information sharing and verification of understanding and knowledge

Boost employee engagement and learning culture

Learning Engagement

© Katja Schipperheijn

that want to increase their learning engagement will share with their target group a great deal of targeted information about the strategy of the department, the company, the market, etc. In addition, they will also share knowledge in a highly targeted manner. And, of course, they will also share highly targeted knowledge that will enable them to perform better in the job. This can be done through formal learning moments with content that is adapted to the target. Finally, we also see that these organizations think about the learning culture that prevails among the target groups within the organization. It may be that salespeople within an organization are motivated by gamification, but this might have the opposite effect on administrative staff or developers. Increasing learning engagement therefore also requires a good understanding of learning culture.

The learning culture

Culture has already been mentioned a few times in this book. The right culture is needed for the learning ecosystem, the LearnScape. Just think about what we discussed earlier in the first part about the future of work and the younger generations for whom culture is an essential component when engaging. We also saw that HiPPOs command and control approach doesn't work with agile teams to capture opportunities faster.

However, in this phase – where we want to improve the building blocks of learning within the organization – we want to be more specific with regard to culture, more specifically the learning culture that is part of the corporate culture, but should not be confused with it. Regarding the aspect of learning culture, I would like to make a distinction between what this means as an employee and as an organization, and how they influence each other.

A learning culture cannot be imposed from leadership. Without understanding why it is relevant to the employee, intrinsic motivation will not emerge and is more likely to be met with resistance. Nevertheless, leaders can take into account the employees they recruit so that they contribute to the learning culture. To do this, they can select committed candidates who take ownership of their own learning from competencies that endorse this such as curiosity, openness, entrepreneurship and resilience, all of which support the growth mindset required for learning. The learning culture of the organization grows out of these learning employees. As part of the corporate culture it consists of the unwritten rules, habits and behaviour of all employees in a given organization. These habits send a positive vibe through the organization and will spread to others and thus gradually contribute to the growth mindset of the learning organization.

Technology alone does not build a social learning culture

In part 2, I highlighted the benefits of social learning strategies through the use of online media or social tools in an organization that leverage knowledge sharing.

LearnScapes, for example, rely on informal learning and finding the experts within the organization to access knowledge more quickly when it is needed. Lean learning via social learning communities supported by what AI has to offer today is the starting point here.

Yet we see that even the most high-performance tools that aim to support social collaboration often fail to stimulate knowledge sharing. The cause is often that we have too many expectations of this technology, or the promises of those selling it, so we fail to take into account the learning culture of the employees themselves as Geert Nijs, learning architect at the Belgian bank KBC and author of the book *The Network Expedition*, also observes.

CASE STUDY
You cannot build a social learning culture with technology alone

Geert Nijs, learning architect KBC and author

The rise of social media has made us think about social learning in a certain way. I've noticed that social learning is always put in a causal relationship with social media or applied within a company: enterprise social networks (ESN). I don't think that's right. Then you're telling the story backwards.

Reality is more complex. Or vice versa. It depends on how you look at it. I came to this insight during a visit to the Agora study centre of the KU Leuven. Peter Verbist was talking the whole time about 'analogue' social learning and made statements like 'seeing learning makes you learn'. There was no technology involved at all. There is a building: an old building that has been cleverly restored and that had a long history for former pharmacy students. This building inspires students to study together, to work together, to experience together. Learning becomes a social activity. Students take each other in tow.

Students from higher years help beginning students. In Agora, it goes beyond studying quietly with fellow students in a library.

You can 'virtualize' this learning environment – once it is there – by providing an enterprise social network where you can 'scale up' this learning environment across physical locations. However, it is wrong to think that this learning climate will be created by providing an ESN. First, you need to work on this climate within an organization. Remember that for a long time, many traditional companies had a culture where only attending formal training was considered 'learning'. The social learning climate where colleagues let each other grow without the intervention of a 'trainer' often does not exist. Enterprise social networks are empty echo chambers in such organizations. You cannot scale up something that is not there (which I believe is the purpose of such an ESN). First, you have to work on a social learning climate. You don't need to erect a building or a study centre for this, but purposefully bring people together who go through the same learning process together for a certain period of time. There is no 'trainer', the group helps each other. Package it a bit like a training, people like to have recognition, but at the same time you can challenge the group to take care of themselves. In the current COVID-19 era, this can even be done virtually, via a video conference.

Little by little, colleagues 'experience' how they can help each other, inspire each other and even encourage each other to learn new skills. And this goes far beyond gaining new 'knowledge'. It is like in the Middle Ages when a teacher taught his apprentices craftsmanship. Introduce this learning culture first and then you can 'scale it up' via an ESN. Here, colleagues take the next step and share their knowledge, but especially their skills, with other colleagues, in other parts of the organization, at other locations... and why not, even outside their own organization.

The above examples all indicate that a strategy will only deliver its results if tools, content and learning culture are aligned. However, this does not mean that they cannot evolve over time. On the contrary. When we approach a project from this holistic approach, we look in this phase for a project that can be rolled out 'now' and in where success can be made measurable.

References

Bersin, J (2019) Josh Bersin, Learning Technology Evolves: integrated platforms are arriving, joshbersin.com/2019/06/learning-technology-evolves-integrated-platforms-are-arriving/ (archived at https://perma.cc/3FTM-NGHL)

EdTech (2022) Database by dealroom.co: All Transactions > Funding rounds, edtech.dealroom.co/transactions.rounds/f/growth_stages/not_mature/industries/anyof_education/rounds/not_GRANT_SPAC%20PRIVATE%20PLACEMENT/tags/not_outside%20tech/years/anyof_2021?showStats=YEAR&sort=-amount&statsType=rounds&_ga=2.64766895.1466635883.1643469687-1785349334.1643469687 (archived at https://perma.cc/8JJD-GKAC)

14

Step 4: Joint execution: no success without cooperation

Collaboration pays off when we think about innovation. Different perspectives and viewpoints sometimes lead to insights that are harder to see alone. That's one of the main reasons the LearnScaper draws inspiration from stakeholders across the ecosystem when looking for opportunities to grow from intelligent collaborations. Collaboration in project execution and implementation is equally important to achieve shared success.

Collaboration in the roll-out of LearnScapes is however multidimensional. We see that the distinct and complementary role of the LearnScaper in relation to the executives has its added value. In addition, the role of the LearnScaper as a central point of contact between the different stakeholders should not be underestimated.

Engaged leaders and the relationship with the LearnScaper

The role of senior leaders in implementing innovative projects that support LearnScapes is sometimes overlooked. The fact that in the first phase the cooperation between the LearnScaper and the leadership team is necessary to align the future vision with the strategy seems obvious. Setting out the strategy is the role of managers, but that role does not stop when the outlines have been set. On the contrary, the real work only begins when a direction has been chosen.

In the third part of this book, I talked about the different types of organizations with regard to knowledge sharing and collaboration. There I deliberately did not take a stand or make statements about certain styles of leadership being better or worse. However, we did see that the communication style, or the example set by senior leaders, set the tone for how knowledge and information were shared within the organization. Peter Somers, my husband, from whom I learned so much, also stated that, 'Every organization is the shadow of its leader'.

We must not forget this role model when we want to implement new initiatives. For example, in the enterprise social network that Geert Nijs talked about, we see the benefits of involving senior leadership and C-level from the start. Their engagement will show the way for others in the organization. When people actually see leaders responding thoughtfully, engaging others in conversations and rewarding participation with a simple thank you, they feel empowered to become more active. Members of those communities feel more open to sharing news, best practices and knowledge, regardless of hierarchical or departmental silos.

In addition to the role model that an executive has, there is another role for the committed leader. As the sponsor of the innovation project, he or she is the ideal sparring partner for the LearnScaper to align the vision of the company with the needs for intelligent collaboration within the organization and the whole ecosystem. This specific sponsor role manifests itself in the provision of resources in the form of budget and staff assigned to the project. Together, they are part of the steering committee, which is supplemented by the various stakeholders within that organization.

In addition, we see that the LearnScaper and sponsor are often complementary in terms of knowledge of innovative technologies and benefit to the organization. It can be said in 93 per cent of situations where managers as described in chapter 1 have no idea of the benefits of intelligent cooperation between man and machine for the growth of the employees, the organization and the ecosystem. Complementarity should therefore be sought with regard to objectives for the organization and their fulfilment through technological opportunities.

A culture of cooperation

In addition to their role as a sponsor for the implementation of innovative LearnScapes, we see that the leader often also has a major influence on the learning culture and the overall culture of the organization.

Earlier I talked about the importance of the learning culture, in this section, I want to focus on the corporate culture in terms of leadership and engagement of all stakeholders to nurture a culture of collaboration. Or as Mark Fidelman described it in his book *Socialized* in 2012; 'a culture where executives make it comfortable to communicate issues, where employees feel it's acceptable to fail fast, to share knowledge in hopes of having people improve upon it, where becoming an expert and helping others is encouraged.'

A positive corporate culture is the foundation for efficient teams and motivated employees. It is therefore worthwhile for leaders to take a critical look at the culture of their organization or team. An empathic leader radiates trust and gives everyone the chance to have an equal say. Everyone's contribution is valued, creating psychological safety that allows for failure and experimentation. In this culture of collaboration, every team member feels safe enough to present ideas, ask questions and be themselves. This trust, as described in part 3, is one of the six pillars on which LearnScapes rests. A premise endorsed by Alain Surkol, culture expert at bpost.

CASE STUDY
Control is good, trust is better

Alain Surkol, culture expert bpost

First, let's go back to the distant past. Have you read the book *Sapiens* by Yuval Noah Harrari? At the start of this book, the author asks the question why we, homo sapiens and not neanderthals, populated the world. Because the latter turned out to be not only stronger but also smarter than homo sapiens. And yet, our species is still there, the others are not. The explanation appears to be the learned sense of cooperation. By working together, homo sapiens succeeded in discovering new areas, killing mammoths and (consciously or unconsciously) driving out and eliminating neanderthals.

What will be distinctive in the future does not differ much from what has been true in the past: our search for and desire for cooperation.

If, as a leader, you want to promote cooperation in a company or organization, the most important building blocks include establishing trust, setting a good example, taking ownership and an irrepressible desire for improvement and innovation. We will go into this in more detail one by one.

The adage used to be, 'trust is good, control is better'. Today, we turn that around: control is good, trust is better'. By giving trust, you also give the necessary autonomy to your employees. This allows them to take new initiatives in a safe environment, make mistakes, try again and fail again before finally succeeding. In short, trust is the cornerstone of a learning culture.

If a leader sets a bad example, it spreads like a virus. Before you know it, everyone behaves like this. Fortunately, that same leader can also prevent the outbreak by setting a good example. Effective leaders therefore ensure that their actions are an extension of their words. Their behaviour casts a positive shadow on others.

Showing ownership is more than taking responsibility. You do not blindly do what is expected of you, but look for new angles, you approach a challenge from a different perspective, you repeatedly ask the 'why' question and you always work towards a positive result. The outcome exceeds expectations, surprises the client, customer, boss or colleague. The possibilities are limitless.

Did you know that companies that have been labelled winners for years have one significant common characteristic? They spend an enormous amount of time, energy and money on research and development. What applies to companies applies equally to individuals. The common will to keep learning, to innovate, to be open to new ideas, to change and thus to improve. Standing still is going backwards. Lifelong learning makes you a future-proof winner.

A future where marketing and learning are one

When I think of the similarities between marketing and learning, three points of contact stand out: influence, technology and data that increasingly blur the lines. When we look at the future of LearnScapes, breaking through the wall between these two departments is therefore a logical step in the transformation of the organization.

Consciously influencing unconsciously

The working methods of marketers and L&D staff are very similar and the question arises whether in the future LearnScapes both departments are not one. Simply put, they do the same thing. They both want to influence external and internal customers respectively, in order to align behaviour with their own objectives. Sometimes this is done consciously, but equally they use techniques that unconsciously induce behavioural change in the form of buying new things or learning new things, unlearning previous habits as well. To achieve this behavioural change through the use of technology, L&D could learn some new tricks from their fellow marketers.

In his book *Influence: The Psychology of Persuasion*, Cialdini described seven principles of influence that help online marketers influence their customers and steer them in the right direction. What he teaches us is that influencing works especially well with people when they hardly need to think. They are subconsciously taught by five star ratings and a high price on an online product that the product is good and of excellent quality.

According to Cialdini, this works through a built-in system in our brains. When we see certain information, it automatically puts a pattern of behaviour into action. With this rapid response, the brain saves time and energy, allowing us to process information and make decisions more quickly.

This technique, which neuromarketers know very well, is also known as the click-zoom principle and plays on our emotions. It makes us act almost automatically and without thinking. The click-zoom principle provides many opportunities in the world of online marketing because it makes it possible to influence buying behaviour without the 'customer' being aware of it.

Another reason why click-zoom is proving its worth in today's world has everything to do with our busy world and the abundance of information. We have literally tuned our brains to respond to impulses that allow us to act more efficiently and quickly in certain situations. We simply do not have enough time or attention left to analyse all the relevant issues that might otherwise prevent us from reacting.

This click-zoom method is therefore increasingly finding its way into online learning applications that respond to lean learning. With adaptive technologies that support lean learning, we provide knowledge at the moment of need.

Given the possibilities that these techniques offer, it seems that cooperation between both departments could prove useful. Not only through techniques, but also through the extra data that can be brought together from internal and external customers and how they deal with online influencing techniques.

According to Anna Tarabasz Dean Teaching and Learning, Head of School of Business and Humanities, Curtin University Dubai, learning experts, can learn, unlearn and re-learn together with our colleagues in Marketing to find the golden key to driving behaviour.

CASE STUDY
Learn, unlearn and re-learn. Be as nimble as only a digital marketer can be

Anna Tarabasz, Dean Teaching and Learning, Head of School of Business and Humanities, Curtin University Dubai

Benjamin Franklin said that the only two sure things we can be about are death and taxes. However, the time comes to contradict. Long before that, Heraclitus of Ephesus is said to have declared that 'the only constant is change'. Coming from a marketing background, and following that way of thinking, I would rather say that 'nothing is as volatile as patterns of consumer behaviour in the digitally-driven world'.

A plethora of stimuli, information overload, and ubiquity of technology, topped up with the complexity of the human mind create together truly an explosive mix. The dream of every marketer is therefore finding the golden key to buyers' purchasing patterns and repetitive actions. Drawing from the consumer decision-making process, marketers can indicate that starting with the problem recognition, followed by information search, evaluation of available alternatives, usually purchase decision will happen along with the post-purchase decision evaluation. Moreover, they will be able to indicate four main groups of factors playing an important role in every purchase decision: cultural, social, personal, and psychological factors. Marketers will therefore adapt their strategies to the first three, whereas the psychological category will make all that is possible to impact the motivations, perception, beliefs, attitudes, and of course the learning process of the prospects.

How this will happen? Carefully observing, they will be drafting omnichannel consumer journeys, indicating touchpoints, and looking for factors triggering the enhanced customer experience. These will become the base point for knowledge acquisition, indicating inclinations, choices and preferences. Subsequently the same will become as the cornerstone of the learning process and contribute to curving up the customer value.

This seems only the beginning of the knowledge gathering process by digital marketers, which could be beneficial for all the learning organizations, whether talking about internal or external customers. Software supporting search engine optimization allows for example to reach the untapped markets and even reach for the new Holy Grail – feature snippet (no-click search). Keyword matching and long-tail keyword search drive model of fulfilling the specific desire, ideally as per the natural language search mechanism. Social media listening enables monitoring the vibes from the market with positive, neutral, or negative sentiment. Big Data fuels the nitty-gritty of consumer insights and enables data analysis on an unparalleled level. Predictive analytics showcases the pathways and facilitates the unprecedented opportunity of looking directly into the minds of consumers and understanding the triggers of their behaviours, before even customers themselves feel the need for purchase.

All that is nicely embedded into the pursuit for excellence in the process of value-added co-creation. Diving into the blue ocean of endless possibilities, marketers put in value, create USPs, and visibly differentiate the products. In this regard gathering data about the customers and the omnichannel journey facilitates microlearning on volatile preferences and underlies the one-to-one marketing communication.

What can we then learn from contemporary marketers? Absolutely everything! Starting from patience, curiosity and perseverance, through lessons of the bitter taste of defeat up to the luxury of uniqueness, boosting consumer desires and providing complete fulfillment. Ability to learn just in case, not just in time. Capability to create the entire ecosystem. Knowledge enabling being the touchpoint between the business and IT. Expertise allowing to drive the digital transformation not only of own brand but sometimes igniting the same for the entire industry.

This journey isn't easy. It is demanding, requires work 24/7, versatility, and a desire for continuous improvement. But it is equally rewarding like the cycle of continuous learning, where the more we know, the more humble we become by quoting Socrates 'I know that I know nothing'. And by telling so becoming capable to do magic, literally: the creation of something, very often out of nothing and driving the skyrocketing sales levels.

What Dr Tarabasz also agrees on is that the future of marketers and L&D practitioners seems to be converging more and more from the techniques they use to the platforms they use. The distinctions between EdTech and MarkTech seem to be becoming increasingly blurred.

MarTech, EdTech... all become one in the learning economy

Where not so long ago, social media channels were used to reach external stakeholders of the organization, we see that they are also increasingly used with employees. These employees are becoming the internal customers of L&D.

More than that, we also see that the ambitions of the various apps already look beyond the walls of learning and marketing. Just think of LinkedIn, which we used to know mainly as a social network for business networking or possibly career planning. Nowadays, however, we increasingly come across them as active sellers of their learning experience platform (LXP) which could fulfil all the learning needs of internal employees. And not only LinkedIn has ambitions to make an inward move in the learning organization ecosystem, also Mark Zuckerberg has his eye on the enormous potential of learning with the introduction of 'his' Meta.

But while we see social apps chasing opportunities in B2B, we also see the reverse happening. Organizations are increasingly sharing their internal knowledge with the ecosystem in order to grow together. A good example of this is organizations that lean on flex and gig workers, as Marc Rummens shared in the first part of this book. In his example, the golden triangle was formed by the LiNK Academy connecting external employees, customers, and the organization itself.

More and more organizations are also trying to take account of their customers and learn from them. For instance, they use reward systems to rate products or share suggestions for improvement with the organization. This is where the boundaries between marketing, product development and learning start to blur even more. Here we see the LearnScape taking its central place in the learning economy.

Innovative cooperation and ICT integrations outside the organization

Collaboration within the organization is one thing, requesting collaboration between partners outside the organization is sometimes a greater challenge. Still, we see that also with regard to technical integrations, optimization must be sought outside the existing frameworks.

Guy Van Neck indicated earlier that he is in favour of cooperation with what would initially be competitors of his. In his example, he indicated that Mobietrain at Azadea plays a role in the bigger picture that is being pursued. They are, as it were, a plug-in in the larger ERP system that connects like an umbrella the whole landscape of technologies that all have the objective to increase knowledge within the organization and stimulate knowledge sharing.

Managing these integrations is not always easy. Many providers are still convinced that their solution must be a *one-fits-all* solution in order to obtain the largest possible market share. They are therefore not very eager to open the gates of their 'unique' solution to others, even if it benefits the customer.

The LearnScaper, supported by their sponsor in the leadership team, therefore also has an important role to play in the larger ecosystem of partners and potential partners. Not only should they internally translate the vision into opportunities for all stakeholders, also external partners should support this vision to go along with it.

These collaborations will often not come about from the first step towards an innovative learning strategy. They are the result of the search for continuous improvement. Not only the technical possibility of integration will be assessed among providers – current and new – but also the willingness of the provider to form a whole of which they themselves are only a small, yet often essential, part.

I dare say here as a personal note that players who are not open to cooperation will in the near future sit alone on their island which will increasingly dry up until nothing is left but their own inward vision.

References

Cialdini, R (2006) *Influence: The Psychology of Persuasion*, Harper Business, New York

EdSurge (2021) As Facebook Changes Name to Meta, Company Wants to Pull Education Into Its 'Metaverse', www.edsurge.com/news/2021-10-29-as-facebook-changes-name-to-meta-education-is-part-of-new-vision? (archived at https://perma.cc/6HX7-3AEN)

Franklin, B (1789) Private letter to Jean-Baptiste Le Roy, *'Our new Constitution is now established, everything seems to promise it will be durable; but, in this world, nothing is certain except death and taxes'*

15

Step 5: Future growth and improvement: never stop learning

Learning never stops. We can always improve if we dare to look to the future with an open mind. A future whose end we cannot see, but which springs from the light. For me, this is the essence of the method of continuous improvement that I discuss in this last part of the book. A vision that I embrace and that the young American poet Amanda Gorman also shared on Capitol Hill before the inauguration of America's new president.

The poem she recited that day in December 2020 left few of us unmoved. Her words of unity, faith and trust inspired me to think about the growth mindset of organizations and the people behind them. Like many others, I was moved by this young poet, not only because of the power of her words, but also because of her message that we must open our eyes to new possibilities. Her poem made me think about the importance of resilience and an open, curious, but critical view of the future. How we can steer our own future from reverse engineering.

The Fibonacci spiral or the golden section is therefore the image that I always use with the method. Not that I set perfection as an ultimate goal, but to continue to grow in search of improvement in which we may also be ambitious. Another link is, of course, with the mathematical sequences that form the basis of algebra and thus the algorithms that intelligent technologies use to add value to our learning and life.

When thinking about LearnScapes, we have already seen in the first step that we need to imagine the future and bring it to the present. Yet looking to the future does not stop there in the process of creating the nimble organization where learning is the oxygen for the ecosystem. From the competencies that characterise the LearnScaper, growth is a process that requires sustained energy. From the steps in the past we look for improvement opportunities in the intelligent symbiosis of human and technology.

Dare to question the legacy

One of the biggest obstacles to innovating with digital technologies is the cost of changing legacy systems. Consider, for example, the ERP system that is the backbone of the organization for many companies. That ERP, the enterprise resource planning, is the software that contains the technology to integrate different processes of a company. These different processes can be very comprehensive and integrate finance, human resources, marketing, procurement, planning, production and more, depending on the organization.

Not only is an ERP system often the backbone, but the costs associated with change and maintenance are not the least of these. For example, a 2019 ERP report found that the average budget per user for an ERP project quickly rises to $7,200. Add in all the unforeseen costs and the cost of a bespoke implementation and you know that for a medium-sized company, the cost runs to somewhere between $150,000 and $750,000. That is indeed a rather broad benchmark, but it all has to do with the specific requirements and integrations needed for optimisation within your organization.

When we talk about LearnScapes where knowledge is the oxygen running through the organization, you cannot do that without taking into account the existing ERP systems. Integration with that planning system is therefore often one of the decisive dimensions in the selection phase, for example via the OODAP methodology. If that ERP system does not keep up with the times, the long-term costs of not changing can be many times greater. These costs are often related to the limitations they impose on innovation and integration. The legacy system then has an impeding effect on the growth of the company.

We also see that certain legacy systems remain in use because they support the habit of working. I am also thinking here of learning management systems or knowledge databases which indeed contain a wealth of knowledge. However, these organizations still work on the basis of the data repository principle: store as much knowledge as possible. Even if it is no longer used or does not flow through the ecosystem, the fear of losing anything when the data has to be transferred is enough to nip any desire for innovation in the bud. This is where the LearnScaper's role is to use empathy to capture fear, channel it and make the benefits for change visible.

Now you may think: why is this coming up now? Surely this is part of the first phase of our project when we start looking for opportunities to support our future growth? Indeed, these opportunities should already have been identified in the discovery phase.

When we think about the premise that in a LearnScape intelligent knowledge sharing and collaboration with technology prevails, quick wins are sometimes easier to be accepted by all stakeholders on the burning platform. When they demonstrate added value in the short term, the next step is to look at what the next step of the transformation might look like.

It is therefore the task of the LearnScaper, together with the working group of the burning platform, to see which steps will be taken first. Is the legacy system only ready after successful first steps to get all stakeholders on board, or is the organization ready for more and is the need now pressing?

From Moore's law to Mendeleev to see the future without end

When we think back to Moore's law in the first part of this book, we know that we are only at the beginning of the accelerating wave of innovations that is coming our way. A crystal ball will not help us to make a prediction. Nor is it possible to select tools now that will be future-proof for years to come.

If we dare to look backwards, we know that in the first months of 2020, more innovations related to learning and collaboration were implemented than what we expected in the coming years. A black swan like COVID-19 has caused this acceleration that no one saw coming, but which technology providers are eagerly jumping on to raise funds and bring new products to market all the time.

What can we do, then, to take the future into account and not have to think that the initiatives we want to launch are already *outdated* on the day they are introduced?

Since I myself often have more questions than answers and that difficult 'why' child in me keeps jumping up, I went to MIT a while ago, hoping to find all my answers there. Funnily enough, it wasn't the answers I was looking for that would open my eyes. Drawing up future-proof digital learning strategies was not the objective of the course I took. However, my competences were strengthened so that I could look for connections that were not there at first sight. Consilience turned out to be one of those competences that made it possible to realize that the future lies where we least expect it. By taking off my blinders and looking for answers in the present, I learned to think more consciously about open human-centered innovation. I did not look for answers in the now, but left empty or connectable spaces where future technologies could find their place.

I have quoted Paul McDonagh-Smith several times, and rightly so, for he has inspired me, and continues to do so, with his stories and insights. It is therefore an incredible honour that he quotes one of his current studies in this book.

CASE STUDY
The table of digital elements

Paul McDonagh-Smith, Senior Lecturer at MIT Sloan School of Management and Digital Capability Leader at MIT Sloan Office of Executive Education

In 1869, Mendeleev had been working for more than a decade on a complex challenge: to identify a universal theory that would order chemical elements. Despite his efforts, he had not yet found the patterns that would lead to his periodic table of elements. His intuition told him that there was a pattern waiting to be discovered, but how to discover it?

One of the things that always inspired me about Mendeleev and his discovery and publication of the periodic table is that he could see the patterns, could connect the dots with less than half of the elements that would eventually fill the table we have today. So I deduce that if you are ever in a business meeting, or in a Zoom call, and a colleague suggests that it is not possible to work with ambiguity, or you need all the data to arrive at a testable hypothesis, you can always refer them back to Mendeleev's discovery.

With 63 elements in front of him, he recognized the patterns and was able to abstract unnecessary details that allowed him to create the algorithm of the periodic table. As in finding games like chess or go with less than half their pieces and boards, he distinguished, recognized and applied the fundamental patterns. The cards and odds were stacked against him and, fascinatingly, that is exactly what history suggests helped Mendeleev make his discovery.

He had an idea. A game that would create perhaps the most famous card game in the history of science, a game of chemical solitaire. He created a set of cards and wrote on each card an element, and its atomic weight. He then laid the cards out to see where there were visible patterns that might suggest how the sixty-three cards, or elements, fit together. Previously, chemists had grouped the elements in one of two ways, patterns based either on their properties or their atomic weight. What Mendeleev did was to unite these two patterns.

I remember reading in Paul Strathern's fascinating book, *Mendeleev's Dream*, that on the evening of 17 February 1869, after days of working without rest, Mendeleev fell asleep at his desk and later woke up after dreaming up the periodic table. It was an incredible breakthrough and one that, like so many others in science and human history owed something to both those who had gone before him and a rare personal determination. It was a rare determination to take on a complex challenge, break it down into its elements (literally in this case), recognize the patterns and combine them, remove the unnecessary information and create a step-by-step solution. Mendeleev's algorithm was the periodic table that I suspect is hanging in every chemistry lab in every school in the world today.

I think there are many lessons we can learn from Mendeleev's discovery, but the one I would like to focus on here has to do with what I call a 'technology presentist'. With this term I want to differentiate from the concept of 'technology futurist' and ask that we all take a page out of Mendeleev's book. Let's work with the technologies we have today and discover the patterns between them to find answers to business problems and open the doors to new knowledge and its application. Let us not wait until tomorrow, or think that all the boxes in our periodic table are filled, before we start experimenting and creating our future. We can start today. History justified the patterns that Mendeleev discovered and combined. We can do the same with the application of digital elements and their critical human counterparts in our organizations today.

It is encouraging that some organizations and educational technology developers are already looking at the gaps they want to fill with innovations that do not yet exist. I notice, for example, that especially in the manufacturing industry people are already looking at the added value of machines to help them think things through and to move from routine assembly line assignments to highly specialized, customized solutions. Where Ford used to make its car available in all black colours, today a car can be configured almost to measure.

Learning at the point of need, in other words when an action needs to be adapted to the customer's expectations, is becoming the norm rather than the exception. There is no time to watch a webinar, let alone to travel for a three-day training course. Learning must become increasingly lean and knowledge is given to us by intelligent cooperation with machines when it can be applied. In the new set-ups that I come across in the manufacturing industry, I see that artificial intelligence is being experimented with in combination with virtual reality and even holograms. Don't have a clue how to integrate the tailor-made engine into the new bodywork? Then you can quickly take apart the virtual version and only then start working on the real pieces.

Learning never ends and the future is full of innovations that can make it easier for us as human beings. Innovations that can make us more human in a world that is becoming faster and more 'high-tech', but also a world where society pays more attention to the wellbeing of people and that of future generations. When we, like Mendeleev, look to the future with an open mind, there is no end to the possibilities, only an open desire to keep growing.

References

Gorman, A (2021) *The Hill We Climb*, Viking Press, New York

Software path (2022) What 1,384 ERP projects tell us about selecting ERP (2022 ERP report) softwarepath.com/guides/erp-report (archived at https://perma.cc/EQC2-RHFG)

Conclusion: next steps

If at this point you are expecting some kind of *trick list* to follow that you can fill in to get to the nimble LearnScape, I have to disappoint you. That *blueprint* does not exist, because no organization is the same. A blueprint would also be against the idea of dealing flexibly with changing circumstances. More than that, I would suddenly promote one of those ideas that I have argued against, a utopian *one-fits-all solution*.

Yet, after reading this book, you can get to work with your team and your organization, starting from yourself. This book will give you a basic understanding of the world we live in and how it impacts on us as lifelong learners. It will hopefully also inspire you to look at technology from a different perspective. Not as a sales pitch that technology is the answer to all problems, or a fear story where machines will oppress people. But as an added value to grow from intelligent cooperation with technology that brings out the best in ourselves.

As a future-oriented lifelong learner, you understand that skills can be learned. That we also need to focus on the competences that make us human. Understanding that is a first step to success, especially if you have ambitions to take the lead as a LearnScaper in the transformation of your team, organization and who knows, if we dare to be ambitious, the ecosystem of which your LearnScape is a part.

I may not want to offer a blueprint that pushes our self-management thinking into a certain corner already, but I do want to point out the importance of a good methodology and structure. The five steps to achieve continuous improvement are all essential. Rushing ahead and skipping steps, as we did with the accelerated innovation at the beginning of the COVID-19 pandemic, will prove unsustainable in the long run and lead to frustration among stakeholders.

It is only when we dare to see the future without allowing ourselves to be trapped by the limits of the present that we can continue to grow from our own strength, as people or as organizations. And we do not grow alone.

If we don't involve our employees and teams in a future strategy, if we can't show them the added value, they will not only drop out but also poison the soil of our LearnScape. Only after we are sure that the soil for transformation is ripe can we grow together, possibly first with small cuttings that we place as low-threshold experiments.

Technological innovation in itself should not drive a transformation project in search of continuous improvement. No technology is a holy grail that gives life to the organization. Only when the LearnScape uses a human-centered approach that connects technologies and teams can the necessary oxygen be provided for growth. Tools and the content we want to share with them may seem cool, but if they don't contribute to lean knowledge sharing, they are worth nothing in this world where abundance of data and knowledge is already overwhelming us.

Better collaboration and growth is the starting point of a LearnScape where knowledge is the oxygen. What is often forgotten is that a transformation needs engaged leaders in a culture that supports collaboration. This is perhaps one of the most difficult challenges you will face if you are reading this book and do not (yet) have a leadership role in the organization. However, when you have read carefully, you will know that the HiPPO is not the leader in a nimble organization, but someone who can see the future and has the competences to translate it into the present together with others.

This book is not a blueprint, but it is a plea to work more with experts who connect the organization, even if they seem to have nothing in common at first sight. It is sometimes said that 'data is the new gold', and marketers and ICT managers are years ahead of many other departments in the organization.

With this book, I hope that you dare to start working with a growth mindset that inspires others to look to the future from the bright light of improvement that you already see. That you inspire and plant seeds that also inspire other organizations to dare to look beyond today's challenges as opportunities for tomorrow.

INDEX

Note: Page numbers in *italics* refer to figures

EU Representative (GPSR)

Authorised Rep Compliance Ltd, Ground Floor, 71 Lower Baggot Street, Dublin,
D02 P593, Ireland

www.arccompliance.com